Paris
to the
Moon

PARIS
TO THE
MOON

Adam Gopnik

RANDOM HOUSE

NEW YORK

Much of the contents of this book was originally published in
The New Yorker.

Library of Congress Cataloging-in-Publication Data
Gopnik, Adam.
Paris to the moon / Adam Gopnik.
p. cm.
3371 3065 5/06   ISBN 0-679-44492-0
1. Gopnik, Adam—Homes and haunts—France—Paris. 2.
Americans—France—Paris. 3.
Paris (France)—Social life and customs—20th century. I. Title.

DC718.A44 G67   2000
944'.3600413—dc21   00-037297

Random House website address: www.atrandom.com
Printed in the United States of America on acid-free paper

4 6 8 9 7 5

Book design by Caroline Cunningham

"I dare say, moreover," she pursued with an interested gravity, "that I do, that we all do here, run too much to mere eye. But how can it be helped? We're all looking at each other—and in the light of Paris one sees what things resemble. That's what the light of Paris seems always to show. It's the fault of the light of Paris—dear old light!"

"Dear Old Paris!" little Bilham echoed.

"Everything, everyone shows," Miss Barrace went on.

"But for what they really are?" Strether asked.

"Oh, I like your Boston 'reallys'! But sometimes—yes."

—*The Ambassadors*

Contents

THE WINTER CIRCUS

(An American family arrives in Paris, is greeted by bombs and strikes, and a good time is had by all.)

Paris to the Moon   3

Private Domain   19

The Strike   28

The Winter Circus, Christmas Journal 1   36

DISTANT ERRORS

(Emigration becomes expatriation, confusion reigns, and serenity is sought in the Luxembourg Gardens.)

The Rules of the Sport   61

The Chill   69

A Tale of Two Cafés   78

Distant Errors, Christmas Journal 2   86

Papon's Paper Trail   106

Trouble at the Tower   123

LESSONS FROM THINGS

*(Food, fashion, and foibles teach their complicated lessons in
the struggle between Administration and Civilization.)*

Couture Shock   129

The Crisis in French Cooking   144

Barney in Paris   166

Lessons from Things, Christmas Journal 3   174

The Rookie   196

A MACHINE TO DRAW THE WORLD

*(Serenity is found in calm and contemplation, and the deep
tragedy of history revealed. All chords are sounded and
the bells rung in the birth of a new French baby.)*

The World Cup, and After   215

The Balzar Wars   228

Alice in Paris   239

A Machine to Draw the World, Christmas Journal 4   253

A Handful of Cherries   271

Like a King   296

Angels Dining at the Ritz   312

One Last Ride   331

The
Winter
Circus

Paris
to the Moon

Not long after we moved to Paris, in the fall of 1995, my wife, Martha, and I saw, in the window of a shop on the rue Saint-Sulpice, a nineteenth-century engraving, done in the manner, though I'm now inclined to think not from the hand, of Daumier. It shows a train on its way from the Right Bank of Paris to the moon. The train has a steam locomotive and six cars, and it is chugging up a pretty steep track. The track is supported on two high, slender spires that seem to be anchored somewhere in the Fifth Arrondissement (you can see the Panthéon in silhouette nearby), and then the track just goes right up and touches the full moon up in the clouds. I suppose the two pillars are stronger than they look. The train is departing at twilight—presumably it's an overnight trip—and among the crowd on the ground below, only a couple of top-hatted bourgeois watch the lunar express go on its way with any interest, much less wonder. Everybody else in the crowd of thirteen or so people on the platform, mostly moms and dads and kids, are running around and making conversation and comforting children and buying tickets for the next trip and doing all the things people still do on station platforms in Paris. The device on the ticket window, like the title of the cartoon, reads: "A Railroad: From Paris to the Moon."

The cartoon is, in part, a satire on the stock market of the time and on railway share manipulations. ("Industry," the caption begins, "knows no more obstacles.") But the image cast its spell on us, at least, because it seemed to represent two notions, or romances, that had made us want to leave New York and come to Paris in the first place. One was the old nineteenth-century vision of Paris as the *naturally* modern place, the place where the future was going to happen as surely as it would happen in New York. If a train were going to run to the moon, that train would originate from the Gare du Nord, with Parisian kids getting worn out while they waited.

But the image represented another, more intense association, and that is the idea that there is, for some Americans anyway, a direct path between the sublunary city and a celestial state. Americans, Henry James wrote, "are too apt to think that Paris is the celestial city," and even if we don't quite think that, some of us do think of it as the place where tickets are sold for the train to get you there. (Ben Franklin thought this, and so did Gertrude Stein, and so did Henry Miller. It's a roomy idea.) If this notion is pretty obviously unreal, and even hair-raisingly naive, it has at least the excuse of not being original. When they die, Wilde wrote, all good Americans go to Paris. Some of us have always tried to get there early and beat the crowds.

I've wanted to live in Paris since I was eight. I had a lot of pictures of the place in my head and even a Parisian object, what I suppose I'd have to call an icon, in my bedroom. Sometime in the mid-sixties my mother, who has a flair for the odd, ready-made present, found—I suppose in an Air France office in Philadelphia—a life-size cardboard three-dimensional cutout of a Parisian policeman. He had on a blue uniform and red kepi and blue cape, and he wore a handlebar mustache and a smile. (The smile suggests how much Art, or at any rate Air France, improves on Life, or at any rate on Paris policemen.)

My younger brother and I called the policeman Pierre, and he kept watch over our room, which also had Beatle posters and a blindingly, numbingly, excruciatingly bright red shag rug. (I had been allowed to choose the color from a choice of swatches, but I have an inability to generalize and have always made bad, over-bright guesses on curtains and carpets and, as it turned out, the shape of future events.) Although we had never gone anywhere interesting but New York, my older sister had already, on the basis of deep, illicit late-night reading of Jane Austen and *Mary Poppins,* claimed London, and I had been given Paris, partly as a consolation prize, partly because it interested me. (New York, I think, was an open city, to be divided between us, like Danzig. Our four younger brothers and sisters were given lesser princi-palities. We actually expected them to live in Philadelphia.)

My first images of Paris had come from the book adaptation of *The Red Balloon,* the wonderful Albert Lamorisse movie about a small boy in the Parisian neighborhood of Menilmontant who gets a magic, slightly overeager balloon, which follows him every-where and is at last destroyed by evil boys with rocks. Curiously, it was neither a cozy nor a charming landscape. The Parisian grown-ups all treated Pascal, the boy, with a severity bordering on outright cruelty: His mother tosses the balloon right out of the Haussmannian apartment; the bus conductor shakes his head and finger and refuses to allow the balloon on the tram; the prin-cipal of the school locks him in a shed for bringing the balloon to class. The only genuine pleasure I recall that he finds in this un-smiling and rainy universe is when he leaves the balloon outside a tempting-looking bakery and goes in to buy a cake. The insou-ciance with which he does it—cake as a right, not a pleasure—impressed me a lot. A scowling gray universe relieved by pastry:

This was my first impression of Paris, and of them all, it was not the farthest from the truth. To this set of images were added, soon after, the overbright streets of the Madeline books, covered with vines and the little girls neat in their rows, and black and white pictures of men in suits walking through the Palais Royale, taken from a Cartier-Bresson book on the coffee table.

Pierre, though, being made of cardboard, got pretty beat up, sharing a room with two young boys, or maybe he was just both smaller and more fragile than I recall. In any case, one summer evening my parents, in a completely atypical display of hygienic decisiveness, decided that he was too beat up to keep and that it was time for him to pass away, and they put him out on the Philadelphia street for the trashman to take away.

I wept all night. He would sit out with the trash cans and would not be there in the morning. (A little later I read about Captain Dreyfus and *his* degradation, and the two uniformed and mustachioed figures got mixed up, so perhaps he had been sent to supply intimations of the other, darker side of French life. They were certainly there to be intimated.) What made me sad just then was the new knowledge that things changed, and there was nothing you could do about it. In a way, that was a Parisian emotion too.

|||

I saw the real—or anyway the physical—Paris for the first time in 1973, when I was in my early teens. I had arrived with my large, strange family, those five brothers and sisters, and a couple of hangers-on and boyfriends. There were eight of us in the back of a Citroën station wagon. I was the one with the bad adolescent mustache. My parents, college professors, were on sabbatical, at a time, just weeks before the oil crunch, when the great good wave that had lifted up college professors into the upper middle classes was still rising. At the time we all lived in Montreal, and my brothers and sisters went to a French private academy there actually run by the French government. The corridors in the school were named after Parisian streets: The Champs-Élysées led the way to the principal's office, and you took the rue Royale to the cafeteria for lunch. I was the only one in an English-speaking school and became oddly, or maybe not so oddly, the only one to fall entirely in love with France. (You can never forget, I suppose, that the Champs-Élysées once led the way to the principal's office.)

We came in through one of the *portes* of Paris, the doors that are now merely exits from the peripheral expressway but that still keep the names of the real gates of the old walled city. It was probably the portes d'Orléans. I saw a girl lean over to kiss a friend on a stopped motorbike on the cheek, twice, *here* and then *there*. The trees cast patterned light on the street. We went out for dinner and, for fifteen francs, had the best meal I had ever eaten, and most of all, nobody who lived there seemed to notice or care. The beauty and the braised trout alike were just part of life, the way we do things here.

We had spent the previous three days in London. Though the taxis were black and the buses red and Regent's Park green, the familiar street names seemed curiously to belong to another civilization, as though the city had been occupied once by another and more vivid, imperial race and had then been turned over to the pallid, gray people on the streets, who ate sandwiches that turned up at the edges. Paris, on the other hand, looked exactly as it was supposed to look. It wore its heart on its sleeve, and the strange thing was that the heart it wore so openly was in other ways so closed—mysterious, uninviting.

We settled in for a long winter. While my parents taught, I spent most of my time going to the movies with my cousin Philippe. You are supposed to be in love with Paris and Philippe and I were both in love. I was in love with Jacqueline Bisset, and he was in love with Dominique Sanda. We went to the movies all the time, looking for them both. I remember finding a fifth-run movie theater someplace in the Nineteenth Arrondissement, deep in a poor Algerian neighborhood, just in order to see Jacqueline's brief, heart-searing part in *The Life and Times of Judge Roy Bean*.

Almost incidentally, in love with Jacqueline Bisset, I fell in love with Paris. Paris—and this is the tricky thing—though it is always and indubitably itself, is also in its nature a difficult city to love for itself alone. What truly makes Paris beautiful is the intermingling of the monumental and the personal, the abstract and the footsore particular, it and you. A city of vast and impersonal set piece architecture, it is also a city of small and intricate, improvised experience. My favorite architectural detail in Paris is the little entrance up the rue de Seine, a tiny archway where, as I have since found out, you can push a *poussette* right through and get to the grand Institut de France. You aren't looking at it; and then you and the *poussette* are *in* it, right in the driveway where the academicians go. For a moment you *are* it. The Institut belongs to you. Ten steps more and you are on the pont des Arts. The passage from the big to the little is what makes Paris beautiful, and you have to be prepared to be small—to live, to trudge, to have your head down in melancholy and then lift it up, sideways—to get it.

What is true for academicians is true for adolescents with a fixation on Jacqueline Bisset. I saw Paris out of the corner of my eye, on my way to the movies, and so a love for Paris came to be one of the strongest emotions I possess. In addition, my father's friend the literary critic and pioneer deconstructionist Eugenio Donato brought me to a seminar that Roland Barthes was giving that spring. I didn't understand a word. (A few years later I met one of the French students in the class, and found out that she hadn't understood a word either.) Then we went home, back to Montreal, where my brothers and sisters returned to that French academy, and I kept my French sharp by reading the sports pages every day about the Montreal Canadiens.

Two years after that first year in Paris, I used the tiny lever of my knowledge of the city to induce—I still won't say deceive—a girl, a real girl, I had fallen in love with into running away to Paris with me. Martha, who became and, twenty-five years later, remains—and I write these words with a stunned disbelief, shared only by her mother—my wife, loved Paris as much as I did, even though many of the advertised attractions—the seminar with my friend Roland Barthes, for instance—that I had promised her were suspiciously missing from our trip. If she noticed this or was bothered by it, she hasn't mentioned it yet. We spent a happy week in the Hôtel Welcome on the boulevard Saint-Germain. The hidden humanism of the classical style, the idea of the intellectual as magician and stylist, and sex in a hotel room: These were the things I took away from a childhood spent continually in a made-up Paris and an adolescence spent, fitfully, in the real one.

|||

For a long time New York intervened. Then, in the late eighties, we began to think about Paris again. We sat on the deck of a rented house in Cape Cod and, listening to old Charles Trenet records, thought . . . why not? (This was neither a hard leap nor an interesting one, since the Trenet songs we were listening to had the theme of Paris pretty much to the exclusion of every other human concept.) We watched *The Umbrellas of Cherbourg* over and over. We visited Paris whenever we could, as often as we could. We weren't Francophiles because we didn't know anything about France, and still don't. We were just crazy about Paris.

When our son, Luke Auden, was born, in September 1994, we knew that we would have to go to Paris soon, or we wouldn't go at all. In five years, everybody told us, he would no longer be "portable." When we were in Paris, we had hung around the parks and gardens, watching the carousels turn and the children play and thinking, This would be a nice place to be a child or have one. We also saw all the aspects of a New York childhood that looked less delightful. You would see the five-year-olds at a friend's house already lost in the American media, simultaneously listening to a Walkman, playing with a Game Boy, and watching a video on the VCR. Perhaps, we thought—however foolishly, however "unrealistically"—we could protect him from some of that if he spent his first five years in Paris.

"You can't run away from (a) reality, (b) American culture, (c) yourself," our friends all said, compositely. "But you can run away," we said under our breaths, and we did. We thought we might stay for good, but we knew that we would certainly stay for the last five years of the century; "We'll stay till the millennium," we could say grandly, and mean it cautiously. *The New Yorker,* where I worked, was ready to hear what I had to say about Parisian scenes and, more important, was willing to keep sending non-Parisian subjects, from Groucho Marx to the Starr Report, my way too, which let us pay Parisian rates. Martha, for her part, had become a filmmaker, and she had the great portable occupation of the late twentieth century, a screenplay to write (and rewrite and rewrite again). So we went.

The New Yorker has had lots of good writers in place in Paris, but it was James Thurber, whose blind eyes in a photograph on my desk stare at me every morning, whose writing moved me most. Thurber, though he hardly spoke a word of French, wrote once that the surface of manners in France seemed to him the most beautiful in the world, and he was right. The romance of Paris was my subject, and if it is a moony or even a loony one, it is at least the one I get, a little.

This was a hard romance to sustain in most of the last five years, when almost everybody else thought that Paris was going straight to hell. When we first started dreaming of coming to Paris, around 1989, long-termist, infrastructure-building Europe, many people said, owned the future. One only had to compare JFK and Charles de Gaulle airports, the one named after the vital young internationalist and the other after the old reactionary, to catch the irony. JFK was decrepit, dangerous, and almost unpoliced; you stumbled off your plane into, of all bizarre things, a linoleum staircase, with a sign above warning you of illegal livery drivers (whose complexions, delicately, had been made neither black nor white but swarthy, like Barbary Coast pirates). You took a taxi over roads so potholed that the infrastructure was visibly rusted out, ruined. At Charles de Gaulle Airport, on the other hand, you came to a breathtakingly modern terminal, full of odd glass corridors and long, radiating, covered walkways, and exited onto a highway so up-to-date that regular announcements of upcoming traffic were posted along with the waiting time for a reservation at the Brasserie Lipp. No one will believe this now, but that is how it seemed then. (Popular memory may be short, but it is nothing compared with the amnesia of experts.)

By 1995 all that had changed, and Paris and France seemed left out of the new all-American dispensation. London, of all places, had become the town where people went to see new art and taste new cooking. For the first time in modern history it was actually possible to live in Paris for comfort and bourgeois security and travel to London for food and sex. (My cousin Philippe had, like so many ambitious Frenchmen of his generation, actually fled Paris for London, where he had made a small fortune in banking and was about to finance his own restaurant.)

The failure of the French model and the triumph of the Anglo-American one is by now a sorry, often repeated fact. For five years hardly anyone wrote about Paris and the French except in a tone of diagnosis: how sick they were, when they got so sick, why they denied that they were sick, and if there was any chance that they would ever get better. (No.) Many journalistic *tours d' horizons* have been written in the last few years—"Whither France?" and "Whether France . . ." and "Weathering France," and "France: How It Withers" and "Withering France." We surf the waves of capitalism, from crest to trough and back again, but the funny thing is that no matter how often we ride the wave, nobody notices that it's wet. When we are on the crest, we believe that we have climbed a mountain through our own virtuous efforts, and when we are in the trough, we believe that we have fallen into a pit through our own vice.

Whatever else might be true, though, in the last five years of the century, as the world became, by popular report, more "globalized" than it had ever been before, France became more *different*. "They order these matters better in France," Sterne's opening line for *his* sentimental journey in France, had a new ring, now. For most of two centuries, after all, what had been so different about France was how central and cosmopolitan it was. Americans had been going to Paris for a couple of centuries to learn a universal diplomatic language and the central artistic culture and even the most influential manner of cooking. Yet in the time we were there Paris seemed to pass from the place where you learned how to do it to the place where you learned how *not* to do it—how not to do it in the ordinary American imperial way, the place where you learned how to do it, as the French like to say, *autrement,* otherly. From the kind of sympathy that labor unions get from their public to the length of time you take to eat lunch, the way it's done in Paris now is not the way it's done in Adelaide or Toronto or Los Angeles or Tempe or Hong Kong or any of the studs on the broad belt of the English-speaking imperium that now encircles the world, with New York as its buckle. Americans still learn about differences in Paris, but now we learn about them not because we are so much closer to the center of things but because we are so much farther away. The light of Paris still shows Americans things as they are (if not as they *really* are) by showing us how things can look different in a different light, but the light it shows them with now is more mysterious and singular, a kind of moral moonlight, a little bit harder to see by.

There was no big story in France at the end of the century, but there were a lot of littler ones, and the littlest ones of all seemed to say the most about what makes Paris still Paris. Princesses died and prime ministers fell and intellectuals argued, gravely, about genuinely grave questions, and I wrote about all these things, but I have left most of that writing out of this book. They are important things, but the things that interested me most, in a time of plenty, were the minute variations, what a professor would call the significant absences, between living a family life in one place and living the same kind of life somewhere else. This is a story of the private life of a lucky American family living in Paris in the last five years of the century, less a tour of any horizon than just a walk around the park. To the personal essays about life in Paris, I have added some private journals I wrote every Christmas. These journals, I see in rereading them, are more pensive and even pessimistic in tone than the stories, perhaps because they are notes sent inward rather than letters sent out. (I have also included a long report on the trial of Maurice Papon because it is about the occupation and collaboration, still the great, unignorable black hole at the center of French life, still sucking in the light even of everyday pleasure.)

Family life is by its nature cocooned, and expatriate family life doubly so. We had many friends and a few intimate ones, but it is in the nature of family rhythm—up too early, asleep too soon—to place you on a margin, and to the essential joy—just the three of us!—was added the essential loneliness, *just the three of us*. What I find is left, after the politics have been removed, are mostly stories about raising a kid in foreign parts. Yet since raising a kid is the one nearly universal thing people do, and since doing it in foreign parts is the one time when you get to see most clearly all the bits of doing it that *aren't* universal—that are inflected and shaped by the local geography and mood and playground equipment—it is in its way, I hope, still a not entirely interior subject.

These stories are also, willy-nilly, about bringing up a kid in foreign parts in a funny time. What made the time funny was that there was as much peace and prosperity in the world as there has ever been and at the same time a lot of resentment directed at the United States, the country where the peace and prosperity, like the kid, came from, or which at least was taking credit for it. Paris, which in the first five years of the century seemed the capital of modern life, spent the last five years on the sidelines, brooding on what had happened. Our son's first five years, and the modern century's last five, five years to the end of the millennium and five to grade one in New York, a small subject and a large one, juxtaposed: These stories take one stretch of time and, as they used to demand in exam papers, contrast and compare.

The stories are mostly about the life spent at home and include a lot—some will think too much—about the trinity of late-century bourgeois obsessions: children and cooking and spectator sports, including the spectator sport of shopping. Yet life is mostly lived by timid bodies at home, and since we see life as deeply in our pleasures as in our pains, we see the differences in lives as deeply there too. The real differences among people shine most brightly in two bedrooms and one building, with a clock ticking, five years to find out how and why. Not just how and why and in what way Paris is different from New York, but how a North American liberal, with the normal "universalist," antinationalist reflexes of the kind, might end up feeling about the idea of difference itself—about the existence of minute variations among peoples: which ones really matter and which ones really don't. (By the end of the decade, a new image of Paris, as a multicultural metropolis with a thriving entrepreneurial culture, was coming into place. This existed—it always had—but it seemed a little too easily pleasing to Americans, perhaps because it was so familiar, not so different after all, and looked to America for inspiration. The young soccer players on the champion French national team carefully imitated Sammy Sosa's finger-kissing when they scored their goals, and French rap, striking though it was, seemed more distinctive from its American sources than really different from them, in the same way that American impression- ism in the nineteenth century was distinctive rather than differ- ent from *its* models. Anyway, while I greatly enjoyed the Sosa finger-kissing, as I enjoyed French rap, I admired even more the way that the great Zinedine Zidane, when asked about a perfect free kick he had taken, calmly said, "I am at the summit of my art.")

I looked for the large in the small, the macro in the micro, the figure in the carpet, and if some big truths passed by, I hope some significant small ones got caught. If there is a fault in re- porting, after all, it is not that it is too ephemeral but that it is not ephemeral *enough,* too quickly concerned with what seems big at the time to see what is small and more likely to linger. It is, I think, the journalists' vice to believe that all history can instantly be reduced to experience: ("Pierre, an out-of-work pipe fitter in the suburb of Boulougne, is typical of the new class of *chômeurs* . . .") just as it is the scholar's vice to believe that all ex- perience can be reduced to history ("The new world capitalist order produced a new class of *chômeurs,* of whom Pierre, a pipe fitter, was a typical case . . .").

What then, the journalist and scholar ask tetchily, what then is exactly the vice of the comic-sentimental essayist? It is of course to believe that all experience and history can be reduced to *him,* or his near relations, and the only apology I can make is that for him in this case experience and history and life were not so much reduced as all mixed up, and scrambled together, they at least become a subject. The essayist dreams of being a prism, through which other light passes, and fears ending up merely as a mirror, showing the same old face. He has only his Self to show and only himself to blame if it doesn't show up well.

Even if experience shows no more than itself, it is still worth showing. Experience and history, I think, are actually like the two trains in that Keaton movie where Buster struggles to keep up with the big engine by pumping furiously on a handcar on the adjoining track. It looks as if the little handcar of experience and the big train of history are headed for the same place at the same speed; but in fact the big train is going where it is headed, and those of us in the handcar keep up only by working very hard, for a little while.

There are two kinds of travelers. There is the kind who goes to see what there is to see and sees it, and the kind who has an image in his head and goes out to accomplish it. The first visitor has an easier time, but I think the second visitor sees more. He is constantly comparing what he sees to what he wants, so he sees with his mind, and maybe even with his heart, or tries to. If his peripheral vision gets diminished—so that he quite literally sometimes can't see what's coming at him from the suburbs of the place he looks at—his struggle to adjust the country he looks at to the country he has inside him at least keeps him looking. It sometimes blurs, and sometimes sharpens, his eye. My head was filled with pictures of Paris, mostly black and white, and I wanted to be in them.

I am aware that my Paris, which began as a cardboard construction wearing a cape and a kepi, in many respects remains one, an invention, a Bizzaro New York, abstract where New York is specific, intricate where New York is short, though not perhaps more soulful, and that my writing about Paris is very much like my writing about New York in the first five years I lived there.

In fact it would have been a lunchtime's work for my old friend Eugenio Donato, who haunts this book as he haunts my memories of Paris, to insist that this book about Paris is *actually* about New York. A lunchtime's worth of work yet not perhaps a dinner's worth of truth. The images contain their little truth too, which I grasped even in remnant form in West Philadelphia. We all see our Paris as true, because it is. It is not an old or antiquated Paris that we love, but the persistent, modern material

Paris, carrying on in a time of postmodern immateriality, when everything seems about to dissolve into pixels. We love Paris not out of "nostalgia" but because we love the look of light on things, as opposed to the look of light *from* things, the world reduced to images radiating from screens. Paris was the site of the most beautiful commonplace civilization there has ever been: cafés, brasseries, parks, lemons on trays, dappled light on bourgeois boulevards, department stores with skylights, and windows like doors everywhere you look. If it is not so much wounded—all civilizations are that, since history wounds us all—as chastened, and overloud in its own defense, it nonetheless goes on. The persistence of this civilization in the sideshow of postmodern culture is my subject, and the life it continues to have my consolation. I don't go on a bus in Paris without still expecting my balloon to be barred and the authority figure who oversees it is still a cardboard policeman in a cape. I see the moon these days from Paris because I once saw Paris from the moon.

|||

My real life in Paris, as in New York, was spent with a few people, and, really, only with two, Martha and Luke, and when I think of Paris, I think of them: Martha and Luke in matching fur hats at the Palais Royal; waiting with Luke in the courtyard of our building for Martha to come down the stairs (in long Russian coat and Tibetan hat, cold girl, in mid-autumn); waiting with Martha in the courtyard of an odd building on the boulevard Raspail for Luke to come from his gym class, peering through the dirty windows and the cagelike grille, one child among many, and then getting a Coca-Cola, five francs from the machine. Cyril Connolly once achieved an unearned poetic effect by reciting the names in wartime of hotels on the Left Bank. I can sometimes achieve a similar one, even more unearned, though not less felt, by reciting to myself the names of restaurants where we ate lunch while Luke slept (or, occasionally, where we wished we could sleep, while Luke ate): Le Soufflé, Le Basilic, Chez André, Le Petit St. Benoît, Laduree. I believe in Le Soufflé, on a Saturday afternoon in December, in the back room, with Luke sleeping in his *poussette,* and the old couple across the neighboring banquette, who had been coming for forty years, there with their small blind dog. The waiters in white coats, the owner in a blue sports jacket, and the smell (aroma is too fancy a word) of mingled cigarettes and orange liqueurs. I am aware that this is what is called sentimental, but then we went to Paris for a sentimental reeducation—I did anyway—even though the sentiments we were instructed in were not the ones we were expecting to learn, which I believe is why they call it an education.

This book is theirs, and I ask them only to share a place at the dedication table with Henry Finder, my first and most patient reader, who had to take what it tasted like on trust.

Private Domain

A bomb went off under my bed the other morning. It was early on a gray Tuesday when I heard a flock of ambulances somewhere near my Left Bank street, making that forlorn, politely insistent two-note bleating all Paris ambulances make. I went downstairs and outside and found—nothing. The street sweeper with the green plastic broom was sweeping; the young woman who keeps the striped-pajama boutique across the street was reading her Paul Auster novel. ("You left New York for *Paris*?" she demanded incredulously when I introduced myself not long ago.) Only in the early afternoon, when *Le Monde* came out, did I realize that the Islamic terrorists who are now working in Paris had left a bomb in an underground train and that, give or take a few hundred yards, it had gone off beneath the second-floor refuge on the Left Bank that my wife and I had found this summer, after a long search. The ambulances were heading for the Gare d'Orsay, where the wounded were being taken.

"*Gardez votre sang-froid*" is the single, self-sufficient impera-
tive posted on the what-to-do-in-an-emergency placard in the
courtyard of our building, and on this occasion people had. The
bombings here, though sometimes murderous in their effects,
haven't caused any panic or even much terror. Though Parisians
believe they are superior by birth, they do not believe, as Americans do, that they are invulnerable by right. But even if our
apartment building had been officially declared the epicenter of
the bombing campaign, I don't think I'd move. Terrorism is part
of life, while a nice apartment in Paris is a miracle.

For the new French prime minister, Alain Juppé, the bombing
campaign has come as a vast, if unadmitted, relief, since he finally has a subject to talk about in public other than *l'affaire des
logements,* which has dominated the news here for four months
and once seemed likely to sink his government. For most of
those months, in fact, Juppé has probably been the only person
more preoccupied with apartments on the Left Bank than I was,
though he and I approached the matter from opposite ends. I
was trying to find one, while he was trying to explain to the
French people why he had so many and what all his relatives
were doing living in them.

Juppé has been prime minister for just under six months. He
is a long-fingered, elegant man of fifty, with the kind of enviable,
aerodynamic baldness that in America only tycoons seem able to
carry off—the Barry Diller, Larry Tisch style of baldness. Juppé
comes from a simple family down in the Landes country. He did
well in school and was eventually admitted to the École Nationale d'Administration, in Paris, the tiny institution that produces nearly the entire French political elite. He came to the
attention of an older fellow *énarque,* Jacques Chirac, and when
Chirac was mayor of Paris, in the 1980s, Juppé became his "financial adjoint"—more or less the city comptroller. Then, when
the conservative parties won the legislative elections two years
ago, Chirac, though he had prudently decided not to seek the of-

fice of prime minister, arranged for Juppé to be named the minister of foreign affairs, in which position, Bosnia aside, he was thought to have done well. So when Chirac was elected president, this May, it seemed inevitable that he would make Juppé his prime minister.

Like all ambitious French politicians, Juppé chooses to present himself as a literary man. He has actually written a book of reflections titled *La Tentation de Venise*—"The Venetian Temptation." Juppé's Venetian temptation was to retire to a house there, where he could escape from political life, admire Giorgione's *Tempestà*, drink Bellinis in the twilight, and think long, deep thoughts. *La Tentation* was regarded as a fighting campaign manifesto, since it is as necessary for an ambitious French politician to write a book explaining why he never likes to think of politics as it is for an ambitious American politician to write a book explaining why he never thinks of anything else. Juppé, ahead of the pack, had written a book asserting not only that he would rather be doing something else but that he would like to be doing it in a completely different country. The romance of retirement is still extremely powerful in France, descending, as it does, from Montaigne, who remains the model here of pensive, high-minded reclusion, even though he spent an important chunk of his life as the boss of a tough town. In Juppé's case, the descent from Montaigne, who supplies the epigraph for *La Tentation,* is easy to show: Juppé is the mayor of Bordeaux, as Montaigne was. (French politicians often hold more than one office at once, just in case.) Among French politicians, in fact, ostentatious displays of detachment are something of a competitive sport. After being succeeded as president by Chirac, François Mitterrand gave an interview to Christine Ockrent, the editor of *L'Express,* simply to announce that he was now taking long walks in Paris and looking at the sky. It was understood as his way of keeping his hand in. Not long ago the former prime minister Édouard Balladur, who had been so busy looking detached from politics that he forgot to campaign for the presidency this time around, sneaked an item into *L'Express* announcing that he too was taking walks and looking at the sky. It was the start of his comeback.

Then, at the beginning of June, the weekly comic paper *Le Canard Enchaîné* revealed that Juppé, when he was the financial adjoint to Chirac, had taken the lease on an apartment in the Sixth Arrondissement that belonged to the *domaine privé* of the City of Paris. The *domaine privé* is a peculiarly Parisian establishment, although even after four months of scandal, no one knows exactly what it is, how the City of Paris came to possess it, or how you get into it. At first many Parisians confused the *domaine privé* with the general stock of public housing that the City of Paris has built since the First World War; most of that housing is on the periphery, and a lot of it is in the less desirable neighborhoods of the Nineteenth and the Twentieth Arrondissements. It turns out, however, that the City of Paris also owns a small, semisecret group of apartments and apartment buildings that are given out at the discretion of whoever happens to be running Paris. These *domaine privé* apartments came into the hands of the Parisian government in all kinds of interesting ways. Many of them are on the beautiful old streets of the Left Bank, near the river, because of various failed city plans that left Paris with a lot of property, which the city fathers eventually started renting to one another. Until 1977 the prefects of the Paris arrondissements controlled the *domaine privé*, but then the system was reformed, which, as often happens in France, managed to make the mechanics of it even murkier. Today no one seems to know exactly how many *domaine privé* apartments there are. One estimate puts the number at about thirteen hundred; another puts it at about fifteen hundred; still another says that there are more than four thousand.

Juppé's apartment, on the lovely rue Jacob, was a lavish spread, complete with garden and terrace, that he had in effect rented to himself for a little less than three thousand dollars a month—well below the market price. When this arrangement was challenged, Juppé announced that he felt "serene" and that he couldn't see what the fuss was about, since anyone could have found out that he lived there by looking at the mailbox. There was something equally off-key about Chirac's later defense of his protégé. During a televised press conference, he declared himself "profoundly shocked" by "the exploitation of a fact that no one should contest." Here, he explained, Juppé was actually paying about three thousand dollars a month in rent, while there were tens of thousands of people in France living in subsidized apartments who did infinitely less service for the nation than Juppé.

As it happened, Martha and I arrived in Paris to look for a place just as the news of Juppé's arrangement broke, and we soon discovered what Juppé obviously knew to be the vital fact but was having a very hard time saying outright: *All* apartments in Paris that you would long to live in belong to the *domaine privé*. This is to say not that they all belong to the city government but that they can be obtained only through membership in one or another of the political or literary or fashionable *keiretsus* that dominate Paris. Though Paris is in many ways a grasping and commercial city, it is not ruled by the market in quite the way that most other Western cities are.

Martha and I, eight-month-old in tow, learned this quickly as we wandered from apartment to apartment. We discovered that apartments came in three varieties: sad apartments that no one would want; interesting apartments that would require *grands projets* to make them work; and nice apartments that had a long private history or, to put it another way, a catch and so were in a *domaine privé* of their own. This one came with a sister in America, who might or might not eventually return. Another was available only if the divorce that had led to its emptying out was concluded. (With tears in his eyes, the previous resident made it a condition that we buy the espresso machine that he and his departed love had picked out in happier days.) That one belonged to a philosopher who had changed his sexual orientation, and it was available with the proviso that if he changed it back, he would need the apartment again. The inwardness of Paris rules out the illusion created by the renting of an apartment in New York, the illusion of renewal, of starting over. An apartment in New York is a blank slate. In Paris it is an already parsed sentence, a string of imperfect verbs, hidden conditional constructions, and long, intricately wrought clauses in the past tense.

Juppé would probably have been able to survive the revelation of his living arrangements if only *Le Canard Enchaîné* hadn't published, a couple of Wednesdays later, the news that when Juppé was a city official, he had taken apartments in the *domaine privé* for his son and daughter as well and that these apartments too were right there on the rue Jacob. Then it turned out that both Juppé's ex-wife and his half brother had apartments courtesy of the City of Paris. (The former Mme. Juppé was lodged across the river, on the Right Bank, presumably out of deference to the sensibilities of the new Mme. Juppé.) At this point *l'affaire des logements* became a little more serious. *Le Canard* published a document apparently showing that Juppé had approved a rent reduction on his son's apartment from seven thousand francs per month to six thousand (a difference of about two hundred dollars). This might have contravened an all-purpose law against ethical backsliding on the part of public officials, a law whose worst penalty, sweetly enough, was that the offender would be prohibited from ever again being elected to office.

Things got so bad that Juppé had to submit to a humiliation that the French had previously considered fit only for American politicians. He had to go on television and answer questions from reporters. (De Gaulle spoke directly to the French people or else in highly choreographed press conferences; Mitterrand would tolerate a few friendly journalists but would explain to them why the questions they were asking were not of a standard that could decently be put to the president of the republic.) Juppé, by contrast, had to give one of those jumpy, undignified, I-have-nothing-to-hide performances beloved of American handlers.

Juppé did his best. He pointed out that members of the French press had been around for dinner at the now-famous apartment on the rue Jacob, and nobody had seemed upset about the apartment then. (This argument was regarded as fighting dirty. The next day *Le Monde* haughtily noted that it was not proper for guests to ask their host how much he paid in rent and who owned his apartment.) Juppé also announced that he had lowered the rent on his son's apartment only because he was afraid of contributing to a general inflation of rents in the city. It didn't help much. In July a local lawyer with Socialist party connections began filing letters of complaint against Juppé with the state district attorney in Paris, Bruno Cotte, who would therefore have to decide whether to go the Italian route and indict the prime minister of France (and, not incidentally, launch his own political career) or go the honored French route and let it all pass.

By this time I had come into possession of what I thought was the lease on an apartment and so found the later stages of *l'affaire des logements* very diverting. There is nothing like being even an honorary, part-time insider to make insiderness look cute. Then, just as we were about to leave Paris to go home and collect our furniture, I got a call from the real estate agent. "I have bad news," she announced. "Your apartment is off the market." She made it sound as though the apartment had won a prize.

Things worked out better for us than they did for the prime minister. We came back to Paris at the end of September and managed, through various routes, to find an apartment at 16 rue du Pré-aux-Clercs in the Seventh Arrondissement. The story with this one was that it belonged to a young man who had just been posted by his bank to Tokyo; the apartment was affordable because he and his wife had left it half renovated and half a wreck. On the other hand, they would want the apartment back when they returned from Japan, at some unspecified date, which makes us leap every time the doorbell rings.

Bruno Cotte has at last offered his judgment on the Juppé case. He declared that he would not indict Juppé for what he had done with the *domaine privé* apartments, provided that the prime minister of France get out of his apartment and rent one someplace else. This may have been a first in the history of jurisprudence: an eviction notice issued by a magistrate against the prime minister of a major Western power. "This was more cruel than an indictment, which at least had the savor of persecution," a veteran Parisian journalist said to me of the Cotte verdict. "An indictment might have been insupportable, but an eviction is merely ridiculous."

Naturally, American and British journalists have tried to analyze *l'affaire des logements* and, interpreting it in the light of Anglo-American politics, have concluded that Juppé has suffered because he was seen as a member of an unduly privileged elite. This is in fact almost the direct opposite of the truth. The Frenchmen who are currently the most enraged at the government—the functionaries who stopped all business in Paris several weeks ago—are not protesting against the accumulated perks of a privileged class. They are the privileged class, protesting on behalf of their accumulated perks. What made them mad about *l'affaire des logements,* and Juppé's conduct, was not that it revealed to them something they hadn't known but that it reminded them of something they knew all too well—namely, that the system of *acquis sociaux*—entitlements—runs so deep in France that to abolish it would be in some sense to abolish French life itself. Every Frenchman who is not outright destitute sits in the middle of a *domaine privé*—that is, within a domain of private benefits that he enjoys by virtue of his place in civil society. The triumph of the Fifth Republic was to have expanded that domain so that it included nearly everybody. But it may no longer be capable of any expansion at all. The people who are left outside now seem to be left outside for good. The North African immigrants, in particular, who fill the Paris *banlieue* that the police have largely abandoned are not just a minority; they are without any entrée at all. They are called, simply, the excluded. Some of them set bombs off under your bed.

Juppé's serenity is certainly gone for good. Already he is speaking plaintively of his fate. "But why have they done this to me? I am honest!" he told an interviewer recently. "Had I known, when I was foreign minister I could have moved to the quai d'Orsay, where I would have had at my disposal two hundred and eighty square meters and a chambermaid, and nobody would have reproached me at all." People agreed that he had a point, but they also noticed the way he was able to rattle off the square meters by heart.

After brooding on this affair, the French elite has decided that the cure for the kinds of hidden deals that fill French public life is transparence, which has become (along with exclusion) the word of the moment here. By *transparence* people just mean that everybody should see everything that is going on. A lot of Parisians would now settle for having a Paris that is transparent the way an ant farm is transparent: with a cutaway front so that you can see the action even if you can't affect it. But what has always given Paris its peculiar grace and favor is that things that are hidden away elsewhere (like, say, adulteries) are all out in the open here, while things that are all out in the open elsewhere are hidden away here (like, say, the way you get an apartment). A Paris you can see right through hardly seems worth having.

The
Strike

The "generalized" strike that the big French labor federations have called—making a fastidious distinction between what they're doing now and the "general" strike that they may yet get around to—has shut down Paris. The commuter and intercity trains haven't run for two weeks, not even the TGV, the famous fast train between Paris and the South. The Métro is closed down (the crickets who live beneath the rails are said to be perishing for lack of the heat they normally get from the friction of the trains running above, and their plight has become a minor cause célèbre here). There are no buses, and the post office has stopped delivering the mail. Even *le Paris touristique* has been snapped shut. The Ritz has had a dropoff in occupancy of 25 percent (at the height of the terrorist bombing campaign, a few months ago, the rate was near normal, which suggests that the rich would rather risk being blown to bits than have a hard time finding a taxi). The Louvre, like a city under siege, has been struggling to stay open and can guarantee only a narrow access corridor, leading directly from the entrance to the *Mona Lisa*. The government has even commandeered the *bateaux-mouches*—those ugly, flat-bottomed open-air tourist boats that ply the tourist sights year-round—and has turned them into ferryboats to get commuters up and down the Seine.

I think that I only really began to grasp just how serious the strike was when the chickens stopped rotating at the outdoor market in my neighborhood. Several poultry merchants there keep chickens and *coquelets* and rabbits and pheasants spitted and broiling on outdoor rotisseries all through the year, even in August and in the quiet days after Christmas. One afternoon a few days into the strike I walked over to the market to check on the progress of a turkey I had ordered from one of the *rôtisseurs*, to be sent up from the country for a belated Thanksgiving, and I noticed that he had unspitted all his birds and turned off the grill. This seemed to me one of those signs that reporters abroad are supposed to treat as portents ("It has long been said in the bazaars that when the chickens stop turning, the government will fall"), and as I approached to ask what he was doing, he gestured grimly in the direction of the boulevard Saint-Germain.

"*Ça commence,*" he said grimly. It's beginning, though what, exactly, was beginning I wasn't sure.

"The turkey, it's still on its way?" I asked, with the stupid inconsequence common to people caught up in revolutions. ("*Rien,*" Louis XVI noted in his diary the day the Bastille was stormed.)

He shook his head gravely, implying, I thought for a moment, that the strike might have spread to the fowl too. Then he gestured again toward the boulevard.

For about ten solid blocks, on each side of the boulevard Saint-Germain a row of tourist buses was parked; that, considering the severity with which the cops normally enforce the no-parking regulations, was in itself a near-insurrectionary sight.

The buses bore on their windshields notices indicating where their journeys had begun—Lyons, Grenoble, Bordeaux—and, in their side windows, little stickers saying "FO," for *Force Ou-vrière*, or Workers' Force. (Despite the militant name, it is the more moderate of the big French labor federations.) Inside, the bus drivers looked bored and sleepy after the long trip in from the provinces. But between the two rows of buses thousands of FO members, from all across France, were marching up the boulevard, three or four abreast. Then came a rear guard of stu-dents armed with batons and occasional bricks. The noise, oddly, was confined, cozily insulated by the parked coaches, a revolu-tion taking place in a bus depot. Farther east on the boulevard, beyond the buses, the French riot police were lined up and wait-ing, in helmets and shields. There wasn't any violence then, and there hasn't been too much since, but around that time it began to seem that the French were trying on, if only for a moment, long-discarded revolutionary roles, albeit in a slightly unreal set-ting: strikers taking buses to the revolution, students relearning the lore of the heaved cobblestone.

The strike had begun, on Friday, November 24, as a one-day job action, led by the railroad workers. The Juppé government was still in a state of self-congratulatory, mildly Gingrichian de-light over the austerity measures that it had announced to reform the expensive social security system of the French state. The *cheminots*, as the railroad workers are called, hated this idea, be-cause a lot of money is put directly into their pension fund by the government, an outright subsidy, which makes the railroad work-ers less employees of a profit-seeking enterprise than subsidized functionaries of a state cultural treasure, like members of the Comédie Française. (Although the train system loses money, it is one of the glories of France.) Perhaps the government doubted whether the *cheminots* could command much sympathy since their specific grievance seemed absurdly small (many of them would no longer be able to retire at fifty at full pay) and since the unions have receded as drastically in France in the past fifteen years as they have in America, maybe more so. One in every ten French workers still belongs to a union, but most of the unionized workers are ensconced for life in the public sector or in subsidized state-run enterprises. What the unions have lost in numbers, though, they have gained in freedom to maneuver and in symbolic force. They are no longer the vanguard of the revolution. Now they are the shock troops of the bourgeoisie.

Meanwhile a strike by university students, which had begun outside Paris, came to town too. The students wanted smaller classes and more money, and the government didn't foresee any possible sharing of interests between them and the *cheminots*; what's more, it didn't see how a student strike could claim center stage in a country that has suffered consistently from 10 percent unemployment. Yet the government underestimated the extraordinary hold that the word *student* has on the French imagination, a little like the hold the word *farmer* has on Americans. In fact the phrase *student movement* has in France much the same magic that the phrase *family farm* has in America, conjuring up an idealized past, even for people who never took part in a student movement or lived on a family farm. For a week the students and the *cheminots* took turns working over the Chirac-Juppé government, like a veteran tag-team wrestling pair going against a couple of beardless innocents. They did such a good job that more groups began to jump into the ring. First, the Métro workers went out, and then the postal workers, and then the employees of France Télécom. No one knows who may go next.

Though the strike has developed a quasi-revolutionary momentum, it doesn't have anything like a quasi-revolutionary ideology; the slogan of the government functionaries at the heart of the strike is, essentially, "Status quo forever." The tone is entirely middle class; it suggests a vast petit bourgeois ghost dance, trying to summon up, by its fervor and intensity, a certainty that the future will be like the *trentes glorieuses*, the glorious thirty years of French prosperity that ended in the late seventies. That is why even French people who don't belong to unions support the strike; a poll taken a week into the strike showed that just over 60 percent of them were sympathetic to it.

A few days after the demonstration, I went back to the *rôtisseur* to see how the turkey was getting along on its way into town. "It does not look good," he said. "The strike prevents him from moving."

"Was he planning to take the TGV?" I asked.

|||

Although workers and students are striking throughout France, the strike is chiefly a Parisian event. That doesn't make it any less national, since France is a completely centralized country. To achieve in America the effect that the strikers have achieved here, it would be necessary to shut down simultaneously the New York subway, the Washington post office, and the Santa Monica Freeway. These weeks have been unusually cold, and that has made the troubles of the strike more difficult. The strike has even produced an iconography of endurance: lots of pictures of bicyclists and Rollerbladers and sailors, carrying on. But in fact the iconography is a little misleading. More typical sights are the endless *bouchons,* or traffic jams, which have made a twenty-minute trip from the Étoile to the place de Clichy last four hours. On the great boulevards and avenues there is a constant press of cars and people, marches one day and solid, immovable traffic jams the next. But if you walk only a couple of blocks away, in any direction, the city looks especially beautiful, and you can have it to yourself. Despite the strike, all the Christmas decorations are up, shiny red and gold ribbon and green garlands draped like bunting around the display windows of the boutiques. Since almost everyone is busy not getting anywhere in a car, you can be all alone with the gleaming glass storefronts and the Christmas garlands and the sight of your own breath.

The motorcyclists have solved the traffic problem by giving up the streets and simply driving on the sidewalks. As you stroll along the boulevard, you suddenly discover a Harley-Davidson bearing down on you at high speed from among the plane trees. The motorcyclists, who would rather run over a few pedestrians than give up their Hogs, are more truly Parisian than the wan in-line skaters, since the French attitude toward any crisis is not to soldier through it but just to pretend that it isn't happening. (It was in Paris, after all, that Picasso and Sartre sat in a café for four years pretending that the Germans weren't there.)

A deeper and more dramatic version of this national habit of pretending that things haven't happened is what has shaped the strike. What the French strikers want to ignore, at least according to their critics, are the economic facts of the end of the twentieth century: "global capital," the "modern service-based economy," the "tough new competitive conditions of the twenty-first century," all of which, the critics say, can be dealt with only by a more "flexible" labor market. When are these people going to grow up and face reality? seems to be the exasperated question that others in Europe are asking. What the French feel is that for the past half century they have done pretty well by not facing reality—or, anyway, by facing it for one moment and then turning their backs on it for another, in a kind of endless inspired whirl through history. France is a uniquely lovely and supple place to live, and there is a reasonable suspicion here that the British and the Americans and the Germans are trying to hustle the French into what is called a liberal paradise, but what no one here is quite convinced is so paradisiacal. Among the nonunionized, petit bourgeois strike sympathizers, in particular, there is an intransigent and rather admirable level of temperamental resistance to the notion of "reforming" France to suit the global economy. Even Bernard Thibault, the secretary-general of the *cheminots'* union, said not long ago that he was willing to negotiate but that his bottom line was "Citizens must never be transported like merchandise."

In France, of course, not even the merchandise is transported like merchandise. When the turkey arrived at last, a week after the strike began, I got an excited call inviting me to come see it, and when I arrived, the *rôtisseur*, showing it off, pointed out to me how different it was from any bird in an American supermarket. It wasn't frozen, pumped full of cooking oil, or raised in a shed. The bird was supposed to have composed what amounted to a suicide note. "I was raised like a savage, in the forest of the Landes," the turkey's last will and testament began. "I fed on pure corn, wandered in the open air, and slept at night alone in the trees. . . ."

We talked about the strike—the *rôtisseur* seemed to have the same ambivalent sympathies as most other Frenchmen—and I sensed then that he believed that somehow the *cheminots'* strike would help him keep out the frozen turkeys, and the supermarkets they sit in, and the big chains that own the supermarkets. This belief may be as false as the belief that a ghost dance could raise the dead and bring back the buffalo, but it is no less fervently held.

|||

The only things that have been working perfectly during the strike are what I suppose have to be called the instruments of global capitalism. The worldwide courier services are still picking up packages and sending them out overnight across the ocean, faxes buzz and communicate, and the one worker who seemed to make it nonchalantly through the streets to our house was the cable TV installer, who hooked us up so that we could watch the strike on CNN. It's that anxious-making globalized economy that the strikers are responding to, however incoherently.

Everyone here likes to compare what is going on now with what went on in '68. The real point may be that while that was, in retrospect, essentially a cultural revolution in the guise of a political one, '95 seems, so far, to be a political revolution in the

form of a cultural ritual—the big student-and-worker strike—
that isn't really appropriate for it. It isn't appropriate because a
strike, by its nature, is unpredictably disruptive, while the emotions behind this one are deeply conservative. The strike is one
more cry of the heart from people who felt blessed for a long
time and now feel threatened. The turkey, not quite incidentally,
was so much better than any other turkey I have ever eaten that
it might have been an entirely different kind of bird.

The Winter Circus,

CHRISTMAS JOURNAL 1

It is the weather reports on CNN that will scare you most. They must come from a studio in Atlanta, like most things on the cable network, but they tell about the European weather, and only the European weather, and they treat Europe as if it were, for CNN's purposes, one solid block of air with dirt down beneath, one continuous area of high- and low-pressure systems bumping into one another over a happy common land, just like the tristate area, or "here in the Southland," or "up in the heart of the North country," or any of the other cheerful areas into which American television stations divide the country.

The job of the European weatherman (or -woman) seems to be pretty low on the CNN totem pole. They keep changing. One day it is a blow-dried midwesterner; the next a corn-fed, nicely Jane Pauleyish woman; the next a portly black guy. Each one points in turn to the big map of Europe, with the swirling satellite photo superimposed, and then, with the limitless cheeriness of an American announcer, calls out the temperature and tomorrow's forecast for every site of the more intolerable tragedies of the twentieth century.

"If you're headed to Warsaw tonight, you may just want to pack that extra sweater, but if business is pulling you over on that quick trip to St. Petersburg"—quick, impish, professional wink—"you'd better make sure that you've got the overcoat. Looking at snow there *all* night long.

"We're looking at sunny weather throughout Italy, from Rome right up to Venice. Looks like another mild night in France, though of course there'll be snow in the mountains around Savoy. In the Basque country, some *really chilly temperatures. Nice* skiing, though. More mild weather in Prague and Budapest, though looking up at Vienna . . ." All the old capitals of Old Europe, the sites of the ghettoes and the massacres and the opera houses, the border with Spain where they turned the refugees away and Walter Benjamin died in despair, all treated in the spirit, with the same sound, that I can recall from every night in my childhood in West Philadelphia, when "Dr." Somebody or other—a "certified meteorologist"—gave the weather for the tristate area and threw in the highs and lows in Atlantic City "for all of you heading for the shore."

We have won as large a victory as any country has ever won—no empire has ever stood in so much power, cultural, political, economic, military—and all we can do is smile and say that you might want to pack a sweater for the imperial parade.

|||

When the cable television man came to hook us up on the first morning of the general strike, you could hear the demonstrators out on the boulevard, singing and marching. But the bland emissary from the age of global information worked on, stringing the wire and hooking up the decoder boxes. He finally handed us three different remotes and then ran through the thirty-odd channels like a priest reciting the catechism. "Here is CNN, news in America. Here is MTV. Here is French MTV," the cable man explained. "Here is Euronews, in English. Here is Euro-sport." A 49ers-Dolphins game was in progress. There it was, truly, the same familiar ribbon of information and entertainment that girdles the world now—literally (really, truly literally) encir-cling the atmosphere, electric rain. All you have to do is hold out a hand to catch it.

Luke, at least, has found a home, shelter from the electronic rain and global weather. He lives in the Luxembourg Gardens. We go there nearly every day, even in the chill November days among the fallen leaves. The design of the gardens is nearly per-fect for a small child. There is a playground; there is a puppet theater, where he is too small to go yet, but outside the puppet theater there is a woman selling balloons, and every morning he points to his wrist and says his all-purpose word, *bu-bel*, which means balloon, ball, whatever it is meant to mean. But then, when we get to the gardens and the po-faced woman goes to tie the balloon to his wrist, he leaps back with fear and demands to have it taken off again. Approach and avoidance with older women.

He rides the carousel, the fallen leaves piled neatly all around it, and though bent-up it is a beauty. The animals are chipped, the paint is peeling, the giraffe and elephant are missing hooves and tusks, and the carousel is musicless and graceless. The older children ride the outside horses. A God-only-knows-how-old carousel motor complains and heaves and wheezes and finally picks up enough momentum to turn the platform around, while the carousel attendant hands a baton to each of the older chil-dren riding the outside horses. Then he unhooks a pear-shaped wooden egg from the roof of his little station, at the edge of the turning platform, and slips little metal rings with leather tags at-tached into the eggs. As the children race around, the little rings drop one after another into the egg and dangle from its base, the small leather tags acting as a kind of target, a sighting mechanism, so that the children can see the rings. The older children try to catch the rings with the sticks.

It looks tricky; it looks *hard*. The kids have to hold the weather-beaten sticks up just so; there's just one angle, one way to do it. As the carousel picks up speed, it gets going whirring fast, and the hand-eye, or rather hand–eye–painted horse, coordination you need looks terrifyingly accomplished. To make things even harder, if two children are mounted one right behind the other, and the first child lances the ring, it means that the next ring, slipping down, only arrives at the base of the wooden egg as the next child arrives, making it just about impossible to aim. If the first child just knocks the ring, on the other hand, the ring starts trembling widely enough to make a good grab impossible. It is a tough game, and what makes it odder is that there is no reward for doing well at it. I have read about this game all my life: going for the Big Brass Ring! It's an American metaphor. But here there are little tin rings, and no reward for getting them except the satisfaction of having done it. You don't even get to keep the tin rings for a moment of triumph—Look, Mama!—to show the cluttered stick, rings on it like plums on the branch of a plum tree. The keeper takes back the batons before the carousel has even stopped.

It is hard for me to imagine Luke ever doing this: sitting up there, skewering his rings. For the moment, for a long moment, we sit together in the little chariots and just spin. He keeps his eyes locked on the big kids with the sticks, who come under the heading of Everything He Desires: a stick, a task, a seat on the outside horse. (For me, the sticks and rings game on the carousel looks more like a symbolic pageant. A Writer's Life: hard job, done intently, for no reason. Cioran used to walk in these gardens. I wonder if he watched this.) The reward for the Parisian children is, perhaps, the simple continuity, the reality that the spinning will never get a prize, but that it will also never stop.

After all, spinning is its own reward. There wouldn't be carousels if it weren't so.

|||

On nice days, when we don't have time to go all the way to the gardens, Luke and I go to the musical horse outside the *Oiseau de Paradis* ("Bird of Paradise"), a toy store on the boulevard Saint-Germain, and he solemnly rides up and down on it while it plays "Camptown Races." On rainy days, we go to Deyrolle on the rue du Bac. It is an extraordinary place. It is on the second floor—almost all of the second story—of one of the old *hôtels particuliers*. It is, I suppose, a taxidermists' supply house and a supplier too of education charts. But it is also one of the great surrealist sites of Paris. Downstairs, at street level, there is the old-fashioned kind of come-hither wraparound window entrance, so that you enter a deep-set door between two vitrines, an architecture that must have been familiar once in Paris—it was the architecture of every South Street shoe store in my childhood—though it is fairly rare now. (Mostly the windows are one sheet of plate glass, with a kind of false front showing the goods and the store behind.) But here you walk past a "seasonal" window, filled with taxidermized animals and bare minimum decor: artificial fallen leaves for autumn, cotton ball "snow" for winter, a few silk flowers for spring. Sometimes the animals inside the windows change too—an ancient, yellowing polar bear right now represents the Spirit of Christmas—but mostly it is the same bunch all year: a fox, a raccoon, a moose. (The polar bear must have been brought down on the same expedition that is celebrated in the window of a lead soldier store on the rue des Ciseaux, which shows an otherwise unrecorded late-nineteenth-century *French* expedition to the North Pole, with the tricolor hanging over an igloo and reindeer entrecôte in a chef's *sauteuse*.)

When you open the door at Deyrolle, there is a moose on your left, and then an odd display case straight ahead, with snake embryos in little jars of formaldehyde. If you go up the stairs—and Luke will only go up the stairs clutching tightly to my chest—you will find at the top an entire bestiary waiting patiently for your arrival, not in casements or vitrines but just standing on all fours on the floor around the casements and vitrines, looking bored and social, like writers at a New York book party. They just stand there. There are several lions, genuinely terrifying in their direct address. They have been taxidermized—*reanimated* is the correct term—not to look fierce but just to look bored—these are French lions, after all—which of course makes them look more fierce.

And then a baby elephant and a jaguar and a gorilla, all just *there,* with all the other natural things—skeletons and skulls and case upon case of butterflies and beetles—all around. The walls are painted a fading blue-green; the cases are all wood and glass. The main showroom is a two-story space, with a balcony up above. They keep the ordinary farm animals, sheep and goats, up there, looking down on the stars, like the extras in *Les Enfants du Paradis.*

There are also—and this is the weirdest touch—lots of domestic animals, family pets, Siamese and Scotties and cockers, who stand there on the floor too, among the lions and jaguars, looking furtive, forlorn, a little lost. Mme. Orlovska, the owner, who has become a friend, explains that they are unclaimed taxidermed pets from the old Deyrolle regime. Apparently year after year people would come in, weeping and clutching the cold bodies of Fido and Minochette, the house pets, and beg to have them taxidermized, restored, revivified. The taxidermists would go to laborious work, and then, two or three months later, when the pet was at last stuffed into its immortality, the owner, consoled with a new living (though mortal) pet, would have forgotten all about it. No answer to calls or bills or what she calls "commands of conscience." So the unwanted permanent pets—

who were perhaps, as pets always are, mere courtesans of affection, feigning a feeling for food—get replaced, as courtesans will, and find themselves at the feet of the lions and elephants.

The big game are themselves souvenirs of a hotter time in Deyrolle's history, when hunters would have their African catches mounted and leave an extra lion or a leftover gnu to the house, as a sort of tip, like gamblers in Monte Carlo in the same period giving a chip or two to the croupier. The house makes its money now, Madame explains, mostly selling bugs and butterflies to decorators. "We can't find any large game anymore," she complains. "The laws are so absurdly tight. If a lion dies in a circus, we cannot touch it. If an elephant falls over in a zoo, we cannot reanimate it. Is it better for a thing of beauty to die and molder away than to be made a work of art?" (The government is worried, as governments will be, I suppose, that if fallen elephants are turned into merchandise, however lovely, then sooner or later elephants will not just be falling. Elephants will be nudged.)

|||

Luke is as frightened (and fascinated) by the small game as he is by the large; he clings to me tightly throughout—and then every day demands to be taken back. I think he feels about it the same way that I feel about the Baudrillard seminar I am attending at the Beaubourg. It's scary, but you learn something.

I've attended this public seminar, given by Baudrillard and friends at the Beaubourg. Jean Baudrillard is, or anyway *was*, the terror of West Broadway back in the eighties. He was the inventor of the theory of "the simulacra," among much else, and famously insisted that "reality" had disappeared and that all that was left in its place was a world of media images and simulated events. ("The Gulf War Did Not Take Place" was his famous slogan, meaning that it was a pure television production.) Before the seminar I imagined Baudrillard as tall and spectral and high-domed as Barthes had been. He turns out to be a stocky, friendly little guy in his fifties, with a leather jacket and a weather-beaten complexion.

The seminar consists of a three- or four-man panel: an economist; a sociologist; Leo Scher, the all-around thinker. Each gives a presentation, and then Baudrillard comments. The other day, for instance, the economist was giving a lecture on exponentiality. "Exponentiality is fatality," he announced grimly, and went on to point out what every first-year biology student is told, that the "exponential" proliferation of biological life—each codfish has a million codfish children; each codfish child has a million of its own children—means that the codfish, or slime mold or antelope or, for that matter, French intellectuals, would cover the world in ten or so generations, unless there were something—several somethings—there to check them.

(The girl in front of me scribbled in her book, in French, of course, "Exponentiality is Fatality.")

"Therefore," said the economist, "I propose that there must exist in the biological sphere a principle, which I will call the Regulon"—he wrote the word in capitals on the blackboard— "which prevents this from happening. I call this principle the Regulon."

No one protested, or pointed out that, as I think is the case, Darwin (among many others) had solved this problem awhile ago without recourse to the Regulon. (Predators eat most of the codfish; the rest just die. Life is hard; the Regulon is called life, or death.) Baudrillard nodded gravely at the end of the exposition. "But yours underlines the point I am making," he added, almost plaintively. He paused and then pronounced: "There is no Regulon in the Semiosphere." (And she wrote it down and underscored it: "There is no Regulon in the Semiosphere.")

There Is No Regulon in the Semiosphere. There is no way of stopping media signs from proliferating, no natural barrier to the endless flow and reproduction of electronic information, no way of keeping the CNN weatherman out of your sky. There is nothing to eat them. There Is No Regulon in the Semiosphere is a wildly abstract way of saying that there is no "natural predator" to stop the proliferation of movies and television; they do overwhelm the world, and with it reality. It is hard to see how you save the carousel and the musical horse in a world of video games, not because the carousel and musical horse are less attractive to children than the Game Boy, but because the carousel and the musical horse are single things in one fixed place and the video games are everywhere, no Regulon to eat them up.

|||

When I lived here with my family, in the early seventies, there was nothing I liked more than walking up the boulevard Beaumarchais to the Cirque d'Hiver, the Winter Circus. It is a wooden octagon, visible from the boulevard, but set well back, on a little street of its own. A frieze, a kind of parody of the Panathenaic procession, runs around its roof: clowns and jugglers and acrobats in bas-relief. Inside, it has a hushed, intimate quality; the hard wooden bleachers are pitched very high. I don't recall that I ever actually went inside when I was a kid—I was too busy with movies—it just seemed like the right place to walk to. But now we've been to a winter circus at the Winter Circus. The Cirque du Soleil, from back home in Montreal, put on its slightly New Age show, and we took Luke and sat in the top rows. They brought the lights down when the circus began, as though it were a play, which struck me as an odd thing. I always think of circuses sharing the light of their spectators. What happened to the summer circus? I used to think that the circuses must have toured all summer and then came into winter retreat on the rue Amelot. But now I suspect that there was a summer circus once too, but they closed it. The Circus. Regulon got it, I guess.

It was a good circus, though a little long on New Age, New Vaudeville, and Zen acrobats and a little short, absent in fact, on the lions and bears I had promised Luke. (We have a standing joke about lions in Paris; as I push his *poussette,* I announce that I am terrified that there may be lions in this quarter of Paris—"and I'm so scared of lions"—and he roars, lustily.) At the end, though, the troupe took its final bow and threw those little glowing green bracelets up into the audience as a favor. A few came up as high as we were. The French fathers, soccer players to a man, snatched at them from the wrist as they flew up, like men slapping futilely at mosquitoes. I stood up and with years of incompetent Central Park softball under my belt, I pounded the right fist into the left and pulled one in like a pop-up. Then I handed it to Luke. The other fathers in the row looked at me with pure hate. I shrugged and have never felt so obnoxious, so proud, so imperial, so American.

|||

We have found Luke a baby-sitter, or I suppose I have to say a nanny. Her name is Nisha Shaw, she comes from Sri Lanka, has long hair in a beautiful braid and beautiful lilting English, and she is the wife of the philosopher Bernard-Henri Lévy's chauffeur. She is lovely and loving, and she sings all day to Luke in a high-pitched soprano, singing songs that seem just out of focus. "Blowin' in the Wind" and a song called "Softly Sings the Donkey/As he goes to hay/If you don't come with him/He will go away." Softly sings the donkey—the theme tune of the American liberal abroad. We have already, in a few weeks, become a strange island of Sri Lankan, Icelandic-Canadian, West Philadelphian, Franco-American civilization within a bigger culture. I imagine these are songs that she's heard over the radio and in school, songs that are part of her own little monoculture, just as we have made up ours.

Every morning as Luke and I wait for Nisha to arrive before I go to work in my office, we look out from the kitchen into the courtyard. Every morning, just at eight-fifteen, a hand emerges, holding at its end a tablecloth or a sheet or something that it shakes out. She is known as the Shaky Lady, the Aurora, or Dawn Goddess, of our home. We made up a song in her honor—Oh, Shaky Lady/Oh, Shaky Lady, be good to me"—and she seems to shake with such authority, such intensity.

The odd thing in making a big move is the knowledge that your life will be composed of hundreds of small things that you will arrive at only by trial and error, and that for all the strikes and seminars you attend, the real flavor of life will be determined, shaped, by these things. The Semiosphere comes at you in little bursts. Where will your hair be cut? What kind of coffee will you buy, and where? We have been searching for the right mocha, everywhere we go: at La Vieille France, a pastry store on the rue de Buci; at Hédiard, on the place de la Madeleine; at Whittard, an English coffee importer that has a counter in the Conran on the rue du Bac. Our old Dean & DeLuca blend is gone now, and we must find a new one. The Shaky Lady will preside over some kind of coffee, but even she cannot know quite which one, not just yet.

|||

We have been trying to furnish our place—we had minimal furniture in the New York loft, really, chairs and rugs and rattraps—and on Sundays we go up to the Marché aux Puces, the flea market, which remains a wonder, though the only fleas in it all have Platinum American Express cards. (It isn't cheap.) The Métro ride up to the porte de Clignancourt is a joy, though, just for the names of the stations in northern Paris: Château Rouge, Château d'Eau—what *was* the Red Castle? what was the *Water* Tower?—Poissonniers, Gare du Nord, with its lovely, thirties, Gabinish overtones. We come up, back home, at Odéon, under the statue of Danton, and a single limb of a chestnut tree hangs over the Métro stairs. It's dark already at five o'clock, the limb silhouetted against the moonlit sky while the crowd presses against you on the stairs. What an old place France is, the attic bursting with old caned chairs and zinc bars and peeling dressers and varnished settees. The feeling is totally different from an antiques fair in America; this is the attic of a civilization.

Today we stop at Le Biron for lunch; the restaurants up at the flea market—Le Biron, Le Voltaire—are among the few real bistros left, in the sense of simple places with some culinary pretension that maintain an air of joie de vivre. The poor madame is terribly overworked, and we feel for her, but lunch, simple chicken, takes an hour and a half. The *tarte tatin* is very good, though. After lunch, on this freezing cold day, faint light raking through the stalls, Luke and I stop at the little bar with a Django-style swing band: two gypsy guitarists with ancient electrics with f-holes, joined by a good-looking blonde with an alto sax. There's a couple smoking endless Gauloises next to us. I ordered, with a thrilling automatic feeling, a café-calva and a grenadine for Luke. They played the old American songs—"All of Me," "There Will Never Be Another You"—some Jobim too, really swinging it. Martha was off shopping at Vernaison for a plain old table. A perfect half hour.

Martha insisted on taking a cab home, declaring it too cold to get on the Métro. The cabbie, observing Luke, began a disquisition on children. Only children—we explained in French that he won't be, or we hoped he wouldn't be—are, he explained, the cause of the high modern divorce rate: The boy arrives, and the man feels jealous; there is another man in his wife's life (well, another being), and this leads to jealousy, a lover; and the whole cycle over again. (Why a second child would cure this . . .) This is why women must have three children and stay home. "The school instructs," he explained, "but the family educates." I couldn't decide whether to give him a large or small tip.

|||

It is odd to think that for so long people came to Paris mostly for the sex. "City of the naughty spree," Auden wrote disdainfully in the twenties, "La Vie Parisienne, Les Folies-Bergère, Mademoiselle Fifi, bedroom mirrors and bidets, lingerie and adultery." These days the city's reputation for naughtiness has pretty much diminished away to nothing. Now the dirty movies get made in Amsterdam; the dirty drawings get sent in from Tokyo; and Oriental and even German towns, of all places, are the places you go for sexual experiment. (Even the bidets are gone from Paris, mostly converted into bizarre plug-in electric toilets, which roar as they chew up human waste, in a frenzy of sanitary appetite, and then send it out, chastened, down the ordinary water pipes.)

Things have become so run-down, or cleaned up, sexually here that France has even reached the point where it is running a bimbo deficit and has to import its sex objects. Just last week Sharon Stone was flown in to Paris to be made a Chevalier of Arts and Letters by the French minister of culture, M. Philippe Douste-Blazy. The award struck many Parisians as ridiculous, but it was, in its crude way, a logical part of a consistent cultural policy. Despite their reputation, the French are not really cultural chauvinists at all. They remain chauvinists about their judgment, a different thing; increasingly their judgment *is* their culture. They want to be free to continue to reinvent American culture in their own image, finding art forms where back home we saw only hackwork and actresses where we saw only bimbos. (The award to Sharon Stone was for "her services to world culture.") They don't mind if the Americans make the movies so long as they get to pass out the medals. Pinning a decoration on Sharon Stone is the perfect way of looking down your nose at U.S. cultural imperialism while simultaneously fondling its chest.

|||

The one exception to the erotic milding of Paris are the lingerie ads, which still fill the boulevards and billboards. The ads—

particularly the ones for Aubade—are sharply, unsettlingly erotic, to a male viewer, and differ from their American counterparts in not seeming particularly modern. Women are, as we would say, reduced to body parts; the Aubade ads isolate breasts or thighs or legs as relentlessly as a prep chef at KFC, each part dressed up in a somewhat rococo bit of underwear, lace and thong, in sculpted-lit black and white, very Hurrell, with a mocking "rule" underneath it—i.e., "Rule Twenty-four: Feign Indifference."

There is something stimulating but old-fashioned about these posters (which, for a week or two at a time, are everywhere, on every bus stop, on every bus). They are *coquettish*, a word I had never associated with a feeling before. For all the complaints about a new puritanism, the truth is that feminism in America has, by restoring an edge of unpredictability and danger to the way women behave and the way men react to that behavior, added to the total of tension on which desire depends. The edgy, complicated, reverse-spin coding of New York life—this skintight dress is not a come-on but its opposite, a declaration of independence meant not for you but for me—is unknown here. Here, the intellectuals wear black, and the models wear Alaia.

The other evening, for instance, we went to a dinner party where the philosopher Bernard-Henri Lévy appeared with his wife, the amazing-looking Arielle Dombasle (who wore a bathing suit in one of those philosophical-erotic-talky French films, from the time when philosophical-erotic-talky French films were the delight of the Upper West Side). She wore a skintight lamé dress. We saw her a week or so later and she was wearing another clinging lamé dress, as though out of obligation to her own image, her own invention. *Désir* in Paris is surreptitious but not ironic; everyone has affairs, but no one has reverse-spin coding. In New York the woman in the clinging dress is probably a professor at Hunter, while the girl in all black with no makeup reading the

French papers may be Sharon Stone. You could tell by the medal, I suppose.

|||

Mostly, we shop at BHV, the department store on the rue de Rivoli, which has become our home, our Luxembourg Gardens. BHV—the Bazar de l'Hôtel de Ville, the City Hall Bazaar—is always called by its initials (bay-aish-vay), and it is an old store, one of the great nineteenth-century department stores on the Right Bank that are the children of the Galeries Lafayette. As I say, it is on the rue de Rivoli; in fact that famous Robert Doisneau photograph of the two lovers kissing is set on the rue de Rivoli just outside BHV. This is doubly ironic: first, because the narrow strip of the rue de Rivoli in front of BHV is about the last place in the world that you would want to share a passionate kiss—it would be a bit like kissing at the entrance to the BMT near Macy's—and of course, it explains why they did it anyway. They are not sundered lovers but a young couple who have managed to buy an electric oven and emerged alive. Anyone who has spent time at BHV knows that they are kissing not from an onset of passion but from gratitude at having gotten out again.

|||

BHV, in its current form, seems to have been invented by a Frenchman who visited an E. J. Korvette's in Cherry Hill, New Jersey, sometime in the early 1960s and, maddened with love, decided to reproduce it down to the least detail. There's the same smell of popcorn, the same cheery help, the same discount appliances stretching as far as the eye can see. It is the Parisian tradition that the landlord does not supply appliances. They must all be bought, and you take them with you when you leave. We had a whole run of things to buy, none of which, as lifelong Manhattan renters, we had ever had to buy before: a refrigerator, an oven, a stove. We *had*, oddly enough, once bought a wonderful French dishwasher, a Miele, silent as a Greek oracle, to add to our old loft. But we couldn't use even this since most of the old appliances run on American 110 volts, and France uses 220 volts. You either have to get the insides of the machine changed or else buy something new.

We became hypnotized, bewitched by the curious selling rhythms of BHV: a mixture of confidence, arrogance, and an American-style straightforwardness, with the odd difference that here the customer is always, entirely wrong. We bought a toaster, which promptly shorted out the first time we used it. We brought it back. "What did you toast in it?" the return man asked, haughty for all that he was wearing a regulation oversize checked vest, the uniform of BHV. "Raisin brioche," we answered honestly. He looked shocked, disgusted, appalled, though not surprised. "What do you expect if you put bread with raisins in it?" he asked. But he let us have a new one anyway.

|||

The week before Christmas I had to go out to buy Christmas tree lights at the Bon Marché, the Left Bank department store. Ours didn't work, for reasons I don't understand, since a lot of the electric lamps we brought with us *do* work. Apparently some American lights shine in Paris, and some don't, don't ask why. (Henry James wrote whole novels on this theme, after all.) Instead of coming in strands that you can wrap around the tree, though, the French Christmas tree lights come in *guirlandes*—garlands—closed circles of lights without beginnings or endings. A thin cord with a plug at the end shoots out from the middle of the garland. (They cost a fortune too: twenty-five dollars for as many lights as you can get on Canal Street for five.) These garlands are packed into the box just the way strands are—light by light in little cardboard notches in a horizontal row—so it's only when you take them out of the box that you realize that what you've got is a ring, not a rope.

This means that the only way to get the Christmas lights on the Christmas tree is to lasso it. You have to get up on a ladder, hold the lights out as a loop, and then, pitching forward a bit, throw the entire garland right over the top of the tree, rodeo style. This is harder to do than it sounds and even more dangerous than it looks. I suppose you could pick up the tree and shimmy the lights on from down below, like a pair of *caleçons*, but this would require someone to pick up the tree so you could do it. I can't really see the advantages of having a garland over a string. A string is easier to use—you just start at the bottom and wrap it right around the tree, merrily ascending—and this seems to me not cultural prejudice but a practical fact. (But then all cultural prejudices seem like practical facts to the prejudiced.) Still, the garlands are all there is. Martha kept sending me back to buy more.

Even then it wasn't finished. I had had the pointed inspiration of buying blue lights for the Christmas tree this year, whereas in New York we always had white ones. Since we had moved, changed cultures, I couldn't think of a better marker, a clearer declaration of difference and a new beginning, than having blue lights on the tree instead of white ones. But when I brought them home and did my Roy Rogers bit again and we turned them on and then turned off the lights in the living room, no one liked the look of them. The blue lights looked, well, blue. I doggedly, painstakingly packed them back into the box, took them back to the Bon Marché, and tried to exchange them for white lights.

The trouble now was that the new white lights I got were white lights that were all twinkling ones. I saw the word *clignotant* on the box, and I knew that it meant blinking, but somehow I didn't associate the word *blinking* with the concept "These lights blink off and on." It was the same thing with the garlands, come to think of it. It said *guirlande* right on the box, and I knew perfectly well what *guirlande* meant; but I am not yet able to make the transposition from what things say to what they mean. I saw the word *guirlande* on the box, but I didn't quite *believe* it. In New York I believe everything I read, even if it appears in the *New York Post*. In France I am always prepared to give words the benefit of a poetic doubt. I see the word *guirlande* and shrug and think that maybe *garland* is just the French seasonal Christmas light–specific idiom for a string. The box says, "They blink," and I think they don't.

I found this out of course only after I had already put the lights on the tree, plugged them in, and watched them blinking. I liked the effect OK, but Martha was having none of it. She thought it looked horrible—*sequiny and vulgar* were her words—so back I went to Bon Marché on the afternoon of Christmas Eve, for the third time, to buy a garland of unblinking white lights. This time the saleswoman gave me a really hard time. It was bad enough not knowing what color you want, but not even knowing if you wanted shimmer or a solid glow? I got them home at last and felt unreasonably proud of the garland of lights: a closed circle, desire and fulfillment meeting in a neat French ring, and just shining.

|||

For all the talk about globalization, the unification of the world through technology, etc., the truth is that *only* information is being globalized (and then only for people who speak English). There *is* a Regulon in the Semiosphere. It is called a plug. The necessities of life—plugs and voltages and battery types and . . . —are *more* compartmentalized, more provincialized, more exhaustingly different now from country to country from what they were a century or even two centuries ago. A chamber pot, after all, was always a chamber pot in whatever country you happened to be sitting; a pen was a pen since a feather was a feather. But to plug in your computer now takes a range of plugs and adapters—three prongs and two prongs and two small prongs with a big prong and three tiny prongs in a row—that look like sexual aids for jaded courtesans in de Sade. We are unified by our machines and divided up by the outlets we use to *brancher* them.

Fish, too. Fish and plugs are the two great differences, the two things that are never quite alike from country to country. Fish are sort of alike but maddeningly not exactly alike. You have to learn the translations. A *bar* is sort of but not quite a sea bass, a *rouget* like a red snapper but actually smaller and more dapper—weirdly *snappier*. A turbot is not a flounder. Even French oysters, the most delicious in the world, have a salty, sea brine, bracing taste, not better than plump, sweet American oysters, but different—far more different from the difference, real though it is, between French lamb and American, or a French chicken and a good American one.

Globalization stops short at the baseboard and the coastline, wherever the electricity and the seafood come charging in. The reason for the differences are plain enough. You can't farm line-caught fish, and the variety of plugs is the consequence of the basic difference in the European decision to have 220-volt outlets where we have only 110. This means that the Europeans worry more about shocks. They add a third plug to ground the charge, the baseboard equivalent of a social safety net. Each one does it a little differently. The French have light, dapper, rounded three-prong plugs with two little cylindrical probes and a third, thicker one; the British have three immensely heavy prongs; and the Italians, I recall, have an odd, all-in-line arrangement. All of them feature that third grounding element to keep the shocks from passing from the surging current directly into the room and the people who live there. Only America remains ungrounded.

To make the transition from country to country, plug to plug, you also need to know more than anyone can—well, anyway, more than I do—about what things have motors and which don't. (Motors aren't adaptable, even with adapters. You have to get converters for them that turn out to be big, heavy black boxes—odd, in this day of the streamlined and transistorized—that do something or other to the current.)

I plugged in my Stylewriter Mac printer the third day here to print something out, and as it began to print, it also immediately began to smoke. Disconcerting plumes of flame shot from it, as though it were being executed in Florida. Horrible sight, particularly as *it kept on printing* even as it destructed, another symbol of the writer's life. So I had to buy a new one, whose software is all in French. I am learning French computerese: *brancher, imprimer, annuler* . . . Even the common language of the bank machine is odd. We got our bank cards from our new bank, but whereas in New York you have to punch out your code—ours was Luke's birthday—here you are assigned your code by the bank, with no appeals. You are 3431, you are 1676, that is it.

There is a separate language of appliance design in France, which we are learning as we wander, pushing the *poussette* in and out of the rows on the second floor of the BHV. Things are smaller, but they are also much quieter and more streamlined. In the kitchen, when you *branché* them, they *hum*, discreetly, impatiently. They all are slim, white, molded, with the buttons and lights neatly small, rectangular, and inset into the white plastic. The hulking, growling American appliances we had at home, with their freezers on top and their sunset brown faces, all were solid, vast and seemed to imply survivalism. You could go cruising in them. The French appliances, with their blinking lights and set-back press buttons on the front, imply sociability and connection.

It is as if all American appliances dreamed of being cars while all French appliances dreamed of being telephones. The French freezer is, in a French refrigerator, always on the bottom rather than the top and is composed of drawers and secret compartments, like an old writing desk; you are supposed to fill it with culinary billets-doux, little extras, like *petits pois,* instead of with the next week's dinner, as you do in an American freezer.

Parisians love telephones, all kinds of telephones. They don't use them the way that Americans use telephones, but they just *love* them, the way that Americans love cars. (This is partly because telephones are newly arriving; when we lived here in the early seventies, a year went by, and we still didn't have a phone.) The cellular phone, which back in New York still seemed to me to be mostly in the hands of real estate agents and salespeople—those who were, in a sense, on call, biddable—is here in everyone's hands. You walk down the boulevard, and everyone is *talking,* a phone clutched to the ear. What you never see, though, is someone walking down the street with a Walkman on, as everyone does in New York. (I miss my walks with my Walkman, in fact, probably more than any other single thing about life here so far: the music, the isolation, the sense of life as a sound track, the pure release of it. Nobody here wants to shut the city out. They are talkers, not silent listeners.)

They don't have answering machines either, or at least don't rely on them to do all the work of protection and sorting and screening that New Yorkers do. If you call people, and they're home, they answer; they have the same law-abiding approach to these calls that Americans have to parking. You park where you're supposed to park, whereas people in Paris will park anywhere. It is not so much that the phone transformed France and the car transformed America as that both fitted right in, as I suppose technologies must, with what people had wanted all along. Not new desires made by new machines but new machines matching the same old needs. The phone replaced the system of pneumatic messages—the *pneus*—that used to race around Paris, and there is something *pneu* about them even now: French telephone conversations tend to be sharp, pointy, rather than expansive.

There is an odd, seemingly purposeful looking-glass quality to a lot of the things we have to buy. The Braun coffeemaker with a thermos that we had in New York is available here, but oddly only in black, whereas the one in New York was available only in white.

Luke loves BHV for the music. All day long it plays excited, taped Christmas shopping announcements, backed with appropriate tunes. Some of the tunes we recognize—it plays the *Looney Tunes* theme, for instance—and some seem vaguely familiar but are hard to name, so we give our own names to them: "The Love Theme from BHV," "BHV's Victory at Sea," and the "BHV Christmas Anthem." His ears undimmed by fifteen years of the IRT, he can hear them all even over the din of appliance shopping, and when he notices a favorite, he rises from his stroller, a cobra in mittens, and sways solemnly back and forth.

About five days before Christmas, BHV was decked out for the holidays, though, with the strikes shutting down transportation, there was hardly a soul in sight. Twenty years ago there was no Christmas in Paris. Oh, there was a holiday, of course, and even the gaunt, Gaullist figure of Père Noël, an ascetic and intellectualized version of Santa. But the great American department store potlatch was unknown. All that's changed beyond recognition now. That central ritual of bountiful capitalism, the department store Christmas, is in late but absurdly full bloom here, and with an American flavor so pronounced that it hardly seems American anymore, just part of an international style. The dome of Printemps, on the boulevard Haussmann, for instance, is this year decorated with stylized Stars and Stripes and life-size figures of Jimmy Dean and Marilyn and Clark and Bogie and even Babe Ruth. Now at BHV there are artificial evergreens, and tree decoration departments, and a Santa—get your picture with the old guy—and boughs of evergreen hung everywhere, and artificial snow, even though it never snows in Paris at all. On this afternoon, the "BHV Christmas Anthem" began to rise from every loudspeaker on every floor. Only now, as Luke swayed in his stroller, I could hear it clearly for the first time, loud and ringing through the almost empty store, and I understood at last why it had sounded so oddly familiar. It was the theme from *Entertainment Tonight*. Maybe there is no Regulon in the Semiosphere after all.

Distant
Errors

The Rules
of the Sport

Late last year the French government assembled a committee to choose a name for the vast new stadium that's being built in a Paris suburb. The committee included an actor, an "artiste," some functionaries, and even a few athletes. It took a long time deliberating over its choice. Names were submitted: Some people liked the idea of naming the stadium after Verlaine or Saint-Exupéry, and lots of others liked the idea of calling it Le Stade Platini, after Michel Platini, the great French soccer player. At last, in December, the committee announced that it had come to a decision, and the government decided to broadcast the verdict on television. The scene was a little like the end of the Simpson trial: the worried-looking jurors filing to their seats, the pause as the envelope was handed to the minister of youth and sports, the minister clearing his throat to read the decision to the nation. The stadium that would represent France to the world, he announced, would be called (long, dramatic pause) Le Stade de

France. The French Stadium. "Banal and beautiful at the same time," one journalist wrote. "Obvious and seductive. Timeless and unalterable."

It wasn't hard to detect, beneath the sturdy, patriotic surface of the new name, an undercurrent of ironic, derisory minimalism. The French are prepared to be formally enthusiastic about American-style stadiums and American-style sports, but they are not going to get carried away by it all. This realization first came home to me when I joined a pioneer health club on the Left Bank and spent four months unsuccessfully trying to get some exercise there.

"An American gym?" Parisians asked when I said that I was looking for someplace to work out, and at first I didn't know what to say. What would a French gym be like? Someone suggested that my wife and I join the Health Club at the Ritz; that was about as French as a gym could get. This sounded like a nice, glamorous thing to do, so we went for a trial visit. I ran out of the locker room and dived into the pool. White legs were dangling all around me—crowded to the edges, as though their owners were clinging to the sides of the pool in fear—and only after I rose to the surface did I see that the owners were all hanging from the edge of the pool, eating tea sandwiches off silver platters. Finally, after we'd done a lot of asking around, someone suggested a newly opening "New York–style" gym, which I'll call the Régiment Rouge. One afternoon Martha and I walked over to see what it was like and found it down at the end of a long, winding street. The gym was wedged into the bottom two floors of an institutional-looking Haussmann-era building. We went in and found ourselves surrounded by the virtuous sounds of Activity—sawing and hammering and other plaster dust–producing noises. The bruit seemed to be rising from a cavernlike area in the basement. At the top of a grand opera–style staircase that led to the basement were three or four fabulously chic young women in red tracksuits—the Régiment Rouge!—that still managed to be fairly form-clinging. The women all had ravishing long hair and lightly applied makeup. When we told them that we wanted to *abonner*—subscribe—one of them whisked us off to her office and gave us the full spiel on the Régiment Rouge. It was going to bring the rigorous, uncompromising spirit of the New York health club to Paris: its discipline, its toughness, its *regimental* quality. They were just in the middle of having the work done— one could hear this downstairs—and it would all be finished by the end of the month. The locker rooms, the *appareils Nautilus,* the stationary bicycles with electronic displays, the steam baths, the massage tables—everything would be not just *à l'américaine* but *très New Yorkais.* Best of all, she went on, they had organized a special "high-intensity" program in which, for the annual sum of about two thousand francs (four hundred dollars), you could make an inexorable New York–style commitment to your physique and visit the gym as often as once a week.

It was obvious that the once-a-week deal was the winner—the closer, in Mamet language—and that though she had a million arguments ready for people who thought that when it came to *forme,* once a week might be going overboard, she had nothing at all ready for people who thought once a week might not be *forme* enough. We asked her if we could possibly come more often than that, and she cautiously asked us what we meant by "often." Well, three, perhaps four times a week, we said. It was not unknown, we added quickly, apologetically, for New Yorkers to visit a gym on an impulse, almost daily. Some New Yorkers, for that matter, arranged to go to their health club every morning before work. She echoed this cautiously too: They rise from their beds and exercise vigorously before breakfast? Yes, we said weakly. That must be a wearing regimen, she commented politely.

She paused, and then she said, wonderingly, "Ah, you mean you wish to *abonner* for an infinite number of visits?" After much fooling around with numbers and hurried, hushed conferences with other members of the regiment, she arrived at a price for an infinity of *forme*. The difference between once a week and infinity, by the way, turned out to be surprisingly small, improvised prices being one of the unpredictable pleasures of Paris life. She opened dossiers for both of us; you can't do anything in France without having a dossier opened on your behalf.

A week later I dug out my old gym bag, cranked up my Walkman, and set off for the Régiment Rouge. When I arrived, the young women in the red tracksuits were still standing there. They looked more ravishing than ever. I picked out our consultant from the group and told her I was ready to get *en forme*. "Alas, the work continues," she announced. I peered down. The renovation seemed to have stopped just where it had been when I saw it before. "The *vestiaires* and the *appareils* will now be installed next month," she said. "However, we are having classes all week long, on an emergency basis, and the Régiment Rouge wishes to make you an award for your patience." Then she gave me a bag of chocolate truffles. (There is a health food store on the rue du Bac that displays in its window its own brand of chocolates and its own marque of champagne. *Tout Biologique!* a sign alongside them proclaims virtuously.) I ate one.

A week after that we got a phone call from our consultant. She proudly announced that things were ready at last, and there would be a crepe party in honor of the opening. "We will have apricot jam and *crème de marrons*," she explained. We went to the crepe party. Everyone—would-be members and the girls in the red tracksuits—walked around eating stuffed crepes and admiring the pristine, shiny, untouched Nautilus machines and exercise bikes and free weights.

A few days later I went back again to try to use the gym, but on my way into the regimen room I was stopped by another of the girls in red tracksuits. Before one could start work on the machines, she explained, it was necessary that one have a rendezvous with a *professeur*. When I arrived the next day for my rendezvous, the *professeur*—another girl in a red tracksuit—was waiting for me in the little office. She had my dossier out, and she was reviewing it seriously.

"Aren't we going to demonstrate the system of the machines?" I asked.

"Ah, that is for the future. This is the oral part of the rendezvous, where we review your body and its desires," she said. If I blushed, she certainly didn't. She made a lot of notes and then snapped my dossier shut and said that soon, she hoped, we could begin.

|||

While all this was going on, I tried to tell Parisians about it, and I could see that they couldn't see what, exactly, I thought was strange. The absence of the whole rhetoric and cult of sports and exercise is the single greatest difference between daily life in France and daily life in America. It's true that French women's magazines are as deeply preoccupied with body image and appearance as American ones. But they are confident that all problems can be solved by lotions. The number of French ointments guaranteed to eliminate fat from the female body seems limitless, and no pharmacy window is complete without a startlingly erotic ad for the Fesse-Uplift—an electrical buttock stimulator, guaranteed to eliminate fat by a steady stream of "small, not unpleasing shocks administered to the area," the ad says. *Votre Beauté,* the *Self* of France, recently had a special issue on losing weight. There were articles on electrical stimulation, on nutrition (raw carrots will help you lose weight; cooked carrots won't), on antiobesity pills, and on something called passive exercise. There was also, of course, a long article on reducing lotions. Finally, buried in the back, among the lonely-hearts ads, was a single, vaguely illicit-looking page of workout diagrams. If all else fails.

Among men, an enthusiasm for sport simply segregates you in a separate universe: You are a sportsman or you are not. The idea of sports as a lingua franca meant to pick up the slack in male conversations is completely alien here. The awkwardnesses that in America can be bridged by a hearty "See the Knicks last night?" exist here, but nobody bridges them by talking about sports. Sport is a hobby and has clinging to it any hobby's slightly disreputable air of pathos. Also, sport is an immigrant preoccupation: Whereas in America it acts as a common church, here it is still low church. There is a daily sports paper here, titled *L'Équipe,* but it is meant for enthusiasts; *Le Monde* devotes one or two pages to the subject, and *Libération* only a few pages more. Paris has one good soccer team (whereas London alone has six), but you could walk the length and breadth of Saint-Germain and not see a single bit of evidence—not a sign in a window, a pennant in a bar, or a sweater on a supporter—that it exists. France has some terrific footballers, but they play mostly in England and Italy. The nearest thing to a Magic-Michael showdown in France is the *affrontements* of the French-born players David Ginola and Eric Cantona, but those take place across the Channel, in the North of England, where Ginola plays for Newcastle and Cantona for Manchester United. Still, Ginola and Cantona are regularly dunned by *L'Équipe* to declare their love of country. "But *la France* I think of all the time! Not only when I play Manchester! She is in my head and in my heart!" Ginola declared recently. It sounded a little forced to me, but apparently *L'Équipe* was satisfied. Legend has it that among Frenchmen sex and food are supposed to take the place of sports ("Did you perhaps see the petite blonde with the immense *balcon, mon vieux*?"), but in fact they don't. What the French do to bridge the uneasy competitive silences that seem to be the price of a Y chromosome is talk about government and particularly about the incompetence of government ministers; which minister has outdone the others in self-important pomposity is viewed as a competitive event. Though the subject is different, the tone is almost exactly the same as that of American sports talk. "Did you see Léotard on the eight o'clock last night?" one Parisian man might ask another. (The news is on at eight here.) Then they both shake their heads woefully, with that half smile, half smirk that New York men reserve for Mets relief pitchers: *beyond* pathetic.

If talking about the bureaucracy takes the place of talking about sports, getting involved with the bureaucracy takes the place of exercise. Every French man and woman is engaged in a constant entanglement with one ministry or another, and I have come to realize that these entanglements are what take the place of going to a gym where people actually work out. Three or four days a week you're given something to do that is time-consuming, takes you out of yourself, is mildly painful, forces you into close proximity with strangers, and ends, usually, with a surprising rush of exhilaration: "Hey, I did it." Every French ministry is, like a Nautilus machine, thoughtfully designed to provide maximum possible resistance to your efforts, only to give way just at the moment of total mental failure. Parisians emerge from the government buildings on the Île de la Cité feeling just the way New Yorkers do after a good workout: aching and exhausted but on top of the world.

|||

A few days after my oral interview I went back to the Régiment Rouge, and this time I actually got on one of the stationary bicycles and rode it for twenty-four minutes. I was in full New York regalia (sweatpants, headband, Walkman) and did it in good New York form (Stones blasting in my headphones, crying out, "One minute!" when there was a minute left to go). By now there were other people at the gym, though the man on the bicycle next to me was going at a speed barely fast enough to sustain life, while the woman beside him, who was on a treadmill, was walking at the right speed for window-shopping on the boulevard Saint-Germain on an especially sunny day when your heart is filled with love and your pockets are filled with money; it was as though she had set the machine at "Saunter."

I got down from my bike perspiring right through my T-shirt—the first person on the Left Bank, I thought proudly, to break a sweat at a gym. I walked back to the desk. "A towel, please," I panted (in French, of course). The girl in the red tracksuit at the desk gave me a long, steady, opaque look. I thought that maybe I had got the word for towel wrong (I hadn't, though), and after I asked again and got the same look in return, I thought it wise to try to describe its function. My description sounded like a definition from Dr. Johnson's dictionary: that thing which is used in the process of removing water from the surfaces of your body in the moments after its immersion. "Ah," she said. "Of course. A towel. We have none yet." She looked off into the middle distance. "This," she said at last, "is envisaged." I looked at her dumbly, pleadingly, the reality dawning on me. Then I walked all the way home, moist as a chocolate mousse.

|||

A couple of days later I went for what I thought would be my last visit to the Préfecture de Police to get my *carte de séjour,* a process that had involved a four-ministry workout stretching over three months. The functionary seemed ready to give it to me—she was actually holding it out across the desk—but then she suddenly took one last look at the dossier the préfecture had on me and noticed something that she had somehow missed before.

"*Alors, monsieur,*" she said, "you have not yet had a physical examination to make sure that you are in sufficiently good health to remain in France."

I didn't know what to say. "I belong to a gym," I said at last, and I showed her my card from the regiment.

"Well," she said, "this will be useful for your dossier." I couldn't argue with that.

The Chill

It was a very cold winter here, and it felt even colder. "It's the dampness," every shivering Parisian explained. But really it was something else. A visitor who has walked bareheaded and oblivious through twenty arctic Canadian winters found that, out for a walk in Paris with the temperature in the high thirties, he was pulling a woolen hat over his ears and huddling in doorways and stopping in cafés to drink hot wine and then quickly heading home.

What has made it seem so cold is the French gift for social dramatization: A cold day is a cold day, and everyone conspires to give it presence. Looking cold is also a way of making it plain that you are feeling miserable, a way to dramatize the "economic horror" that has overtaken Paris. In the chill a series of smaller social pageants have been played out, including a hostage taking, a craze for a strange book on economics, a growing conviction that the way out of the crisis is for everyone to stop working, a campaign against immigrants that led to mass civil disobedience by intellectuals, and visits by two foreigners bringing messages of deliverance.

The hostage taking at the Crédit Foncier de France, a semi-public, or state-supported, mortgage lender, was the first and the most improbable of the economic dramas. The Crédit Foncier was practically bankrupt, and the government decided to fob off parts of it on anybody who wanted bits of a failing bank. Its employees then decided that the best way to persuade the government to reconsider this plan was to go to the top and kidnap the president, a M. Jérôme Meyssonier. Not only did M. Meyssonier stay on as a hostage, but he supposedly made it the only condition of his imprisonment that no photographer be allowed to take a picture of him sleeping on a cot in his office. The employees agreed, and even decided to keep the bank open for business while the boss was being held incommunicado. Then they too decided to sleep in the building, presumably as an act of solidarity with the boss they had just imprisoned.

Hostage taking of this kind has become more or less routine here, kidnapping the boss being to the French economic crisis what firing the employees was to the American one. Over the past few years a number of French bosses, including some at Moët et Chandon, have been held hostage. There's actually a nice word for telling the *patron* to go to his room and stay there: He is merely being "sequestered," which, as euphemisms go, seems a fair trade for the Anglo-Saxon *downsizing*.

The hostage takings, naturally, are almost entirely symbolic: If M. Meyssonier had really wanted to leave, he could have left. The melodrama of the "sequestration" was nonetheless mistaken by some foreign observers for the real thing. It's easy to exaggerate the scale of the French crisis; the French do it themselves. The secondary, or symbolic, point of an action is often as clear as the primary, or practical, reality, and sometimes a lot clearer. At Christmastime in 1995 many journalists were enthralled by the masses of ordinary people who were out on the streets every day in the tens of thousands, symbolically showing their solidarity with striking Métro drivers. It was easy to miss the real point, which is that what everybody was doing on the streets was walking to work.

One economic problem is especially acute here: Unemployment—or *chômage,* as it's called—has hovered around 12 percent for the last two years. Most of the other problems, the ones that create the sense of crisis, are anticipatory. They grow out of the fear that the right-wing government's tentative attempts at reform will eventually corral France into an "Anglo-Saxon" economy, where an unleashed free market will make everybody do awful jobs for no money, forever. No one is reassured by the stridently triumphal tones of American free-marketers. After a recent trip to New York one French journalist remarked that leafing through a copy of *Forbes* or *Fortune* is like reading the operating manual of a strangely sanctimonious pirate ship.

These days one popular solution to the economic crisis is for everyone to stop working. The movement to lower the universal retirement age to fifty-five is the closest thing to a mass economic uprising that the country has seen; without the support of even the labor unions, to say nothing of the bemused parties of left or right, it is sweeping the country. It started last November, when striking truck drivers blockaded highways and ports to secure their right to retire at fifty-five. The government, faced with a choice between calling out the army and giving in, gave in. There was a general feeling that social justice had been done: Truck drivers work long hours, away from their families, and letting them stop for good at fifty-five seemed fair.

Several weeks later people started to realize that after all, the truck drivers' lot wasn't that much harder than everybody else's, and the idea of universal retirement at fifty-five really took flight. In January one of the public transportation unions decided to demand universal retirement at fifty-five, and despite the opposition of the respectable left, by mid-February a poll revealed that almost 70 percent of the population was in favor of stopping work at fifty-five.

The *folie* for fifty-five can be seen as a nice populist rebound on an idea first put forward by employers. For years businesses had been able to draw on a public fund (the Fonds National pour l'Emploi) in order to encourage workers to take early retirement. At the same time, the idea of reducing the length of the workweek has been debated; many people, for instance, had proposed moving to a four-day week, so that a few young workers might be shoehorned in on Fridays. In the minds of many working people, though, the debate about a shorter workweek got mixed up with the truck drivers' retirement coup, and the two together produced a sweeping, simple, plausible-sounding solution to the *crise*: Since the unemployed would benefit if everyone worked a little bit less, wouldn't they benefit even more if everyone stopped working a lot sooner?

|||

The national craze for early retirement may be an employees' twist on an employers' gimmick, but its roots are cultural. Retirement isn't scary here. In America one unmentioned aspect of the Social Security debate is the feeling people have that to stop working is, in a sense, to stop living. It is the vestibule of death. In France there is no equivalent anxiety—and there are no great Florida-style gulags for the elderly. One of the striking things about Paris is that it is filled with old people who actually look old: bent, fitted out with canes, but dining and lunching and taking the air and walking their small, indifferent dogs along with everybody else. The humiliations visited on old people in America—dressed up like six-year-olds, in shorts and T-shirts and sneakers, imploding with rage—aren't common here. The romance of retirement is strong. The right-wing daily *Figaro*, for instance, though editorially opposed to the move for very early

retirement, ran a series of pieces about the "young retired"—
people still in their forties or fifties who have managed to stop
working. The series described people who at last have time to
"reflect"; it was written in exactly the same admiring spirit that
an American daily might use for a series about old people who
are as busy as all get-out.

For Parisians the pleasure of quitting isn't far to seek. Many of
them come from the country—or, at least, feel attached to a particular village—so the idea of *returning* has a certain appeal.
They are not being sent to Florida; they are just going home. People who remain here in town find that life becomes interesting
when they stop working. Everyone who attends French public
lectures knows that the most visible, and most audible, element
in the crowd is the phalanx of the retired. Sometimes they
present a bit of a problem, since they tend to be contentious, and
when the subject comes within their purview—if it's the Third
Republic, say, or the Second World War—they feel free to speak
up and correct the lecturer.

|||

Not long ago somebody referred to the debate on Social Security
in America as being distorted by "black helicopter" thinking. In
France there is something that might be called "white helicopter" thinking. The American populist belief is that there is a
secret multinational agency ready to swoop down from the skies
and make everybody work for the government; the French populist belief is that there is a secret government agency that may
yet swoop down from the skies and give everybody a larger
pension.

L'Horreur Économique, the extreme manifesto of white helicopter thought, is the most successful book of the last several
publishing seasons. A treatise by the novelist and essayist Vi-
viane Forrester, it has sold a couple of hundred thousand copies
in six months, and in November it won the Prix Médicis, which

is a little like a French Pulitzer Prize. Forrester is a minor bellet-trist whose earlier work included popular studies of Virginia Woolf and van Gogh. Not surprisingly, in *L'Horreur Économique* she has produced a work of political economy with all the economics, and most of the politics, left out. Unburdened by pie charts, statistics, or much else in the way of argument or evidence, the book is written in a tone of steady, murmuring apocalyptic dissent, with an occasional perky nod to a familiar neoliberal argument. The total effect is of a collaboration between Robert Reich and Rimbaud. Barely into the first chapter the author flatly announces that the logic of globalization will lead to an Auschwitz of the unemployed. "From exploitation to exclusion, from exclusion to elimination," she writes. "Is it such an unlikely scenario?"

The reader eventually comes to the realization that Forrester is not arguing against the free market, or even against globaliza-tion, but against the original sin of commerce—against buying and selling and hiring and firing and getting and spending. Her book is a pure expression of the old French romance of a radical alternative, with the ancient Catholic prejudices against usury, simony, and the rest translated into a curious kind of dinner party nihilism. Of course, the trouble with reviving the romance of the radical alternative is that the only radical alternative remaining is the extreme right-winger Jean-Marie Le Pen, who isn't romantic at all.

Laurent Joffrin, the editor of the left-wing daily *Libération*, likes to say that Forrester's book is a "symptom." "The fears are ir-rational, psychological, but they are real," he says. He himself is a kind of neo-Keynesian, and like many other sensible people here, he thinks that for all the hysteria, the economic *crise* is not really very deep and could be soothed by a little deficit spending. But the Keynesian medicine is forbidden by the rules of the Maastricht Treaty, which is to lead to European economic union and which, for the sake of German confidence, prohibits new deficit spending.

In any case, there's something emotionally unsatisfying about the Keynesian message. It is like going to the doctor in the certainty that you're dying of tuberculosis, only to be told that your trouble is that your shoes are too tight. In America, and even more so in England, the triumphant free market has a rhetoric, and even a kind of poetry, of its own, visible in the *Economist* and the *Spectator* and the *Telegraph*: witty, trumpet-sharp, exuberant, hardhearted. In France there is a knack of small shopkeeping and a high rhetoric of the state, but there will never be a high rhetoric of shopkeeping.

|||

By the end of February a new social movement was sweeping the papers and the streets. This one came from the left, in reaction to a new bill that attempted to appease Le Pen supporters by jumping up and down on illegal immigrants. The most obnoxious aspect of the Debré bill—named after the interior minister— was a requirement that people who had foreign guests in their homes inform the police when the foreigners left. This provision was so reminiscent of the Vichy laws, which made denouncing Jews a social obligation, that the entire French intellectual class launched a series of petitions against it. Famous artists and directors announced (theatrically, and as a dare-you-to-do-something-about-it principle, rather than as actual fact) that they were lodging illegal immigrants. The petitions flooded the newspapers and were signed by groups: directors, actors, philosophers, and even dentists. A massive demonstration was held, drawing as few as thirty thousand people (the government counting the marchers) or as many as a hundred thousand (the marchers counting themselves).

The provision was immediately withdrawn, but everyone agreed it was depressing that the government had been swayed by Le Pen's absurd notion that France's economic problems have to do with the presence of immigrants, legal or illegal. Many people, including numerous petition signers, also thought there was a depressing element of coercive self-congratulation about the marchers. The protest reached its climax when protesters, got up as deportees, arrived at the Gare de l'Est to reenact the deportations of the forties. This struck even many sympathetic watchers as being in *mauvais goût*.

|||

On a recent Saturday, at the first children's concert of the season at the beautiful new Cité de la Musique, the union of part-time artists, which had been threatening to strike over *their* pension predicament, decided instead to educate the audience. Before a Rameau pastorale began, a representative of the union harangued the five-year-olds for fifteen minutes on the role of itinerant workers in the arts, and about the modalities of their contributions to the national pension fund, and how the government was imperiling their retirement. The five-year-olds listened respectfully and then gave him a big hand.

In the midst of the economic gloom Bill Gates came to France. Not since Wilbur Wright, back in 1908, has an American arrived in France quite so imbued with the mystique of American inventiveness, industry, and technological hocus-pocus. Bill Gates came here with a masterpiece, the *Leonardo Codex,* and it has gone on display in the Musée du Luxembourg, but his visit seems unlikely to produce a masterpiece, as Wilbur Wright's did. Wright became the subject of one of the great portraits by the boy genius Jacques-Henri Lartigue, the Mozart of photography, which summed up the early-twentieth-century French view of American technological wizardry; grave, dignified, pure. Bill Gates doesn't have the bone structure, and anyway, the French cult of Gates is strangely indeterminate. He is described, variously, as the father of the Internet and the creator of popular computing—as anything except what he is, which is the head of a gigantic corporation. He is a symbol divorced from his invention, an aviator without an airplane.

Nonetheless he is presumed to know something. "What France needs is its own Bill Gates," the governor of the Bank of France announced. Gates's message to the French, which is essentially that buying Windows will lead to mass happiness, was symbolically linked with that of another celebrated recent visitor, the German philosopher Jürgen Habermas. Habermas is the last of Europe's "master thinkers," and he gave a series of lectures at the Collège de France. His books and lectures have been the subject of reports in *Le Monde* and *L'Express* and on the television news. It seems that Habermas has replaced his old theory of the state, which was that there is no natural basis for it outside of a bunch of human conventions, with a new theory, which is that the natural basis for the state is the human habit of arguing about whether or not it has one. The argument is somewhat opaque, but it has produced a nice catchphrase, "social communication." That, rather than the social contract, is to be the basis of the new society, and a hope now faintly glimmers that between Habermas and Gates—between the German philosopher who tells you that you need only connect and the American businessman who will sell you the software to let you do it—a new, comprehensive social theory is around the corner.

Some people just get fed up waiting. After five days in mostly happy captivity at Crédit Foncier, Jérôme Meyssonier decided that he'd had enough. "*Ça sufit,*" the president announced to his employees, and that afternoon he went home. Curiously, he had become, in the interim, a kind of hero to the very people who were keeping him locked up. "Meyssonier is with us!" the employees of the Crédit Foncier cried as their boss emerged into the light. (Later in the week they added to that slogan an even better one: "The semipublic will never surrender!") On television Meyssonier was seen smiling weakly. He looked worn out and about ready to quit, but then perhaps this should not be a surprise. M. Meyssonier is fifty-five.

A Tale
of Two Cafés

I have been brooding a lot lately on what I have come to think of as the Two-Café Problem. The form is borrowed from the old Three-Body Problem, which perplexed mathematicians late into the nineteenth century, and which, as I vaguely understand it, involved calculating the weird swerves and dodges that three planets worked on each other when the force of gravity was working on them all. My problem looks simpler, because all it involves is the interaction of a couple of places in Paris where you can eat omelets and drink coffee. It's still pretty tricky, though, because what fills in for gravity is the force of fashion—arbitrary, or arbitrary-seeming, taste—which in Paris is powerful enough to turn planets from their orbits and make every apple fall upward.

I began to brood not long ago, on a beautiful Saturday in October, when I arranged to meet my friend Nicole Wisniak at the Café de Flore, on the boulevard Saint-Germain, for lunch. Nicole is the editor, publisher, advertising account manager, and art director of the magazine *Égoiste* and is a woman of such original chic that in her presence I feel even more ingenuous and American than I usually do, as though pinned to the back of my jacket were a particularly embarrassing American license plate: "Pennsylvania: The Keystone State" or "Explore Minnesota: 10,000 Lakes."

When we got to the Flore and looked around, upstairs and down, we couldn't find an empty table—that kind of Saturday— so we went outside and thought about where to go. I looked, a little longingly, at Les Deux Magots, just down the street, on the place Saint-Germain-des-Prés. The two cafés are separated only by the tiny, narrow rue Saint-Benoît. I turned to Nicole. "Why don't we just go in there?" I said.

A smile, one of slight squeamishness mixed with incapacity, passed across Nicole's face. "I don't know," she said, at a loss for the usual epigrammatic summary of the situation. "We used to go there, I think . . . twenty years ago. . . ." Her voice trailed off, and again she got a funny smile on her face. She couldn't say why, but she knew that it was impossible.

A taboo as real as any that Malinowski studied among the Trobriand Islanders kept us out, though why it existed and how it kept its spell I had no idea. Still, one of the things you learn if you live as a curious observer (or as an observed curiosity) on the fringes of the fashionable world in Paris is that the Flore remains the most fashionable place in Paris, while the Deux Magots was long ago abandoned by people who think of themselves as belonging to the world, to *ce pays-ci*—this country here, as the inhabitants of Versailles called *their* little fashionable island. Somehow, at some point, in a past that was right around the corner but—to Nicole, at least—was irretrievable, something had happened to make the Café de Flore the most fashionable place in Paris and the Deux Magots the least.

|||

In Paris explanations come in a predictable sequence, no matter what is being explained. First comes the explanation in terms of the unique, romantic individual, then the explanation in terms of ideological absolutes, and then the explanation in terms of the futility of all explanation. So, for instance, if your clothes dryer breaks down and you want to get the people from BHV—the strange Sears, Roebuck of Paris—to come fix it, you will be told, first, that only one man knows how it works and he cannot be found (explanation in terms of the gifts of the romanticized individual); next, that it cannot be fixed for a week because of a store policy (explanation in terms of ideological necessity); and, finally, that you are perfectly right to find all this exasperating, but nothing can be done, because it is in the nature of things for a dryer to break down, dryers are like that (futility of explanation itself). "They are sensitive machines; they are ill suited to the task; no one has ever made one successfully," the store bureau-crat in charge of service says, sighing. *"C'est normal."* And what works small works big too. The same sequence that explains the broken dryer also governs the explanations of the French Revo-lution that have been offered by the major French historians. "Voltaire did all this!" was de La Villette's explanation (only one workman); an inevitable fight between the bourgeoisie and the aristocrats, the Marxists said (store policy); until, finally, Fou-cault announced that there is nothing really worth explaining in the coming of the Reign of Terror, since everything in Western culture, seen properly, is a reign of terror (all dryers are like that).

"It's a good question," a friend who has been a figure in the French media since the forties, and who eats lunch at the Flore every day, told me when I quizzed him about why, and when, ex-actly, and how the Flore had outstripped the Deux Magots. We were sitting, as it happened, at the Flore, eating good, wildly overpriced omelets. The downstairs room was as pleasantly red and melancholy as it always is, with its square, rather than round, tables, which give the impression that all the tables are corner tables.

In the week or so since my first inquiry I had been doing some reading. The Deux Magots and the Flore had, I knew, existed beside each other for more than a century. The Flore had long had a white marquee with green lettering, the Deux Magots a green marquee with gilt lettering. The interior of the Flore had always been decorated in red leather—what the French call moleskin— and the Deux Magots in brown. But I had only just learned that like so many timeless things in Paris, they got timeless right after the horror of the Franco-Prussian War. Although there had always been a church at Saint-Germain, the topography of the place Saint-Germain—the square itself—dates back only to the 1870s.

The Deux Magots is the modest inheritor of a silk lingerie store of that name that stood on the spot for decades, until the 1860s, when the growth of the big department stores across the river drove it out of business. The owners eventually rented out the space to a *café liquoriste,* which kept the name and started serving coffee. No one knows exactly when the two famous statues of Chinese mandarins—the Deux Magots—were installed; Anatole France, in his memoirs, written at the turn of the century, speaks of a big picture of three *magots* that used to hang in the lingerie store. The Flore, on the other hand, has no prehistory; founded in 1870, it was always a café and was called the Flore because of a statue of the goddess Flora that used to stand outside. Then, in 1880, Léonard Lipp, an Alsatian who had fled the German occupation of his province, opened a *brasserie* across the street, and the basic topography of the new square was in place.

For many years the Deux Magots was the more famous and fashionable of the two cafés. It was there that Oscar Wilde went to drink after he left England; he died about five blocks away. And it was there that Joyce went to drink Swiss white wine, with everybody except Hemingway, with whom he drank dry sherry, because Hemingway wasn't everybody. (That's how Hemingway tells it, anyway.) The presence of so much history ought to be unmanning or even just embarrassing. In Paris it isn't, not because the past is so hallowed but because it doesn't seem to be there.

The unsentimental efficiency of French commonplace civilization, of which the French café is the highest embodiment, is so
brisk that it disarms nostalgia. History keeps wiping the table off
and asking you, a little impatiently, what you'll have now.

Not until the 1940s—I had learned a lot of this in the course
of reading Olivier Todd's excellent new biography of Camus, one
of the big books here this year—did the triangle of the two cafés
and the Brasserie Lipp at Saint-Germain-des-Prés become leg-
endary. This was when the group of *résistants* came into being,
and a culture to go with them—when Camus and Sartre and Simone de Beauvoir, as the cliché has it, brooded in one corner of
the Deux Magots while Juliette Greco sang sad songs in another.
The odd thing is that the cliché is almost entirely true. It was at
the Deux Magots, for instance, that Sartre saw his famous philosophical *garçon,* of whom he wrote, "His movement is quick and
forward, a little too precise, a little too rapid. He comes toward
the patrons with a step a little too quick. He bends forward a little too eagerly, his eyes express an interest too solicitous for the
order of the customer." (I still get waiters like that.)

Yet fifty years after the classic period, one café is more fashionable than ever and the other is not fashionable at all. You
might not see this at once. At the Flore the fashionable people
are spread out among the tables rather than concentrated in one
spot or area; they occupy the place clandestinely, following the
law of Inverse Natural Appeal. The *terrasse* of the Flore, even on
a sunny and perfect day (*especially* on a sunny and perfect day),
is off limits; the inner room, with its red moleskin banquettes, is
acceptable; but by far the most OK place to sit is upstairs (I was
sitting there now, with my friend), and the banquettes are made
of an ugly tan leatherette. (The law of Inverse Natural Appeal is
at work: The outlawed *terrasse* is, as it happens, an extraordi-
narily pleasant place to sit; the inner room is a very pleasant
place to sit; and the upstairs room is reminiscent of the cocktail
lounge of a Howard Johnson's.)

The sounds of the higher French conversation, with its lovely murmur of certainties and, rising from the banquettes, the favorite words of fashionable French people, resonated all around. *Perversité,* which means "perversity" but is used as a word of praise, suggests something—a book, a dish, a politician—that is aristocratic. *C'est normal,* which means something like "No problem" and can also refer to any political or literary situation, is different from the American phrase in that its emphasis is not on a difficulty surmounted or evaded but on the return to a familiar, homeostatic atmosphere of comfort: Something that happens may seem unusual (say, the revelation that a former defense minister might have been an East Bloc agent) but, properly understood, is not shocking at all; it's *normal,* even if a little deplorable. And from table after table, like the sound of a tolling bell, rises the connective *donc,* which just means "so" or "therefore," but, when used in literary and worldly conversation, and rung with sufficient force, means "It must therefore follow as the night the day" and always sounds to me as conclusive as Gideon's trumpet.

"But it all has to do with the character of two men, Boubal and Cazes," my friend said. Paul Boubal was the owner of the Flore from 1939 to 1983—he died five years later—and Roger Cazes was the owner not of the Deux Magots but of the Brasserie Lipp, across the street. "That is to say, both Cazes and Boubal were from the Auvergne—they were countrymen—and though each thought the other was running a sneaky business, each respected the other and frequented the other's place. This produced, in the fifties, a natural compact, a kind of family feeling between the two places. I mean family feeling in the real sense—of dependence and suspicion and resentment. The owner of the Deux Magots was a much more timid fellow. He was left out of the compact." So the real force working was that of the Lipp; it was the third planet, perturbing the orbits of the two others.

There it was, the explanation in terms of the romantic individual in almost perfect form, along with the bonus of a touch of *terroir,* the French affection for a bit of native land. Then someone suggested that I speak to the essayist and editor Jean-Paul Enthoven, who is the author of the season's most winning collection of literary essays, *Les Enfants de Saturne.* Enthoven, I was told, would be sure to have an explanation; he could explain anything Parisian.

"Here is my hypothesis," he announced when I reached him on the phone at his office, at the publishing house of Grasset. "You must go back to the twenties and thirties, when the Flore became identified with the extreme right and the Deux Magots, by default, with the left. Charles Maurras, the founder of Action Française, used the Flore as his home base." Maurras was simultaneously one of the most important stylists in French literature—a member of the French Academy, and a crucial influence on T. S. Eliot, among other modernists—and a right-wing anti-Semite. "Before it was anyone else's place, it was Maurras's. His most famous polemic was even named after the café: 'Au Signe de Flore.' Maurras was a malevolent force, in that everything he touched was simultaneously disgraced and hallowed."

Enthoven went on to say, "This meant that by the time of the occupation, when Sartre and Simone de Beauvoir came to Saint-Germain and began their *résistance,* they had to avoid the Flore like a plague, since it had been contaminated by Maurras. But then the tourists began to crowd into the Deux Magots in order to look at Sartre and de Beauvoir. The place became overcrowded, and eventually the intellectuals noticed the emptiness of the Flore next door. By then Maurras was gone, the occupation had passed, and confronted with a choice between the pollution of Maurras and the pollution of tourism, the intellectuals chose to remake the emptiness rather than abide with the many. So they went across the street and have never returned." He stopped for a second, as if readying himself for an aphorism, and then said, "The Deux Magots was sacralized by Sartre, desacralized by the tourists, and then left vacant by history." Eighteen-seventy, 1940, I thought. Like so many lovely things in Paris, the two cafés were given shape by the first German invasion and then in one way or another were deformed by the second.

It was left to another, more dour friend to supply the futility-of-explanation explanation, over coffee at a lesser, more despairing café—neither fashionable nor unfashionable, just a place where you go to talk. "There is nothing to explain here," he said. "The explanation is a simple, Saussurean one." He was referring, I realized after a moment, to the father of modern linguistics, who was the first to point out that signs get their meanings not by being like the things they stand for but by being different from other signs: A sign for black means black because it isn't like the sign for white.

"The fashionable exists only in relation to something that is *not* that way," he went on. "The relationship between the modishness of the Flore and the unmodishness of the Deux Magots isn't just possibly arbitrary. It's *necessarily* arbitrary. If you place *any* two things side by side, one will become fashionable and the other will not. It's a necessity determined by the entire idea of fashion. A world in which everything is fashionable is impossible to imagine, because it implies that there would be nothing to provide a contrast. The reason that when you place any two things side by side, one becomes chic and the other does not is that it's in the nature of desire to choose, and to choose *absolutely*. That's the mythological lesson of the great choice among the beauties: They are all beautiful—they are goddesses—and yet a man must choose. And what was the chooser's name? Paris. *C'est normal.*"

Distant Errors,

CHRISTMAS JOURNAL 2

My fax machine, which was made by the French state, always blames someone else when things go wrong. It is a Galéo 5000 model, and it is made by France Télécom and is therefore an official, or French government, product; even its name carries with it the nice implication that 4,999 other models were attempted before perfection was at last achieved by the French fax machine ministry.

You even have to go to a government telephone outlet to buy a new ribbon for it. It's a plain paper fax (you have the same expression in French, *papier ordinaire*, ordinary paper) with all the usual features. It's really very nicely designed—much better designed than its American equivalents, with that streamlined, intelligent Philippe Starck look that the French seem magically able to give to everything they make. It's reasonably efficient too—perhaps a little overtricky in loading in the sheets and unduly inclined to *bourrage de papier*, paper jams—but still . . .

It has a little glowing window on its face where it *affiches,* or posts, the events and troubles of its day, its operating life. The window flashes, for instance, a shocked, offended *Pas d'identité!*—no identity!—when the fax machine at the other end doesn't "identify itself," which for some reason or another most American machines don't seem to.

But the favorite, all-purpose *affiche* of my fax machine is *erreur distante*—distant error—which it *affiches* all the time, no matter where the error actually originates, far away or right in its own backyard. Whether the error comes from a fax machine in Lille or Los Angeles, it says that it is a distant error. When the machine itself has run out of paper, it is still a distant error. When I have forgotten to clean the ribbon heads, an error has nonetheless taken place, at a distance. Jams and overflows, missed connections, and faulty plugs: all are *erreurs distantes.* When it really *is* a distant error, it is still just another distant error. This is the French fax machine's way of getting through life. The error is distant; the problem lies someplace else; there is always somebody else to blame for your malfunctions.

French intellectuals and public people, I have on certain occasions come to the mordant, exasperated, and gloomy conclusion, share the same belief, *affiche* the same accusatory message, banding together and flashing *erreur distante,* whenever they run out of paper or ink or arguments. This morning, for instance, I saw the economist Emmanuel Todd being interviewed about his book on the economic "stagnation" of industrialized economies. He blandly announced that the U.S. economy was just as stagnant as France's, in fact was worse because its "cultural level" (by which he meant the level of education) was so much more depraved. Also, the United States manufactured less than it once had. Economic stagnation was the problem of all the industrialized economies, France was simply sharing in it, and the United States was really to blame. His debating opponent, an intelligent economist named Cohen—very poorly dressed in a brightly colored blazer and bad tortoiseshell glasses—tried to explain that this wasn't so, that the fall in manufacturing was in fact a sign of the renovation of the American economy, and that whatever its flaws in equality, the growth in America was real, that the one thing you *couldn't* call the American economy was stagnant. Todd, who looked terrific, hardly bothered to argue with him; he just made the same assertions again: The American economy is stagnant. He just *affiched,* like my fax machine *erreur distante,* and the host, terrified, nodded.

A while ago I was on a panel broadcast for France-Culture, the radio station, at the Sciences Po, the great political science school, along with Philippe Sollers and other French worthies, and we talked about the influence of American culture on France. Everyone took it for granted that the American dominance in culture was a distant error or, rather, a distant conspiracy organized by the CIA and the Disney corporation. (I was there, the sole American on the panel, to be condescended to as the representative of both Michael Eisner and William Colby, with mouse ears on my head and a listening device presumably implanted inside them.) The clichés get trotted out—that Jackson Pollock and the abstract expressionists got put over by the CIA, etc.—with a complacent certitude, and it was taken for granted that the relative decline of the prestige of French writing and painting has nothing to do with the actual decline of the quality of French writing and painting. (And yet when we got down to particulars, much of these prejudices vanished: Sollers and I actually had a reasonable debate about Roth and Updike. No American Sollers would have been able to *name* two French novelists, much less debate their value.)

What was maddening was not the anti-Americanism, which is understandable and even, in its Astérix-style resistance to American domination, admirable. What is maddening is the bland certainty, the lack of vigilant curiosity, the incapacity for critical self-reflection, the readiness to *affiche erreur distante* and wait for somebody else to change the paper.

|||

A wise man, an old émigré artist, when I told him, gaily, that we were going to move to Paris, said soberly, even darkly: "Ah. So you have at last decided not to forgo the essential Jewish experience of emigration and expatriation." I thought it was a joke, a highly complicated, ironic joke, but still a joke, since what could be less traumatic, in the old-fashioned émigré's sense, less Cioran and Benjamin and Celan, than moving to Paris with a baby? But of course, what he said was true, or contained a truth. The reality is that after a year here everything about moving to Paris has been wonderful, and everything about emigrating to France difficult. An immigrant is an immigrant, poor fellow: Pity him! The errors arrive, and they tell me I brought them with me.

The loneliness of the expatriate is of an odd and complicated kind, for it is inseparable from the feeling of being free, of having escaped. Martha, the other day, spent the morning watching Luke open and shut the little gates that lead into the interior gardens at the Palais Royal. He would open the gate, she explained, walk through, watch it shut, and then walk back through again, with the rows of violet flowers in the background. She felt, she said, as if she had died and gone to heaven—but with the strange feeling that dying and going to heaven mean parting, leaving, and missing the people you left behind on earth. No wonder ghosts at séances are so blandly encouraging; they miss you, but they are busy watching someone else.

There is the feeling of being apart and the feeling of being a *universe* apart—the immigrant's strange knowledge that the language and lore that carry on in your own living space are so unlike the ones right outside. (This is particularly true of our odd Canadian-American-Jewish–Sri Lankan–Franco-American ménage, with the two-year-old at its center.) There is also the odd knowledge, at once comforting and scary, that whatever is going on outside, you are without a predisposed opinion on it, that you have had a kind of operation, removing your instant reflexive sides-taking instinct. When French politicians debate, I think, well, everybody has a point. After a year the feeling that every-thing was amusing, though, bombs and strikes an act in the Winter Circus, does begin to fade, to seem less amusing in itself. When *Le Canard Enchaîné*, the satiric paper, comes out on Wednesday mornings, I buy it and generally enjoy, am even beginning to understand, most of the jokes and digs; what was largely incomprehensible to me at first is now self-evident: who is being mocked for what and why.

But I don't actually care about who is being mocked. I am simply pleased to register that what I am reading is mockery. And the slightly amused, removed feeling always breaks down as you realize that you really don't *want* to be so lofty and Olympian— or rather, that being lofty and Olympian carries within it, by tra-dition and precedent, the habit of wishing you could be down there in the plain, taking sides. Even the gods, actually looking down from Olympus in amusement, kept hurtling down to get laid or slug somebody.

|||

After a first winter in Paris, when the lure of the chimney and cigar smell holds you in thrall, you become accustomed to them, and then all you notice is the dark. From November to April, hardly a single day when you see the sun. The light itself is beau-tiful, violet and gray, but it always looks as if it were planning to snow, and then it never does.

We had the seasonal pleasure of buying a (by Canadian stan-dards, insanely overpriced) Christmas tree. We bought it from a Greek tree-and-plant dealer on the Île de la Cité. It's a nice tree, a big fir, green and lush, but, at our insistence, without that crazy wooden cross that the French insist on nailing to the bottoms of their Christmas trees, so that you can't give them water. Ours is open, with a fresh cut, and sits in its watery pedestal, a red-and-green tripod, which we brought all the way over from Farm and Garden nursery down on Franklin Street in TriBeCa.

The logic (or fantasy) of the wooden cross on the bottoms of the trunks of the French Christmas trees, as the bemused dealer explained it to me, is that it "seals" off the tree's trunk and keeps the sap inside, keeps it from drying out. The opposed American logic, our logic, of course (or is it our fantasy too?), is that an open cut will keep a dead and derooted tree "fresh" for as long as you need it, for as long as you give it water and the season lasts.

Or is the cut cross, after all, really a kind of covert, symbolic, half-hidden reminder on the part of a once entirely Catholic country of the cross-that-is-to-come, of the knowledge that even Christmas trees can't be resurrected without a miracle? Americans persuade themselves that a dead tree is still fresh if you keep pouring water on it; here there is a small guilty stirring of Catholic conscience that says, "It's dead, you know, the way everything will be. You can seal it up, but you can't keep it going. Only a miracle will bring it back to life."

|||

Naturally none of the Christmas tree garlands I bought last year works this year. Though Martha packed them away neatly when we took the tree down, they have managed to work themselves into hideous tangles, the way Christmas lights always do. If the continued existence of the Christmas tree light garlands, even though they're obviously impractical compared with strings, is proof of the strength of cultural difference, their ability to get themselves tangled is just as strong proof of cultural universality. The strands did it in New York, the garlands do it here, and there is no explaining how they do. The permanent cultural differences are language, the rituals of eating, and the habits of education; the permanent cultural universals are love of children and the capacity of Christmas lights left in a box in a closet to get themselves hopelessly tangled in knots.

|||

The American Christmas came to Paris while I was away in New York; Halloween came this year for the first time, right while we were watching, right under our noses. Linus waiting for the Great Pumpkin couldn't have been more shocked, more pleased than we were to see Halloween rising before us like a specter, an inflato raft. The shops were suddenly filled with pumpkins and rubber masks and witches and ghost costumes and bags of candy. Apparently the American Halloween has been sneaking up bit by bit for a little while, but everyone agrees that this year the whole thing has really happened, and for the most obvious of reasons: It is a way for small shopkeepers to sell stuff before Christmas comes. *Le Monde,* sensing this brisk commercial motive, published a piece about the coming of Halloween, predictably indignant.

The essentially creepy, necrophile nature of the holiday, invisible to Americans, was harder to hide from the French. Our friends Marie and Édouard, whose two children, Thomas and Alexandra, live across the courtyard, were dubious: The children dress up as the dead and the horrific and then demand sweets at the price of vandalism? The pleasure is located *where* exactly? Our friend Cassie says that her French mother-in-law, seeing the grandchildren dressed up as skeletons, let out a genuine shriek of distaste.

Of course, it is incumbent on Americans to reassure, gently, that it is not really a holiday of the dead at all, that like all American holidays, it is a ritual of materialism, or, to put it another way, of greed, a rite designed to teach our children that everything, even death, ends with candy. It is just *fun. Fun* is the magic American word (Our motto "Let's have fun!" is met by the French motto "Let's be amused.") Though Halloween arrived and caused parties and sales, the tradition of trick-or-treating has not really caught on here, and so Martha and several other mothers decided to have a Halloween party in her friend Cassie's apartment, where the mothers hid behind doors, so that the children could knock and get their candy. It was trick-or-treating made into an indoor sport. The French children in the party, she tells me, just didn't get it. What was the point, the French children, disconsolate as ghosts and skeletons and witches, seemed to wonder, waiting behind their doors, to be all dressed up, with nowhere to go?

|||

Luke has mounted up onto the horses on the carousel this year, although he needs to be tied on, like a parcel. To my delight, though not really to my surprise, I discovered this year that the carousel has been turning in the same manner, offering the same game, and drawing the same bemused, fascinated attention of foreigners for at least seventy-five years. I found a passage in the travel writing of Joseph Roth, the German novelist, who visited the Luxembourg Gardens in 1925 and wrote about the *"manèges de chevaux de bois pour enfants."* He describes the rings and sticks, exactly as they are today: "The owner of the merry-go-round holds in his hand, at the end of a stick, little rings lightly hung and easy to detach. All the children on the horses and in the tiny cars are armed with wands. So that when they pass before the rings, they try to unhook them, which is to say slip them onto their wand. Whoever gets the most gets a prize. They learn quick action, the value of the instant, accelerated reflexes, and the trick of adjusting one's eye." "The value of the instant . . ." Doubtless Cartier-Bresson and the rest of the "decisive moment" photographers rode on such horses, caught their rings, learned there's only one right moment in which to do it.

Roth admired the game endlessly, because it seemed so un-German, such a free and charming way to educate, without the military brutality of Teutonic schools. The funny thing is that there are now no more prizes—the same game, same carousel, but no more prizes. Nothing left to teach. You get the ring for the pleasure of having taken it. I wonder which child when won the last prize.

|||

The differences are tiny and real. Cultures don't really encode things. They include things, and leave things out. There is, for instance, the exasperation of lunch. Lunch, as it exists in New York, doesn't exist here. Either lunch is a three-course meal— i.e., dinner, complete with two bottles of wine—or else it is to be had only at a brasserie, where the same menu—croque monsieur, omelet, salad Niçoise—is presented almost without any variation at all, as though the menu had been decreed by the state. A tuna sandwich, a bran muffin, a bowl of black bean soup—black bean soup! Yankee bean! Chicken vegetable! It is soup, beautiful soup, that I miss more than anything, not French soup, all puréed and homogenized, but American soup, with bits and things, beans and corn and even letters, in it. This can shake you up, this business of things almost but not quite being the same. A pharmacy is not quite a drugstore; a brasserie is not quite a coffee shop; a lunch is not quite a lunch. So on Sundays I have developed the habit of making soup for the week, from the good things we buy in the *marché biologique* on the boulevard Raspail. Soup and custard on Sunday nights, our salute to the land of the free.

|||

My favorite bit of evidence of the French habit of pervasive, permanent abstraction lies in the difficulties of telling people about fact checking. (I use the English word usually; there doesn't seem to be a simple French equivalent.) "Thank you so much for your help," I will say after interviewing a man of letters or politician. "I'm going to write this up, and you'll probably be hearing from what we call *une fact checker* in a couple of weeks." (I make it feminine since the fact checker usually is.)

"What do you mean, *une fact checker*?"

"Oh, it's someone to make sure that I've got all the facts right, reported them correctly."

Annoyed: "No, no, I've told you everything I know."

I, soothing: "Oh, I know you have."

Suspicious: "You mean your editor double-checks?"

"No, no, it's just a way of making sure that we haven't made a mistake in facts."

More wary and curious: "This is a way of maintaining an ideological line?"

"No, no—well, in a sense I suppose . . ." (For positivism, of which *New Yorker* fact checking is the last redoubt, *is* an ideological line; I've lived long enough in France to see that move coming. . . .)

"But really," I go on, "it's just to make sure that your dates and what we have you quoted as saying are accurate. Just to be sure."

Dubious look; there is More Here Than Meets the Eye. On occasion I even get a helpful, warning call from the subject after the fact checker has called. "You know, someone, another reporter called me from the magazine. They were checking up on you." ("No, no, really checking on *you*," I want to say, offended, but don't—and then think he's right: They *are* checking up on me too; never thought of it that way, though.) There is a certainty in France that what assumes the guise of transparent positivism, "fact checking," is in fact a complicated plot of one kind or another, a way of enforcing ideological coherence. That there might really *be* facts worth checking is an obvious and annoying absurdity; it would be naive to think otherwise.

I was baffled and exasperated by this until it occurred to me that you would get *exactly* the same incomprehension and suspicion if you told American intellectuals and politicians, postinterview, that a theory checker would be calling them. "It's been a pleasure speaking to you," you'd say to Al Gore or Mayor Giuliani. "And I'm going to write this up; probably in a couple of weeks a theory checker will be in touch with you."

Alarmed, suspicious: "A what?"

"You know, a theory checker. Just someone to make sure that all your premises agree with your conclusions, that there aren't any obvious errors of logic in your argument, that all your allusions flow together in a coherent stream—that kind of thing."

"What do you mean?" the American would say, alarmed. "Of course they do, I don't need to talk to a theory checker."

"Oh, no, you don't *need* to. It's for your protection, really. They just want to make sure that the theory hangs together. . . ."

The American subject would be exactly as startled and annoyed at the idea of being investigated by a theory checker as the French are by being harassed by a fact checker, since this process would claim some special status, some "privileged" place for theory. A theory checker? What an absurd waste of time, since it's apparent (to us Americans) that people don't speak in theories, that the theories they employ change, flexibly, and of necessity, from moment to moment in conversation, that the notion of limiting conversation to a rigid rule of theoretical constancy is an absurd denial of what conversation *is*.

Well, replace *fact* (and *factual*) for *theory* in that last sentence, and you have the common French view of fact checking. People don't speak in straight facts; the facts they employ to enforce their truths change, flexibly and with varying emphasis, as the conversation changes, and the notion of limiting conversation to a rigid rule of pure factual consistency is an absurd denial of what conversation *is*. Not, of course, that the French intellectual doesn't use and respect facts, up to a useful point, any more than even the last remaining American positivist doesn't use and respect theory, up to a point. It's simply the fetishizing of one term in the game of conversation that strikes the French funny. Conversation is an organic, improvised web of fact and theory, and to pick out one bit of it for microscopic overexamination is typically American overearnest comedy.

|||

"Does this bus go across the river?" the man from Chicago demands of the Parisian bus driver, who looks blank. "I said, this bus goes across the river, or doesn't it?" I myself have been in this position, of course, more times than once, in Venice and in Tuscany, but (I choose to believe, at least) I try to make up for it with the necessary abasing looks of ignorance and sorrow and multitudes of thank-yous and head ducks, as the Japanese do here. The American in Paris just *demands*, querulously—"Now, you remember that pastry I showed you in the window. Now, I want that one"—in English, and expects the world to answer.

Sometimes the French response is muttered and comic. "Hey, does this bus go across the river?" the woman from California says, mounting onto the steps of the 63. "I wouldn't come to your country and not speak in your language," the driver says, in French. A sensitive listener would detect some frost in the manner, but the American woman doesn't: "No—I asked you, does this bus go across the river?" Or, worse, Americans ordering in English at French menus, specifying precisely, exigently, what they want in a language the waiters don't speak.

For it turns out that there is a Regulon in the Semiosphere stronger even than the plug, more agile than the fish. It's language. Language really does prevent signs or cultures from going universal. For all the endless articles in the papers and magazines about the force of globalization and international standardization, language divides and confuses people as effectively now as it ever has. It stops the fatal "exponentiality" of culture in the real world as surely as starvation stops it in the jungle. It divides absolutely, and what is really international, truly global, is, in this way, very small.

The real "crisis" in France in fact is not economic (France is in a cyclical slump; it will end) or even cultural (France is in a cyclical slump; it will end) but linguistic. French has diminished as an international language, and this will not end. When people talk about globalization, what they're really saying is that an English-speaking imperium now stretches from Adelaide to Vancouver, and that anyone who is at home in one bit of it is likely to feel at home in the other bits. You can join this global community by speaking English yourself, but that's about all. The space between the average Frenchman (or Italian or German) and the average American is just as great as it's ever been, because language remains in place, and it remains *hard*. Even after two years of speaking French all the time, I feel it. We breathe in our first language, and swim in our second.

|||

Yet there *is* a kind of authority associated with the American presence right now that is both awe-inspiring and absurd. At the Bastille Day fireworks, for instance, over on the champ-de-Mars, there is always a nice big picnic feeling, but no one pays minimal respect to the notion that people ought not to stand up in front of other people when other people are trying to watch fireworks. As happens so often in France, it is a designated bacchanal, like the playground in the Luxembourg Gardens. At the Bastille Day on the champ-de-Mars this July, in the midst of the anarchy— over on the fringes, of course, there were *flics, gendarmes,* busy arresting the vendors of those glow-in-the-dark necklaces; now, there was a *real* crime—a single American woman rose to bring order to the multitudes. She was the kind of big-boned East Coast woman you see running a progressive day camp, or working as the phys ed instructor at Dalton or Brearley, high-flown but (as she would be the first to tell you) down-to-earth. She just started ordering people around: Sit down, you down there (all this in English, of course), now make room so the little kids can see, etc. And people, at least the few hundred in earshot, actually did it. They *obeyed,* for a little while anyway.

The French believe that all errors are distant, someone else's fault. Americans believe that there is no distance, no difference, and therefore that there are no errors, that any troubles are simple misunderstandings, consequent on your not yet having spoken English loudly enough.

|||

It is, still, amazing to see how vast a screen the differences of language can be—not an opaque but a kind of translucent one. You sort of see through it, but not quite. There is a book to be written, for instance, on small errors in subtitles. In the Fred Astaire musical *Royal Wedding,* for instance, the English girl he falls for, played by Sarah Churchill (daughter of Sir Winston), is engaged to an American, whom we never see but who's called Hal—like Falstaff's prince, like a good high Englishman. That English *H,* though, was completely inaudible to the French translator who did the subtitles, and so throughout the film the absent lover is referred to in the subtitles as Al—Al like a stagehand, Al like my grandfather. If you have the habit of print addiction, so that you are listening and reading at the same time, this guy Al keeps forcing his way into the movie. "But what shall I say to Hal—that I have never loved him?" Patricia says to Fred. Down below it says, *"Et Al—qu'est-ce que je vais lui dire?"*

My other favorite subtitle was in some contemporary comedy that we went to see—we see about a movie every six months, where once I saw three a day—in which there was a reference to American talk shows. "And what do you want me to do: go on Oprah, Geraldo, or Sally Jessy?" the character asked. The translator did fine with Oprah and Geraldo but could make nothing of the last, so Sally with her glasses became a non–non sequitur question. *"Oprah, Geraldo—et sale est Jesse?"* the subtitle read— "Oprah, Geraldo—and Jesse is dirty?" This network of distant errors obviously occludes itself in front of us all the time, every day, and mostly we don't know it.

|||

There are at least three moments a month when you are ready to leap across a counter or a front seat to strangle someone: the woman at France Télécom who won't give you the fax ribbons that are there on the counter in front of her because she can't find them on the computer inventory; the chair restorer who looks at your beautiful Thonet rocker and then announces, sniffily, that it isn't worth his time; the woman who sells you a poster and then announces that she has no idea where you might go to frame it; the bus driver who won't let an exhausted pregnant woman off the front door of the bus (you're supposed to exit from the rear) from sheer bloody-mindedness. It affects Martha much less than me, leading me to suspect that it is essentially a masculine problem. My trouble is that I think like a Frenchman: I transform every encounter into a competition in status and get enraged when I lose it. As Cioran said, it's hard for me to live in a country where everyone is as irascible as I am.

At the same time, I find myself often reduced to an immigrant helplessness. We went to BHV, for instance, earlier this year to frame our *Paris to the Moon* engraving. I have had it up in my study, an icon to write under. There's a nice do-it-yourself framing shop up there, and lacking a framer to go to, we thought we just ought to, well, do it ourselves. Back in New York we knew a framer who did our frames, and I prided myself, within limits, on having learned a thing or two about what made the right edge for the right picture. We began to sort around with simple white mats and black wooden frames. As we were doing it, a lady came up to us: a Frenchwoman in her seventies, with pearls and a strong jaw and silver hair. She had a couple of handsome flower prints that she was framing for herself. "No, no, children," she said. "You are doing that quite incorrectly. This, you see," she said, "is a nineteenth-century print. It needs a nineteenth-century mat, a nineteenth-century frame." She took the white-and-black frame away from us—put them right back—and chose a cream mat and a fake, "antiqued" gold frame. "There," she said. "*That* is the French nineteenth century," she said, and took the frame and the print and the mat all up to the counter for us. We looked at each other sheepishly and went ahead and bought them. I used to know something about art, or thought I did, I muttered to myself, all the way home. The print actually looks pretty nice in its gold frame. When I remember the moment now, I remember my utter helplessness and how she smelled of a wonderful tea-rose perfume.

|||

The other side of French official arrogance is French improvised and elaborate courtesy. The men from the department store Bon Marché, the deliverymen, called last night, to deliver the wicker kitchen organizer. "We have to be there early, because it's a small street. Six-thirty."

"It's a little too early for us," I said. "Let's make it later."

"Ah, no. It's impossible. Six-thirty or nothing."

"All right," and I hung up the phone, silently cursing French arrogance and the lack of any kind of service ethic.

Then, the next morning, at six forty-six, I was just awakened by the sound of the gentlest possible knocking on the front door—so butterfly quiet that at first I imagined that it must have been Luke Auden stirring in bed. But then there it was again, quiet but insistent. I got up, put on my robe, got to the front door, and stared out the spyglass. There were two work-men in the hallway, leaning over gently, knocking with their knuckles, as lightly as ghosts. I slipped the door open and got not a smile, but a look of acknowledgment, and they brought the kitchen organizer in with balletlike light-footedness. "Thank you," I said, "the baby is sleeping." They nodded. *We know.* I signed the invoice, and they were gone, and I went back to sleep.

|||

And then there is the chair. It started by accident one rainy Monday, after we had been to the Musée d'Orsay, and I had failed to get Luke much interested in my old favorites, Monets and Manets. I still find going to the Musée d'Orsay an infuriating, maddening experience. (Apparently, despite my superficial essays at amused blandness, I realize, reading this, that I'm a real pepperpot, a hothead, Billy Martin in France.) That vast, handsome railroad station so horribly done over in Wiener Werkstätte fashion by Gae Aulenti; the stupid, unquestioned dominance of the worst *pompier* art of the nineteenth century in the main hall as though saying, *here* are our real treasures. And the greater pain that only the *pompier* official art could look any good in such a vast and frigid space. I no longer find the taste for nineteenth-century French academic art, which can be amusing if seen small on a slide screen, the least bit likable. It is horrible, depressing beyond words, the revenge of official culture on life and youth, on reality itself. I swear to God I would take a razor to *The Romans of the Decadence* without a moment's hesitation.

And then having to take the escalator up all the way to the far upper floors—a garret, in museum terms, in order to see the great pictures, every one of which looked incomparably better in the old Jeu de Paume. It is a calculated, venom-filled insult on the part of French official culture against French civilization, revenge on the part of the academy and administration against everyone who escaped them. French official culture, having the upper hand, simply banishes French civilization to the garret, sends it to its room. What one feels, in that awful place, is violent indignation—and then an ever-increased sense of wonder that Manet and Degas and Monet, faced with the same stupidities of those same academic provocations in their own lifetimes, responded not with rage but with precision and grace and contemplative exactitude.

Paris is marked by a permanent battle between French civilization, which is the accumulated intelligence and wit of French life, and French official culture, which is the expression of the functionary system in all its pomposity and abstraction. Perhaps by French civilization I mean the small shops; by French official culture I mean the big buildings. There is hardly a day when you are not wild with gratitude for something that happens in the small shops: the way that Mme. Glardon, at the pastry shop on the rue Bonaparte, carefully wraps Luke Auden's chocolate éclair in a little paper pyramid, a ribbon at its apex, knowing perfectly well, all the while, that the paper pyramid and ribbon will endure just long enough for the small boy to rip it open to get to the éclair. And hardly a day when you are not wild with dismay at something that has been begun in the big buildings, some abstraction launched on the world in smug and empty confidence.

|||

In any case, I couldn't, as it happened, get Luke much stirred by Manet or Monet (not that he was stirred by the Couture either, I'm glad to say), but searching for something that *would* stir him, I came across the handsome side chapel devoted to Daumier's portrait busts. They are caricatures of the political men of the mid-nineteenth century. Luke loved them. I held him up, and he stared at their faces behind the Plexiglas boxes and imitated each one. We guessed at the character of each one: who's mean, who's nice, who's conceited. The scary thing is that the faces are *exactly* the faces of French politicians today: Philippe Séguin, with his raccoon-circled eyes; Le Pen, with his obscene, smiling jowliness; Bruno Megret with his ratlike ordinariness. You could find the men of the left; too: Jospin's fatuous cheerfulness—they're all there.

After the success of the Daumiers, I thought of going to the park, as a release, or back to Deyrolle, for the umpteenth time, but it was raining hard, and we needed something new. "Do you want a soda?" I said, and we went over to the Courier de Lyons, the nearest thing our *haut* neighborhood has to a workingman's café. After he had a grenadine, and I a *grand crème,* and we had shared a *tarte Normande,* I noticed that there was a pinball machine—a *flipper,* as it is called in French. So I dragged a chair over, so that he could stand up on it and work the left flipper, and took control of the right flipper myself. It was an "NBA all-star" pinball machine, a true old-fashioned, pre-Atari, steel ball pinball, but with extra ramps and lights that let you shoot the ball up into hoops, get extra points, make model players jump up and down. (Luke, of course, had never seen a basketball game.) We started playing, and he loved it: the ping of the hard metal balls, the compressed springiness of the release, the fat thwack of the bumpers, above all the bounce of the flipper, hitting the ball back up, keeping it in play, making it go. We played three times, rushed home, and he told his momma about it. "It goes . . ." he said, and at a loss for words, he just raced his eyes, back and forth, rolled them back and forth crazily—*that's* how it goes.

Since then we go once a week to play pinball, always prefaced by a trip first to the Musée d'Orsay to look at the funny faces (while Daddy seethes at the nineteenth-century academicians and the small boy counts the minutes to the Courier de Lyons.) The funny thing is that the café changes the pinball machine every month or so, and it is always, *always,* an American machine with an American theme. Each machine has an automated bonus, something weird that happens if you get enough points, and there is something rapt and lovely, in this day of virtual everything, about the clockwork nightingale *mechanicalness* of the pinball machines, about the persistence of their metallic gears and simple slot-and-track devices. So far we have been through major-league baseball, Star Wars (Hans Solo gets blasted into that carbon sheet), Jurassic Park (an egg glows and opens, and a baby dinosaur appears), Gopher Golf (a kind of parody golf, with little chipmunks that jump up, bucktoothed), and, our favorite, Monster Bash (Dracula comes out of his coffin, on a little metal track; Frankenstein, to the accompaniment of suitably stormy music—the lights on the machine actually first go off, a lovely touch—*sits up*). All the instructions on the machines are in English, of course, as are all the details. ("I love these machines, compared to video games," another aficionado at the café said to me once, sincerely, as we scored big and watched Dracula creaking out on his mechanical track. "They are, well, *so real*.")

We go once a week, always get the same grenadine-coffee-pie combo, leave a ten-franc tip; I am sure that it is illegal for a three-year-old to play pinball, and I am paying protection. After a month or so, though, I noticed something odd. When we began to play, I would always discreetly drag a café chair over from the table and put it alongside the machine for him to stand on. But after we had done this five or six times, over five or six weeks, I noticed that someone had quietly tucked that small café chair under the left flipper, for Luke to stand on. The chair, the little bistro chair, was pushed under the pinball machine, on the left, or Lukeish, side. There was no talk, no explanation; no one mentioned it, or pointed it out. No, it was a quiet, almost a grudging courtesy, offered to a short client who came regularly to take his pleasure there. Nothing has changed in our relation to that café: No one shakes our hands or offers us a false genial smile; we pay for our coffee and grenadine as we always have; we leave the tip we have always left. But that chair is always there.

Papon's
Paper Trail

Bordeaux is the town where France goes to give up. It was where the French government retreated from Paris under fire from the Prussians in 1870, and again from the kaiser's armies in 1914, and where, in June 1940, the French government fled in the face of the German advance and soon afterward met not just the fact of defeat but the utter depth of France's demoralization. A. J. Liebling wrote of those days that "there was a climate of death in Bordeaux, heavy and unhealthy like the smell of tuberoses." He recalled the wealthy men in the famous restaurants like the Chapon Fin, "heavy-jowled, waxy-faced, wearing an odd expression of relief from fear." Though the bad peace was ruled from the spa town of Vichy, Bordeaux is the place that gave the surrender its strange, bitter, bourgeois character: a nation retreating from cosmopolitan Paris back to *la France profonde*.

Bordeaux has always been a trench coat–and–train station, 1940s kind of town, and despite the mediocre, concrete modern architecture it shares with nearly all French provincial capitals, it remains one. The Chapon Fin is still in business, but it is not deathlike—merely nervous and overwrought, in the way of French provincial restaurants since the capitalists trimmed down and the only market left was German tourists.

In the spring of 1998, Bordeaux was invaded again, this time by battalions of lawyers, broadcasters, historians, and journalists, who had come to attend or participate in the trial of Maurice Papon—the former secretary-general of the Gironde, of which Bordeaux is the capital—for complicity in crimes against humanity fifty-five years ago, during the occupation. The Papon trial was the central, binding event of the past year in France, a kind of O.J. trial, without television or a glove. It was the longest, the most discouraging, the most moving, at times the most ridiculous, and certainly the most fraught trial in postwar French history.

On the last day of the trial, Wednesday, April 1, the invasion of the media became an occupation; what seemed like every European journalist resident in France, and a lot of Americans too, descended on the little square outside the Palais de Justice. The convenience of having La Concorde, a stage-set grand café right across from the Palais (doors open to the spring weather, bottles of good wine lined up on the wall), gave the end of the trial a strangely hilarious, high-hearted, yet self-subduing party spirit— a combination of Swifty Lazar's Oscar party and the Nuremberg trials.

Despite the mob, the national allegiance of every journalist was instantly recognizable. French journalists wear handsomely tailored jackets and share with English rock guitarists the secret of eternal hair: It piles up. Americans, rumpled and exhausted before the day begins, seem to be still longing for Vietnam. Even walking up and down the steps of the *palais,* they looked as though they were ducking into the backwash of a helicopter rotor, weighed down by invisible dog tags. What really depressed them was the knowledge that their stories about the *procès Papon* would sneak into the paper only "between blow jobs," as one said bitterly. The British alone were exhilarated, bouncing around in bad suits. They all speak French, they all knew they would be on the front page, and secretly they knew too that their readers would not be completely unhappy with a story whose basic point was that all foreigners were like that.

The great Nazi hunter Serge Klarsfeld waited outside the courthouse too. He is in his sixties, spreading at the middle, and was dressed in a black jacket and cloth cap. "If Papon is found guilty, then the *appareil* of the state will be held responsible," he was saying to another journalist. "The French people will be saying that there is a limit, you must act on your conscience, even if you are a man motivated not by hatred but by procedures." Behind him, members of his group, the Association of Sons and Daughters of the Deported Jews of France, were reading out the names of Jewish children whom Papon was charged with having sent to their deaths.

A few moments later three British journalists rushed into La Concorde, having just heard the accused man's last speech. Like all of Papon's interventions during the trial, this one was sonorous, unremorseful, and full of literary and artistic reference. As soon as he finished, the three judges and nine jurors had gone to deliberate 764 questions of guilt or innocence, with a tray of sandwiches to see them through the night. The three Brits now sat down and ordered wine and roast chicken, and one began reading his translation of the speech as the others ate: "He said that it was a double scandal, something about Camus in here. Oh, yes, his wife's favorite writer was Camus." The reporter looked down at his notes and deciphered. "They killed his wife . . . I think." Papon's wife of sixty-six years had died, at the age of eighty-eight, the week before the trial was to end. " 'In their desperate . . . desperate search,' I think you'd put it, 'for a crime, they have killed her with . . . *petits esprits.*' What would you say? Small guns? Small steps? Little blows? Little blows. De Gaulle gave her a *Légion d'Honneur*."

" 'With his own hands,' " one of the other journalists added, consulting his notes.

"Oh, yes. God, yes. 'With his own hands.' Then there was . . . Oh, yes. Here's when he turned to the prosecutor: 'Sir, you will go down in history—but through the servants' entrance!' " The reporter looked up, his eyes amused. "Well, that's not bad. Now something here about the absence of Germans. Oh, yes: 'Throughout the stages of this strange and surreal trial, there has been a notable absence of Germans.' A Notable Absence of Germans—sounds like a Michael Frayn play. Then something odd about Abraham sacrificing Isaac in Rembrandt, a ray of light? Staying his hand. Anyone get that?"

Everything came to a halt as a crowd of journalists who had gathered around the table tried to call to mind the light of an early Rembrandt, struggling to keep up with the tight web of cultural allusion spun by a French war criminal.

"Well, anyway," the British reporter resumed, "he called it the most beautiful light in painting. I still don't get it. He's comparing himself to the Jewish child about to be killed? Well, it's a point of view. Anyway, he stayed the hand. So that's it. Camus, his wife, no Germans, servants' entrance, bit about the light, Rembrandt, and then the sandwiches were sent in," he concluded decisively.

"Anyone see what kind of sandwiches?" an American reporter asked anxiously. The Brits laughed. But a little later the man from the *L.A. Times* said that he had seen the sandwiches go in, and he was confident that they were ham.

|||

When the French government in Bordeaux surrendered, in 1940, it was replaced by the right-wing Vichy government under the direction of Maréchal Pétain, the great French hero of the

First World War. The Vichy regime passed anti-Jewish laws that summer, before the Germans even demanded them. Two years later, at the Nazis' demand, Vichy began deporting Jews, including children, from all over the country. Although "only" 25 percent of the Jews in France were sent to death camps, this is, as the historian Robert Paxton has pointed out, a derisive figure: Jews in France were the most assimilated in Europe. If there had not been fiches and dossiers in place at the prefecture, the Germans would have had a hard time finding Jews to kill.

No one disputes that from 1942 to 1944 Maurice Papon, the secretary-general of the department of the Gironde, signed documents recording the arrest, assembly, and deportation of more than 1,500 Jews, including 220 children. The *rafles* took place between July 1942 and May 1944. The documents show that the deportees, some French, some refugees from the East, were to be sent to the transit camp of Drancy, outside Paris. Then they were to go to a *destination inconnue*. The unknown destination was Auschwitz.

Papon's history after the war is also public knowledge. By the end of 1943 Papon had begun to cooperate quietly with the resistance, and even sheltered an important Jewish *résistant*. Then, at the liberation, he delivered the prefecture to the resistance and, despite the complaints of a few locals, began a spectacular rise in the postwar French bureaucracy as an *haut fonctionnaire*. In the late fifties he became the head of the prefecture of police in Paris and, in the seventies, budget minister in the government of Giscard d'Estaing. (The division between *hauts fonctionnaires* and politicians in France is fluid; there were five *hauts fonctionnaires* in the cabinet that signed the armistice with the Germans. Today, 41 percent of the members of the National Assembly are civil servants on leave.)

Then, in 1981, Michel Slitinsky, a Bordeaux Jew who had escaped the deportations, met a historian named Michel Bergès, who had been doing work on the role of the local wine negotiants during the war. Bergès had stumbled on some interesting documents recording what the prefecture under Papon had been doing at the same time. Slitinsky eventually helped deliver the documents to the satiric newspaper *Le Canard Enchaîné*. Later, two more Bordelais, Maurice-David Matisson and René Jacob, made formal accusations against Papon. (A Frenchman can bring a charge against another Frenchman to the attention of a magistrate, who may then investigate it.) President Mitterrand did everything he could to delay the trial. French justice is under the control, or anyway the influence, of the president; Mitterrand must have felt that opening old Vichy cases was not in anyone's interest, especially his. It was only in 1995 that a formal indictment was handed down. Last October, Papon was brought from his house outside Paris to Bordeaux to stand trial.

The trial began in October and was expected to end in December, but it went on until the *poisson d'avril*—April Fools' Day. The cast of characters in the courtroom, as the trial was reported in manic detail in the Paris papers, seemed noisy and fantastic. French courtroom decorum allows far more time than would be acceptable in an American or British court for free questioning, speechifying, digressive material, and moral instruction directed by whoever is in the mood to give it toward whoever he thinks deserves to get it. This lent the event an interestingly literary air. There was the lawyer for the accused, Jean-Marc Varaut, the author of grandiloquent books on famous trials: one on Oscar Wilde, one on Jesus. There was a stream of historians: Bergès, now bizarrely on the side of the defense; the universally admired American Robert Paxton, the greatest of Vichy historians; and Henri Amouroux, "of the Institute," the most well-known historian to appear for the defense.

There was Serge Klarsfeld, whose son Arno was one of the leading civil prosecutors in the trial. (In a French courtroom, four or five separate prosecution teams—some civil, some from the government—can all argue the same case, each in its own way.) Arno drove the other prosecutors crazy. At the last minute he pleaded for a lesser penalty for Papon than *perpétuité*, the life sentence, demanded by the *parquet*, the prosecuting government authorities. And during the trial he led a move to have the presiding judge barred, on the ground that a relative of his had been among the deportees. (This may have been a preemptive strike, to keep the defense from raising the same point.) Then, after the motion failed, he took it on himself to disassociate Papon from other, worse war criminals, like Paul Touvier and Klaus Barbie, whom his parents had also helped bring to justice, announcing that, unlike them, Papon had merely signed papers. Since the whole point of the trial was to establish that signing papers was itself a crime, the other prosecutors understandably developed an even more intense dislike of Arno. Arno became the event of the trial. Out of the black robe and white kerchief that French lawyers still wear, making them look like perpetual Daumier drawings, he could often be seen in jeans, with his shirt hanging out. He is handsome, but in a modelish way, with too much hair and too open a collar. For a while before the start of the trial, he lived with the model Carla Bruni and had been photographed in *Paris Match* with her on a romantic vacation in Venice. Most days he arrived at the Palais on Rollerblades. Even in America this would have been controversial. In France it was regarded as just short of mooning the judges.

Above all, there was Papon himself, pompous and aging and erect and unrepentant. For the first time in a French war crimes trial, there was a figure of sufficient Mephistophelian stature to excite a moralist. Papon may have been evil, but he was certainly not banal. According to the rules of French trials, he was allowed not just to speak but to pontificate, and from the courtroom came daily dispatches recording, in the sonorous, Gaullist tones of the high estate, his views on the trial and the witnesses brought against him. "This testimony is moving in both its nature and the dignity with which it was given," he said of one witness. Or again, "I cannot help but express my emotion in the face of this sober, painful account. It brings back heart-wrenching memories."

The trial failed to clarify its subject, for reasons that were partly complicated and French, partly universal and human. The universal and human reason was that Papon was an old man being tried as an accomplice to murder. Complicity is hard to prove in any courtroom, and old men make bad culprits. Papon was sick—too sick, the doctors said, to be held in prison during the trial—and his wife was even sicker; after he went home for her funeral, there were those who thought that he might not come back. Whenever it seemed that the accusers had assured the necessity of his conviction, Papon stumbled, or fell sick, or a confused memory intervened, and one was reminded that here was a very old and decrepit functionary. Whenever one wanted to leave the verdict to the historians, one was reminded by some piece of heartbreaking evidence—a few words about a wife, a mother—that here in person was the instrument by which the French state casually delivered children to their murderers. We will have justice, said the ghosts. I will soon be one of you, said the guilty man. The trial went on for six months—too short a time to try Vichy, someone said, and too long a time to try Papon.

There is an idea, beloved of American editorialists, that the Vichy regime itself was on trial in Bordeaux and that France was finally "confronting its repressed past." This is a myth. The French have been obsessed with the details of Vichy for at least twenty-five years. Almost every bookstore keeps a shelf of books devoted to these four years of France's thousand-year history. Frenchmen of the left and of the right long ago accepted that Vichy was made possible by the German army but followed homegrown right-wing ideology, and was broadly popular.

What was on trial in Bordeaux was not Vichy but something more: *l'état*, the state itself, through the acts of one of its most successful representatives. The French war crimes trials of recent years, from Barbie the Gestapo man to Touvier the militia-man to Papon the *fonctionnaire*, have been moving closer to the heart of the French identity. The idea of *l'état*, the state, and its representatives, the *hauts fonctionnaires*, has a significance in

France that is incomprehensible to Americans, for whom it means, at best, the post office. *L'État* suggests far more than the mere sum of the civil service. It has the authority that the Constitution has in America, that the monarchy until recently had in Britain. (Serge July, of the newspaper *Libération,* has even referred to "the religion of the *fonction publique.*") The state is the one guarantor of permanence in a country where neither the left nor the right can quite accept the legitimacy of the other side.

In France the state intervenes between the nation, the repository of racial memory, beloved of the right, and the republic, repository of universal rights, beloved of the left. Its presence lets them coexist: The state keeps the nation from becoming too national, and the republic from becoming too republican. In France the state suggests the official, disinterested tradition of service; it means the functioning and unity of the country; it means what works. When one of the lawyers at the trial, trying to give an interview in English, was prompted with the term *civil servant* as a translation for what Papon had been, he repeated it and then visibly gagged, as though he'd swallowed a bad oyster; the idea of associating the word *servant* with the social role he was describing was just too weird.

The cult of the state makes France run. Yet every cult comes at a price. The price of constitution worship, as in America, is to make every personal question a legal question—so that every pat on every bottom, every swig on a bottle, and every pull on every cigarette seem likely to have, eventually, a law and a prosecutor of their own. The price of state worship, as in France, is that real things and events get displaced into a parallel paper universe; the state is possible only because everything has been neatly removed from life and put in a filing cabinet.

The abstraction extends into every corner of French life. The girl at the France Télécom store who is asked for a new fax ribbon finds it, places it on the counter beside her—and then spends fifteen minutes searching through her computer files, her inventory, for some evidence that such ribbons do in fact exist. The ribbon on the counter is an empirical accident; what counts is what is in the system. The reality is the list; the reality is the document. This French habit of abstraction, unlike, say, the German habit of blind obedience, is difficult to criticize, because it is linked to so many admirable things. It is linked to the French gift for generalization, for intelligent living, for the grand manner, the classical style. It not only makes the trains run on time but makes them run on time to places one would like to visit. But it was this national habit of abstraction, with its blindness to particulars, that was, in a way, on trial.

The irony was that a French courtroom attended by the French political classes was the last place to defeat, or even to test, the compulsive habit of abstraction. The language of French lawyering, like the language of the institute and the academy, is an *étatiste* language. Inside and outside a French courtroom, abstractions pile on abstractions, and by the end you are so distracted that you are unable to face plain facts: children in a cattle car being delivered to a death camp. It was not just that you could not see the trees for the forest. It was that you could not see the forest because it was covered by a map.

So the documents involving deportations that bear Papon's signature might have been official orders authorizing actions, but—crucial difference—they might have been official memorandums, recording for the benefit of the regional prefect, Maurice Sabatier, who was Papon's boss, actions already taken, a type of document that belongs in a different filing cabinet. Bergès, the historian who found the documents, was persuaded to testify that this was in fact the case. Papon was, in his own words, a mere *téléphoniste*—a receptionist, taking messages and creating memorandums. Then what to make of Sabatier's delegating to him, among other things, responsibility for Jewish affairs? Ah, but—understandable, though lamentable, confusion—this Department of Jewish Affairs was a recording bureau, not to be confused with the governmental Department of Jewish Affairs, which organized the deportations and the convoys. Papon was responsible for Jewish affairs only in a secondary sense. Anyway, he did whatever he could to protect Jews; look at the memos in which he struggles to see to it that Jewish children are sent to their parents! But those children were being sent to parents who were already dead and were therefore being sent to their own deaths. Where on paper can that be shown to have been understood? Within the paper universe of the prefecture, the unorthodox act of attaching children's files to their parents' was an act of respect for families, whatever the sad distortion in the world outside. And Papon actually insisted that the cattle cars, *wagons à bestiaux,* be replaced with passenger cars. But if he was capable of ordering the change of cars then . . . No, here again you are confusing the technical decisions of the prefecture with the policy directives of Paris—or, in this case, of Paris and Vichy. In any case, Maître Varaut, Papon's lawyer, demanded, seizing on the prosecutors' uncertainty about how hard to press their case, how could one talk about degrees of guilt in a crime against humanity? Either one was implicit in mass murder or one was not. Any other claim was illogical. One could not be 60 percent guilty, or 30 percent guilty. The paper chain proved guilt or it did not.

Only the victims seemed quite real. Marcel Stourdze, a deportee who traveled back and forth from Paris to Bordeaux every day, in order not to miss a day, testified, "When I went back to Auschwitz after the liberation, I saw that in an enormous vat they had saved all the hair. I thought that I saw the hair of my wife. Today all that hair has become white. But at the time it still bore the color of those we had loved."

|||

One of the shocks the trial offered involved the events not of 1942 but of 1961. At that time, when Papon was the head of the Paris police, the city and federal police had taken part in a mas-

sacre in which approximately two hundred Algerian demonstrators died. It was toward the end of the Algerian War, and Algeri-
ans in Paris, sympathetic to Algerian nationalism, broke a curfew
and marched to the center of the city. There had been Paris policemen killed in the preceding month, and as the march pressed
on, a kind of murderous free-for-all began. Many of the demonstrators, bound hand and foot, were drowned in the Seine. (The
details of this atrocity, which took place in the center of Paris, remain murky and obscure.) A partial glimpse of the records of the
crime appeared only last fall, in the newspaper *Libération*.

This was regarded as good news for the defense—it showed
that Papon had nothing particular against Jews—but it was also
seen as an attempt by the left to equate the mistakes of the
Gaullist regime during the Algerian civil war with the crimes of
Vichy. What came to fill the gap of real issues was, inevitably,
contemporary politics. The first people to feel the sting of the
Papon trial were the Gaullists, and Philippe Séguin, the leader of
the remaining Gaullist party, was the first political leader to de-
nounce the trial. De Gaulle himself, Séguin felt, had come
under attack. Papon, after all, had been allowed to continue in
the *fonction publique* and had been regularly promoted by
Gaullist politicians.

The right discovered a response in an 850-page book called *Le
Livre Noir du Communisme,* the Black Book of Communism,
which appeared last November, shortly after the Papon trial had
begun. It is an encyclopedia of Communist atrocities around the
world, from 1917 to the present, all scrupulously recorded and
presented, with a tally of a hundred million deaths. The Black
Book became the subject of a polemic, focused indirectly, as
everyone understood, on the *procès Papon.* Were the crimes of
the Communists really comparable to the crimes of the Nazis?
And if they were, didn't that make the entire apparatus of international communism, including, of course, the French Communist party and its intellectuals—slavishly Stalinist for so

long—"complicit" in another way too? Were the fiches in the prefecture the only ones that mattered or could acts in that other paper universe, of poems and manifestos, be complicit in murder too?

|||

After the jury retired, the journalists waited for the verdict at La Concorde. The wine was good, a generic Merlot, and every table was taken. Nine o'clock became ten, the clouds of smoke thickened, and the gaiety rose as, one by one, filing deadlines for the next day's paper passed. Twelve o'clock and the French journalists are off the hook; three o'clock and the Brits are off! Only the Americans are going to have to file late tonight, no matter what. But then, around three-thirty, the big news comes in. The Paula Jones case has been dismissed; whatever anyone files is now set for page 2. Mildly annoying to the newspapermen, this news is disaster for the independent television crews. "I can hear them now," one cameraman says moodily, deep in his cups. " 'Ship it, ship it.' " ("Ship it" meaning "Don't even try to put it on the satellite" is the TV equivalent of "We'll call you.")

The owners of La Concorde had learned, over the months of the trial, that American journalists cannot be outdone in their pitiless pursuit of truth and blank restaurant receipts. To cries of "Fiche, fiche, fiche," the waiters slap one down with every order. A gloomy Dutch newspaperman at one table is telling stories about how often he has broken big stories, but in Dutch. "No one knows. No one cares," he says. "Cheesus could come back tomorrow, but if he comes to me, they'll know it only in Amsterdam."

The British journalists, deadlines gone, drink whiskey and begin to reminisce about other, kinder war crimes trials, where you didn't have to stay up all night for the verdict. "Take the Barbie trial," one says. "Everyone knew what the verdict would be, but the jury waited until just after midnight to announce it; that way they got an extra day's pay, six hundred francs. We all went out and got drunk with the jury and the lawyers, and then we filed and were all on the boat train home and back in London in time for dinner. Now, that was a trial for crimes against humanity that wasn't a crime against humanity."

The Klarsfelds wander in and out, waiting for the verdict like everyone else. They have been cast as wreckers, loose cannons, pursuing some odd, private agenda. Seeing them together, certainly, one finds the connection between stolid, impassive father and mercurial son hard to grasp. Daniel Schneidermann, a television journalist who has written a book about the trial, argues that the horror of their family history—Serge's father was a deportee who died in Auschwitz—has left an "emptiness" inside Arno, the emptiness of a world that, since the Holocaust, has been abandoned by God. It is probably true that Arno's aggressive gestures—the Rollerblades, the jeans, the rude interjections in court—are meant to show a certain distaste for the whole pompous system, for the parallel paper universe in all its dignity. But it is also possible that metaphysics aside, the Klarsfelds just have a shrewder take on the possibilities of the trial than their more sophisticated confreres. They understand that only an "intermediary" penalty, only some finding of guilt for Papon clearly distinguished from the great guilt of the real killers, will seem plausible to a Bordeaux jury. They are struggling to articulate, in the rhetoric of the courtroom, that there are gradations of guilt, styles of complicity, even in the Holocaust. To treat Papon as though he were equivalent to SS killers, like Barbie, is, in a sense, to draw a line again around the killings, with pure evil on one side and innocence, by implication, safely on the other.

Among the people and the talk and the stories, one bald, hard-looking man in his seventies, drinking his cognac and coffee, never leaves his table. "Who is he?" a newcomer asks.

"Nobody knows," one of the women from the wire services answers. "He's been here every day since the trial began. He hassled some of the women, but then he gave it up." She lowers her voice. "A lot of us think he may be the man from the FN." The FN, the neo-Fascist National Front, is the phantom of Vichy that everyone wishes would go to sleep.

At four-thirty in the morning it was announced that the verdict would arrive at eight. A lot of the American reporters went back to their hotel rooms, opened their windows to let in the French spring air, and turned on CNN to watch the news about the Paula Jones dismissal. It was hard, one reporter commented afterward, not to think about the extravagant good fortune of a country that had trials like that to worry about. Another, watching James Carville and Susan Carpenter-McMillan on *Larry King*, said that he found it hard, particularly after months of trying to decode French verbal combat, to remember which was which: Did the two Americans on TV actually hate each other, despite the smileyness and forced good humor? Or was the hatred the pretense, and the reality the professional prizefighter's camaraderie? He had, he said, been away from America too long to remember.

By eight everyone was back at La Concorde. Serge Klarsfeld was waiting too. Someone asked one of the Brits, who had been there all night, if anyone had any instincts about what was to happen.

"None," he said.

"No one was persuaded?"

"No one was sober," he replied.

Shortly after nine a middle-aged woman rushed into the café. She was stout and squarely built and was bent over as she ran. She had both palms held out straight in front of her, fingers spread. It was a strange, lamenting posture, like that of a Greek mourning figure.

She ran over to Klarsfeld. He nodded and wept briefly, and they held each other. Ten! The spread fingers meant that Papon had been given ten years. "And everyone against us," Klarsfeld muttered. It was a victory for him and for Arno; the jury had found Papon guilty of complicity in crimes against humanity, but not of mass murder.

Outside, the children of the deportees came to meet Klarsfeld, clasping one another and kissing cheeks. They were stout and old and plain; evil may sometimes be banal, but virtue, to its credit, always is.

In front of the courthouse the argument had already begun. "It isn't enough of a penalty!" someone cried. "You go serve ten years," Klarsfeld said, pushing him gently. The stout lady kept saying, "It was double or nothing, the *parquet*"—the government prosecutors—"wanted double or nothing." She said "double or nothing" in English. Klarsfeld said, "He was not Touvier, and he was not Barbie. The ultimate *responsables* were the Nazis. After you have looked a real Nazi in the eye, you know the difference with Papon." For the most part, the civil parties and the reporters who had been with them for six months were disappointed. "Ten years! Ten years is what you give a housebreaker," one exhausted French journalist said.

Somehow, back in Paris, the verdict seemed more tolerable. Paradoxically, the trial had concentrated so exclusively on Papon's role in Bordeaux in the forties that it had redrawn his picture, making him once again a mere prefect. In reality, he had not been one more face among the *fonctionnaires* but one of the highest, one of the great men of state, a cabinet minister. But this was a Paris reality, not a Bordeaux one, and it was only back in Paris, where the ministerial Papon could be recalled, that the scale of the achievement in Bordeaux registered. A great man of state, protected by the state, had been pursued for crimes by pitifully ordinary people—and despite that, he had at last been held responsible. It wasn't the victory over abstraction that Camus had died dreaming of. But this time nobody gave up.

In a way, the jury in the Palais de Justice had even, over sandwiches, used their imaginations to make some necessary retrospective law, and they had done it well. By saying that Papon didn't know where the trains were going, and also saying that he was guilty of crimes against humanity, they were making the right and courageous point. To deliver a child to the secret police is as large a crime against humanity as you ever need to find, no matter where you think he is going or what kind of car he is going to travel in. The men with stamps and filing cabinets now couldn't plead procedure any more than soldiers could plead orders; the *appareil* of the state would have to understand that their fiches represented people, whether they were Jews or Algerian demonstrators or refugees yet to come. The parallel paper universe now had a window.

|||

I had explained to Luke, over the course of the trial, what was going on and why I was away: A bad man had long ago done wicked things to little children, and now he would be put in jail for it. When I came home, he asked if they had put the bad man in jail, and I said, well, yes, they had. "And when the bad man got put in jail, did all the children come out?" he asked.

Of course, they hadn't even really put the bad man in jail. Papon remained free for almost another two years in various appeals—unusually so for a convicted man in France—and then, on the eve of his incarceration, fled to Switzerland. It seemed clear from the circumstances of his flight that he had some kind of internal help from the French functionary state. But he was found, quickly, within days, and brought back to France and locked up at last. In his flight he had taken the alias of La Rochefoucauld, the great French skeptic, a man of culture to the end.

Trouble at the Tower

Paris in July is pretty much left to the tourists and the people who look after them, while everyone else goes south, or west, or, in any case, away. An incident at the Eiffel Tower—which left a tourist sore, the tower closed tight for a couple of days, and an elevator operator out of a job for a while—told you everything you needed to know about what happens when you leave the tourist and his handlers alone to sort things out. What happened, if you missed it, was that a lady tourist got on the "up" elevator of the tower with a ticket for the second platform and then decided to get off at the first platform (because she felt dizzy or because she didn't, or just because she was exercising her fundamental right to get on and off an elevator whenever she felt like it). She was kept from getting off the elevator by a French elevator operator (who either gently dissuaded her or handled her a bit roughly, or else launched into a Joe Pesci–in-a-Scorsese-film attack). The woman (an American? No, a Brit! Finally the French papers settled on calling her an Anglo-Saxon) was, it turned out, a successful writer with a profound sense of indignation and a lawyer. She complained, and the company that runs the tower—it's a private business—had the elevator guy fired. But then the rest of the tower employees went out on strike in solidarity, closing down the tower and leaving a lot of indignant American and British tourists on the ground, furious at being denied their chance to be manhandled by the elevator operators.

The incident produced a certain panicky, just discernible exchange of meaningful glances for the rest of the week between the tourists and the touristed. ("So that's what they want—our lives!" "So that's what they want—our jobs!") Naturally, sympathy in France gathered quickly around the wronged operator and his striking friends, while sympathy on the Anglo-American side gathered around the roughed-up lady. This distribution of sympathy wasn't merely tribal, though. The Eiffel Tower Incident of the Summer of '97 illustrates a temperamental and even intellectual difference between the two cultures. Most Americans draw their identities from the things they buy, while the French draw theirs from the jobs they do. What we think of as "French rudeness," and what they think of as "American arrogance," arise from this difference. But she was just trying to have a good time, we think. But he was only doing his job, they think. For us, an elevator operator is only a tourist's way of getting to the top of the Eiffel Tower. For the French, a tourist is only an elevator operator's opportunity to practice his métier in a suitably impressive setting.

The metaphysics of consumerism are much studied, of course, since it seems to be the century's winning ism. (Americans have shown that whole art forms can be made through creative browsing.) Producerism, its surprisingly hardy French counterpart, is much less well diagnosed. The Eiffel Tower itself is a prime example of pure producerism, of métier mania: a thing built by an engineer as a self-sufficient work, whose only function is to stand there and be admired for having been engineered. The French ideal of a world in which everyone has a métier but no customers to trouble him is more practical than it might seem. It has been achieved, for instance, by the diplomats inside the quai d'Orsay, who create foreign policy of enormous subtlety and refinement which has absolutely no effect on anyone outside the building. It has also been achieved by IRCAM, the modern music institute, which sponsors contemporary composers who write music that so far no one has ever heard. (When the waiter at the café finally deigns to shake your hand, it does not mean that you are now a valued client. It means that you are now an honorary waiter.)

The elevator operator dreams of going to the top of the tower alone in his elevator, while the Anglo-Saxon tourist, in her heart of hearts (and he knows this; it's what terrifies him most), dreams of an automatic elevator. When the two ideals—of absolute professionalism unfettered by customers and of absolute tourism unaffected by locals—collide, trouble happens, pain is caused. Americans long for a closed society in which everything can be bought, where laborers are either hidden away or dressed up as nonhumans, so as not to be disconcerting. This place is called Disney World. The French dream of a place where everyone can practice his métier in self-enclosed perfection, with the people to be served only on sufferance, as extras, to be knocked down the moment they act up. This place, come to think of it, is called Paris in July.

Lessons
from
Things

Couture
Shock

I suppose you could say that my introduction to the rites and spells of Parisian haute couture occurred early on a Sunday morning, at the Valentino show, when the ladies in the front row suddenly, and pretty much in unison, folded their programs over and began to fan themselves ferociously with the gold and brown paper. The Valentino show was being held at nine-thirty in the morning for reasons of protocol so complicated that they resembled one of those nineteenth-century diplomatic negotiations, like the Schleswig-Holstein question, comprehensible to only three people in Europe. The cream of the fashion press had turned up anyway, although Anna Wintour and Suzy Menkes and the rest had the pained, *aren't*-you-a-clever-boy-to-wake-me-up-this-early smiles otherwise seen only on parents of two-year-olds. The music had begun, Stella Tennant had come out (head angled, shoulders thrown back, hips a little forward, rolling the works) in ivory wool and silk chevron trousers with two patch pockets, an ivory blouse with matching lace, and a beige cash-mere shawl bordered in lace, looking game despite the hour and all that lace. Then the ladies in the front row, the rich clients, began to fan. They fanned hard, expertly—my God, it's hot in here—just the way veteran *dé-flé* watchers always do. And this was odd, because it was freezing cold inside the Salon Opéra at the Grand Hôtel: the coldest July in Paris anyone could recall; cassoulet and topcoat weather. But the ladies fanned as they al-ways do, in the gasping heat of July at the collections.

I turned to a friend sitting next to me, a French television journalist, and directed at her my version of the French shrug-and-frown that means, Why on earth? She, in turn, made the French O with her mouth that means, Please, my friend, discard this elaborate pretense of naiveté. Then she shrugged too. "They are at the collections. It is July. They fan," she said. She thought for a moment. "It is a reflex. We watch, therefore we fan. No. I fan, therefore I am." Then she looked around the salon and made the encompassing shrug-and-pout-and-flex-your-hands-from-the-wrist French gesture that in the context meant that the ap-parent absurdity of the act of fanning yourself in the cold is no more absurd than the whole enterprise of traveling to Paris to look at clothes that you will never wear, displayed on models to whom you bear no resemblance, in order to help a designer get people who will never attend shows like this someday to buy a perfume or a scarf that will give them the consoling illusion that they have a vague association with the kind of people who do at-tend shows like this—even though the people who attend shows like this are the kind who fan themselves against July heat that happens not to exist. It is these formulations—packed tight with contradictions that spiral around, turn in on themselves, bite their own tails, and eventually come out dressed in taffeta and lace tulle—that give haute couture its charm, or, anyway, help it cast its spell.

Participating in the haute couture is more like entering a

yacht in the America's Cup than it is like opening a Seventh Avenue showroom: The collections are overseen by the Chambre Syndicale de la Couture Parisienne, which demands, among other things, that its members maintain a working atelier in Paris, and put on a show each season of no fewer than fifty costumes each. Belonging is an expensive, exacting business, and every year one more house just drops out. This season there were sixteen shows—about a thousand outfits, from Stella's silky pants to the wedding dress at Saint Laurent. First an event and then a theme dominated the five days of the shows. The event was the separation of Gianfranco Ferrè as head designer from the House of Dior, which was significant because it threw a major house into a "crisis," and the theme was the crisis of haute couture. Of course, haute couture is always in crisis, like Cyprus or the New York theater. But by now the crisis has become almost existential; not even a hit will help. Even very, very rich women don't buy bespoke clothes in Paris anymore, and the widely understood, though never openly articulated, justification for losing money in couture for the past twenty years or so—the loss leader justification—no longer works. By now, most fashionable people feel, the average woman who buys, say, a box of Pierre Cardin handkerchiefs is probably buying them less because of the glamorous association of Pierre Cardin haute couture than because of the glamorous association of Pierre Cardin socks and Pierre Cardin sunglasses. (As a consequence, Pierre Cardin, who seems to have figured this out, doesn't even show his haute couture line in the *défilés*.)

Fashionable people have two contradictory theories to explain the persistence of couture despite its troubles—theories usually mentioned in succession and often in the same sentence. The first—a kind of Tang and Teflon explanation, which is promoted by the *chambre*—is that haute couture is the R&D wing of the fashion business, an investment in its future, since the "techniques" and "styles" that the designers wheel out today will somehow affect the kind of clothes that people wear tomorrow. (Veteran explainers offering this view can make it sound as though the *défilés* were taking place in a particle accelerator.) The other, contradictory explanation is that haute couture is the living memory of French fashion, where vanishing standards of workmanship, craftsmanship, and imagination are kept alive as a necessary act of filial piety. When you point out that both these explanations can't be true at the same time, you generally get in response a kind of Paris Zen. "Ah, you are right. Both things cannot be true at once. That is the point of haute couture," one fashion prince explained to me. Then he walked off seraphically.

|||

The haute couture remains a rite. There are the photographers, who push to get inside, and who form, on their bleachers, a little island of happy heterosexual lust amid two seas of becalmed aestheticism. They're the only free men at the collections; they whoop, whistle, and call out to the models anything they feel like calling out to the models. ("They could come out dressed in paper bags for all I care," one photographer said that morning as he looked over the Valentino program. "Well, *plastic* bags anyway.") Then there are the models themselves, who can undress and dress again so quickly that when the show is over, they climb out of the last evening dress and are on the street, wearing jeans and T-shirts and Prada knapsacks, getting a taxi before the applause has stopped. And there are the fashionable people, lining up in order not to be allowed in. (The shows never start on time, or near it, but everybody comes to the security desk and waves the invitation anyway.)

It's the clothes, of course, that differ from show to show. At Valentino the collection soon settles into a look—clothes in colors that the regular guy might describe as "sort of brown," although a fashionable person might call them chestnut, chocolate, beige, coffee, and bronze. The sequence of styles is fixed. Day wear comes first, then what are still called, touchingly, cocktail dresses, and then evening wear. Usually a wedding dress comes last, but Valentino replaced it with a long red chiffon sheath. As the models come out, almost everyone in the room begins one task of translation or another. The press has the simple job of translating the descriptions of the clothes, which are written in fashionese, into ordinary language. Valentino's program was relatively taciturn compared to most. Lacroix, for example, later in the week showed a " 'cold dawn' shot razimir spiral sheath dress with 'apricot' and 'melon' kick pleat"). Still, even Valentino's "Mordoré silk laminated ottoman pinstriped pantsuit, gold lace polo T-shirt, black cashmere shawl bordered in gold lace" became, in the margin of one journalist's program, "beige slacks." The garment industry people are looking for something—a range of colors, a shape, a new line—that they can translate from cashmere and laminated ottoman into cottons and synthetics and sell. They sketch shapes, which to the unpracticed eye all look more or less the same. A tight bodice with a big skirt represents evening wear; a short, tight jacket with big pleated flowing pants stands in for day wear. The few unattached, noncommercial, nonbuying spectators in the room are waiting for what they call a couture moment—a moment, the newcomer is assured, that is roughly equivalent to the moment in opera when the clouds of shlock lift and something crazily artificial becomes transporting.

Only the top fashion editors—at whom all the expense is in a way directed—cannot sketch or make notes, for fear of seeming rude. They leave that to their underlings and try to look interested and amused as each costume passes by. A haute couture *défilé* is an oddly heart-lifting occasion, inflected with hope. The fashion editors are hoping that one of the models' dresses will give them a point, a theme, something to write about. The fashion merchants are hoping that one of the models' dresses, suitably adapted, will make them a fortune. The aficionados are hoping that one of the models' dresses will supply a couture moment. The photographers are hoping that one of the models' dresses will fall off. The press scribbles. The photographers hoot. The ladies fan.

|||

Most of the collections are shown either in the ballroom of the Hôtel InterContinental, which is long and narrow and mock grand siècle, or, like the Valentino show, in the ballroom of the Grand Hôtel, which is high and circular and Second Empire. On Sunday afternoon, though, every fashionable person has to find a taxi or get a lift all the way out to the periphery of Paris, where John Galliano is showing his fall collection for Givenchy at the Stade Français—the old French indoor sports arena. What no one at Givenchy has considered, though, is that holding the show in a stadium means holding the waiting period before the show outside the stadium—in the open air, where few fashionable people are inclined to spend a lot of the day and, as it happens on this Sunday, in a steady Paris drizzle too.

Things get ugly fast. "It is insupportable!" one distinguished-looking dowager is crying as the rain pelts her perfectly constructed face. "I have been a Givenchy client for decades, and now I am being made to stand outside, exposed to the wind, naked to the rain!"

"In the rain! *In the rain!*" the lady next to her cries out, and she goes on, "I too have been a client for a period of time." She resists saying "decades," despite its obvious pathetic force; she is a little younger than the first lady. "The thing is insupportable."

"No! It is worse! It is a scandal!" the first lady cries, definitively. *Insupportable* is a bitter word in French, but *scandal* is a fighting one. Even the Givenchy guards at the chain-link gate, in their double-breasted jackets, are beginning to get uneasy. When the crowd gathered outside the Bastille, the trouble began after some old lady said the thing was a scandal.

At this point the fashion editor André Leon Talley comes up, pushing people aside on his way to the ritual "No, you see, *I've* been invited. What! You mean these people have too?" moment. André Leon Talley is a big guy, and for a second or two it seems likely that the guards are going to let him in. This makes the dowagers, standing behind me, plain crazy, and they charge, blind to the consequences. We are storming the Givenchy gates when the guards just give way: They open the gate and let everyone walk across the lawn toward the stadium. We file in, feeling vindicated, and take our seats. At least thirty more minutes pass before anything happens.

The Givenchy show, appropriately, takes as its subject the ever-popular fashion themes of decapitation and mass murder. Inside the stadium Galliano has constructed a Fragonard-like forest of feathery trees and dark ferns. Then, instead of sending the models one by one down a runway, he sends them out in groups, to wander around the artificial forest. The setting is meant to recall eighteenth-century French aristocratic life, and the dresses what became of it. The dress worn by Inès de la Fressange, for instance, is frankly described as an "ivory lace Empire Trench with blood pre-guillotine velvet sash." All the girls are meant to look as if they were on their way to the tumbrels, and in fact the Revolutionary-era Empire dresses, with their long, columnar lines and soft, clinging bodices, in beaded ivories and reds and champagnes and olives and emeralds, *are* quite unreal in their loveliness. They are by far the most memorable "pure" design of the week and, toned down and deblooded, the obvious tip to become this autumn's look.

||||

Haute couture, everyone says, no longer has much to do with what normal women normally wear. The besetting sin of haute couture, though, is not unreality but corniness: not that it looks like things no women would actually wear but that it looks exactly like what your aunt Ida *always* wears "for best"—that shiny black thing, say, covered with sequins and accompanied by a little shoulder-hugging jacket.

This is a thought that occurs on Monday afternoon, at the Ungaro show—a collection of pantsuits and long dresses so standard and uneventful that it gives you a lot of time to think. There is a reason, you realize, that even women who could afford to do not wear what the models in Ungaro are wearing: dresses of floor-length flowing lace. The reason is that fancy clothes look fancy, and fanciness now looks primitive. So many of the clothes, in their elaborately ostentatious materials, just seem regressive, overrich, brutally obvious. In feeling, they date back to a time when a complicated display of expensive materials was meant to be crushing evidence of wealth. Now wealth, wanting to crush, likes subtler evidence; that's why more wealthy women buy Brice Marden squares than haute couture evening clothes.

Ungaro, though, has intelligently taken his show off the runway too and put it on the floor—in principle, so that you can see the detail work on the clothes, but with the side effect that you can also see a lot of the models inside them. None of the big-name girls are here—not Linda or Naomi or Claudia—but it is the B, or nonname, models who are the most thrilling to look at. This is partly because the name models are phoning it in; Linda Evangelista, at the Givenchy show, had exactly the smug "I don't have to do this for a living anymore" look that Shecky Greene and Buddy Hackett used to have when they "dropped in" on Merv Griffin. The B list models, on the other hand, *work*: They throw out their hips, they flirt with their eyes, and when the photographers call out to them to smolder, they smolder. A great deal of time is spent—by regular guys anyway—explaining to themselves why the haute couture models are not really as desperately beautiful as you might think when they are even more beautiful than you can imagine. The trick—or, to put it another way, the consolation—is that their beauty has become so familiar that it is not so much a commodity as a commonplace. Looking at Kate Moss modeling Givenchy, you don't think, There's a heartbreakingly beautiful girl. Instead you just think, There's Kate Moss. The projected fantasy bangs up not against her inaccessibility but, paradoxically, against her familiarity. She offers not a limitless horizon of love and elegance and great clothes but the reality of a known life. (You would have to avoid talking about Johnny Depp. You would have to tell her how thin she looks, or, rather—for it is the New Kate—how zaftig.)

But they are perfect! A twelve-year-old American boy who was visiting Paris that week had come equipped with his skateboard, and, to his shock, discovered in Paris not a skateboard hell but a paradise of broad, flat avenues and, at the place du Trocadéro, vast, flat concrete plazas. "How do you find Paris?" he was asked.

His eyes went round and reverent.

"*Smooth*," he said.

I find the models smooth too.

One new girl in particular is so perfectly beautiful that she seems a composite of various imaginary smoothnesses. I later learn that her name is Honor Fraser, that she is English, and that she is being tipped by the fancy as the Next Great Model; she will be Miss England in next year's Pirelli calendar. I feel like a novice horseplayer who has just picked the Kentucky Derby winner.

When the shows were over, I spoke with her about what it is like to be on the runway, instead of watching what happens there. She turned out to be a poised student of her own craft. "I love modeling couture," she said, with a passionate eagerness. "It's the only pure expression in fashion—the one part of the fashionable world where there are no commercial compromises at all. There's something terribly moving about being an element of it—being its vehicle. The purity and the exactitude that the designers devote to every tiny detail of your clothing and accessories, as though they were working from some image deep in their minds, which they're trying to approximate with you, the way people exhaust themselves in pursuit of an ideal—it's really very moving. It's quite extraordinary to be backstage, being made up for two hours, being transformed from who you are into this ideal of beauty that the designer keeps in the back of his mind.

"I love couture modeling too, because you have such a pure feeling of control and power when you're out there. For a tiny period of time—three or four seconds—you have the chance to hold the entire room. This may seem like a strange comparison, but I'm fascinated by comedy, and I imagine that modeling couture must feel very much like being a comedian; it's just you out there, having to win over an audience, with nothing except yourself and your attitude to do it. And then I, for one, find the clothes so lovely—those Valentino colors that aren't quite colors and yet register as though they were. I feel lucky to have been a part of it." I had never before come across someone who was articulate and knowing about her craft, was big enough to start at power forward, and looked great in a black velvet military coat with rhinestone buttons, black satin trousers, and a black silk top embroidered with black jet. (She had been wearing that, for Valentino, the first time I saw her.)

|||

Tell about the pathetic collections. A certain number of the collections seem intended to be pathetic. Olivier Lapidus's is my specimen pathetic collection. The house is full, and the B list girls do the modeling, and Olivier, who is the son of the designer Ted, looks like a very nice guy. But it is held at the Carrousel du Louvre, a place designed specially to hold collections—it is big and well lit and clean—which means, naturally, that absolutely nobody wants to show there. Olivier Lapidus comes onstage to point out that his collection is a mixture of past, present, and future and includes the first solar-paneled jacket ever made. He shows it off. You can control the solar panels, turning the heat up or down, and it also has a built-in plug that could *brancher* you right into the Internet, the first haute couture garment equipped to go on-line. The poor model has to take the plug out of the pocket and show it to the audience. Then you hear the theme from *Star Trek*. Nobody knows which way to look.

|||

Tuesday night is Christian Lacroix. The show is held in the ball-room of the Grand Hôtel, and it is by far the most intently at-tended *défilé* I have seen yet; even Mme. Chirac is here. Lacroix is of the moment. I associate his clothes with the tasteless things about the eighties, the Ivana Trump era—clothes to wear for the big settlement. Tonight, when the lights go down, Linda Evange-lista comes out in the ugliest dress I have ever seen. Even the program's words can't disguise its ugliness: "silk-crêpe dress stamped with a mauve-and-ochre-green 'reptile' design." I am settling in for a good long bath of contempt.

But then something happens. First, the music begins to take hold. In most of the collections the music is either generic "so-phisticated" soprano and synthesizer pop—the kind you associ-ate with the singer Sade—or classical chestnuts, like Albinoni and Mozart. Lacroix, though, has had someone (the program credits a Laurent Godard) with an uncanny eclectic ear arrange his music. We begin with the breathless, chimelike sounds of the Swedish group the Cardigans and switch to Joe Jackson and then, without missing a beat, land in a Bellini aria. Lacroix works through his day wear and moves into the cocktail dresses and then the evening wear. In the program he announces that he has been spending all his time lately "with Vermeer." He seems to have taken a wrong turn in the museum, for what you see is Goya: Goya's duchesses, in their mantillas and black satin dresses, but wildly remade, as though for a Balanchine ballet of the life of Goya. There are lots of satins and silks in dark colors—navy blue satin and vermilion satin and black chiffon. The layer-ing is ecclesiastical. For once, the program description actually describes the clothes: a long, lined black crepe sweater-dress tucked up over a crepe underskirt with a fuchsia faille bustle at the back, accented by a pistachio satin knot. The crepuscular colors mute the ostentation, so that it doesn't look like ostentation at all but, rather, like art, like old painting. The music turns to the Beatles' baroque period: the string part from "Eleanor Rigby" and then a long cello and harp version of "For No One." The lovely sad yet modern tunes, the twilight, and the dresses themselves create, against all odds and probabilities, something touching, and even—Honor Fraser's word is right—moving. The dresses aren't really dresses at all; they are little buildings of crepe and silk and taffeta. The girls look out from them, like Spanish ladies looking out from a second-floor window. When a model named Victoria appears in a black satin corset with Elizabethan sleeves of tulle and worn over a deep lavender-blue skirt flecked with black lace—she looks like an actress dressed up as Viola for an impossibly beautiful production of *Twelfth Night*— the audience applauds, genuinely, not politely. When Karen Mulder comes out in a silver lace dress with an iced pearl bodice, I make exclamation points in my program.

It's all too much, and that's where the loveliness—the couture moment—begins. The clothes are extravagant and unreal, but they don't seem camp. They don't seem artificial or out of this world, just symbolic of a common human hope that the world could be something other than it is—younger and more musical and less exhausting and better lit. It proposes that the little moments of seduction on which, when we look back, so much of our life depends could unfold as *formally* as they deserve to, and all dressed up. It is as if we were wishing that the rituals of sex, those moments of painful sizing up, which begin with the thought That's a nice dress, could pass by more consequentially, slowly—love walking down a runway instead of just meeting you outside the movie theater.

Couture is a romantic cartoon. It's a caricature of the romantic impulse, with a cartoon's exaggerations but a cartoon's energy and lighthearted poetry too. The thing you feel in a couture moment isn't "What a wonderful dress" or, as you do with higher kinds of art, "What a good place the world is," but, more simply,

"I'm in love." The point of haute couture may be any one of a hundred things, ninety-nine of them sordid or silly, but its subject is women wearing clothes and all the emotion that rises from women wearing clothes. Offering romance in cartoon form, couture helps preserve the habit of romance. The best moments at Lacroix or Givenchy, far from being giddy or empty, were familiar and held out the promise of the beginning of a whole familiar cycle. Soon the fantasies, translated, will become purchases— This Fall's Dresses—and these will become photographs, the kind you look at five years later (God, that dress is so mid-nineties!) to find that they have become a little piece of your time, a peg to hang a good memory on ("Remember that kind of satiny Lacroix knockoff thing you had? You looked great in that"). The sequence, one of the last romantic sequences we can count on, starts in these hotels; that they happen to be places where rich ladies cool themselves off in the cold seems a small price to pay to keep that emotion in circulation.

The emotion passes quickly, of course. In a minute Love walks back up the runway, changes into her jeans and T-shirt, and is on the phone to her agent. Still dazed by Lacroix, I stumbled across one beauty outside the hotel with her cell phone clutched in her hand. I heard her mutter, firmly, "I know I said I'd do it, but I can't. It's only Tuesday, and already I've got taffeta coming out my ass."

|||

Yves Saint Laurent, on Wednesday morning, is the last important collection, and the most "classic." Here, for once, is a really well-organized show, where everybody slips inside on time. Lacroix is the haunt of the new Gaullist French government establishment; Saint Laurent is still the favorite of the old Socialist aristocracy, and they all turn out. Jack Lang, the former culture minister, is here, looking as though he owned the place. (The Socialists loved Saint Laurent because his clothes promised the pleasures of modernity without the sacrifices of modernism; that was the Mitterrand dream.) Saint Laurent just shows Saint Laurent, beautiful clothes that he could have shown in 1980 or 1990 just as well. The music is standard opera arias. Everything gets a hand.

The big news for the photographers is that Claudia Schiffer has come to YSL, having been snubbed by Karl Lagerfeld at Chanel, and she gets the first-desk position. Claudia, though, is not what you would call a team player. While the other models only occasionally respond to the photographers' pleas for more, Claudia stands at the end of the runway for what seems like ten minutes at a time, making love to every camera in sight. The other girls, held up at the head of the runway and waiting for her to get through, give her exactly the look you see on the face of an impatient commuter at the Holland Tunnel who is stuck in the exact change lane behind a woman who has entered it on a hunch.

Then the blond, Botticelli-faced Karen Mulder comes out in the costume that every photographer has been dreaming of for years: *robe de soir courte de mousseline et satin noir*—a sheer dark silk nightgown that, for one reason or another, provides an undergarment below but not above. Karen holds one fingertip precisely in front of each breast, demurely, as she walks down the runway. The photographers go crazy. "Karen! Karen!" they moan. "*Give* us something." Karen smiles. Nothing doing. She walks right to the end of the runway—right into the heart of the photographers' lair—smiling, keeping her fingertips in place, not embarrassed but not giving anything away, either, and then she walks right back. The photographers groan, in disbelieving unison, as she disappears. You could have heard them out on the place Vendôme. "There was a fortune in it for all of us," one of them says mournfully. I notice Claudia, on her way in, giving Karen a look. You have the feeling that Claudia would have dropped her hands, pulled off the gown, and jumped off the runway to autograph the negatives.

Afterward, in the Saint Laurent dressing room, I see that, while every other outfit, on every other girl's card, includes three or four accessories, cover-ups, or undergarments, the *robe de soir,* listed on Karen Mulder's card, is, by design or mistake, all by itself—nothing to help her out at all. For the first time all week, someone had left a fashionable vacuum. She had filled it with her fingertips.

The Crisis in
French Cooking

Nine o'clock on a Friday morning, and David Angelot, the *commis* at the restaurant Arpège, on the rue de Varenne, has begun to braise tomatoes for dessert. The *tomate confite farcie aux douze saveurs* is one of the few dishes in the Michelin red guide whose place on the menu has to be clarified with a parenthesis (*dessert*), indicating that though it sounds like a veggie, it eats like a sweet. It is a specialty of the kitchen of the great chef Alain Passard, which a lot of people think is the best and most poetic in Paris, and probably all France; it requires a hair-raising amount of work by the *commis*, the kitchen cabin boy; and many people who care about French cooking believe that it is a kind of hopeful portent, a sign that the creative superiority of French cooking may yet be extended indefinitely. Normally a braised tomato becomes tomato sauce. ("The limitations of this insight," one of Passard's admirers has noted gravely, "describe the limitations of Italian cuisine.") To make a tomato get sweeter without falling apart not only is technically demanding but demonstrates, with a stubborn, sublime logic, an extremely abstract botanical point. Tomatoes are not vegetables; they are fruit.

For David, who may not see M. Passard all day long, they are work. David, who is eighteen and who studied cooking at a government school just outside Lyons, cuts the tomatoes open (about fifty of them, from Morocco, in the winter), scoops them out, and makes a *farce,* a stuffing of finely chopped orange and lemon zest, sugar, ginger, mint, pistachios, star anise, cloves; then he makes a big pot of vanilla-scented caramel and braises the stuffed tomatoes in it, beating the caramel around the tomatoes vigorously for forty-five minutes without actually touching them. The tomato is a fruit and can be treated like one, but it helps to beat a lot of caramel into its body, to underline the point.

While he works, he thinks about his girlfriend (who is also a cook, and with whom he lives in an apartment in north Paris), his future, and his desire to visit Japan someday. He works in a tiny basement room in the small, two-story space of the kitchen, and he shares that room with another, more experienced assistant, Guilhem, who spends his mornings making bread. (All the bread at Arpège is made by hand.) Guilhem, while he works, thinks of going back to Washington—he calls it D.C.—where he has been before, where there is a constant demand for good French food, and where he has an offer to work in a French bakery. If David's job at Arpège embodies one of the principles of high French cooking—the gift of making things far more original than anyone can imagine—Guilhem's embodies the opposite but complementary principle: the necessity of making things much better than anybody needs. This morning he will make three kinds of bread: a sourdough raisin and nut loaf; trays of beautiful long white rolls; and a rough, round peasant bread. All the bread will be sliced and placed in baskets to be presented upstairs in the dining room, and then mostly pushed around absentmindedly on the plates of people who are looking at their menus and deciding what they really want to eat. This knowledge makes Guilhem a little bitter. He thinks about D.C.

In the main kitchen, a short flight up, Pascal Barbot, the sous-chef, is keeping things under control. The atmosphere there, with eleven serious short men in white uniforms going about intricate tasks in a cramped space, does not so much resemble the bridge of a nuclear submarine in an action movie as it does the bridge of a nuclear submarine in an action movie after it has been taken over by the Euroterrorists led by Alan Rickman: that kind of intensity, scared purposefulness, quickness, and heavy, whispered French. The kitchen is white and silver, with a few well-scrubbed copper pots hanging high up—not like the lacquered copper you see in rusticated, beam-heavy restaurant interiors but dull and scrubbed and penny-colored. The richest colors in the kitchen are those of French produce, which is always several glazes darker than American: The birds (chickens, pigeons, quail) are yellow and veined with deep violet, instead of the American white and rose. The assistant chefs start at nine o'clock and will remain at their *stages* until one o'clock the next morning. When the service begins, around twelve-thirty, they will experience an almost unendurable din, which, after a few days of work, they learn to break down into three or four distinct sounds: the *thwonk* of metal in water hitting the sides of a sink as a pot is washed by one of the Malinese *plongeurs*; the higher, harsh *clank* of one clean saucepan being placed on another; the surprisingly tinny, machine-gun *rat-a-tat* of a wire whisk in a copper pot; and the crashing, the-tent-just-fell-down-on-your-head sound of hot soiled pans being thrown down onto tile to be washed again. (In a good kitchen the pans are constantly being recycled by the *plongeurs*.)

The kitchen crew includes three Americans. They have worked mostly at California and New York restaurants of the kind that one of them describes as "grill and garnish joints." They are all converts to Passardism. There is never anything entirely new in cooking, but Passard's technique is not like anybody else's. Instead of browning something over high heat in a saucepan and then roasting it in an oven, in the old French manner, or grilling it quickly over charcoal, in the new American one, Passard cooks his birds and joints *sur la plaque*: right on the stove, over extremely low heat in big braising pans, sometimes slow-cooking a baby *gigot* or a milk-fed pig in a pot for four or five hours on a bed of sweet onions and butter. "He's just *sweating* those babies," one of the Americans marvels under his breath, looking at the joints on the stoves. "Makes them cook themselves in their own fat. It's like he does everything but make them pluck their own feathers and jump into the pan. Fucking genius."

Downstairs, another of the Americans is slicing butter and teasing Guilhem about his D.C. plans. "Look at this butter," he says to himself. "That's not fucking Land o'Lakes." He turns to Guilhem. "Hey, forget about D.C.," he says. "It's cold. There are no women. Where you want to go is California. That's the promised land. Man, that's a place where you can cook *and* have a life."

Guilhem looks genuinely startled and turns to speak. "You can?" he says, softly at first, and then louder, calling out to the back of the American cook as he races up the stairs with the butter pats for the dining room. "You *can*?"

|||

Most people who love Paris love it because the first time they came they ate something better than they had ever eaten before, and kept coming back to eat it again. My first night in Paris, twenty-five years ago, I ate dinner with my enormous family in a little corner brasserie somewhere down on the unfashionable fringes of the Sixteenth Arrondissement. We were on the cut-rate American academic version of the grand tour, and we had been in London for the previous two days, where we had eaten *steamed* hamburgers and fish-and-chips in which the batter seemed to be snubbing the fish inside it as if they had never been properly introduced. On that first night in Paris we arrived late on the train, checked into a cheap hotel, and went to eat (party of eight—no, party of nine, one of my sisters having brought along a boyfriend), without much hope, at the restaurant at the corner, called something like Le Bar-B-Que. The prix-fixe menu was fifteen francs, about three dollars then. I ordered a salad Niçoise, trout baked in foil, and a cassis sorbet. It was so much better than anything I had ever eaten that I nearly wept. (My mother, I am compelled at gunpoint to add, made food like that all the time too, but a mother's cooking is a current of life, not an episode of taste.) My feelings at Le Bar-B-Que were a bit like those of Stendhal, I think it was, the first time he went to a brothel: I knew that it could be done, but I didn't know there was a place on any corner where you could walk in, pay three dollars, and get it.

That first meal in Paris was for a long time one of the few completely reliable pleasures for an American in Europe. "It was the green beans," a hardened New Yorker recalled not long ago, remembering his first meal in Paris, back in the late forties. "The green beans were like nothing I had ever known," he went on. He sat suddenly bolt upright, his eyes alight with memory.

Now, though, for the first time in several hundred years, a lot of people who live in France are worried about French cooking, and so are a lot of people who don't. The French themselves are, or claim to be, worried mostly about the high end—the end that is crowded into the Passard kitchen—and the low end. The word *crise* in connection with cooking appeared in *Le Monde* about a year ago, with the news that a restaurant near Lyons, which had earned three Michelin stars, was about to close. Meanwhile, a number of worrying polls have suggested that the old pyramid of French food, in which the base of plain dishes shared by the population pointed upward to the higher reaches of the *grande cuisine*, is collapsing. Thirty-six percent of the French people polled in one survey thought that you make mayonnaise with whole eggs (you use only yolks), 17 percent thought that you put a *travers de porc* in a pot-au-feu (you use beef), and 7 percent believed that Lucas Carton, the Paris restaurant that for a century has been one of the holiest of holies of haute cuisine, is a name for badly cooked meat. More ominously, fully 71 percent of Frenchmen named the banal *steak-frites* as their favorite *plat*; only people past sixty preferred a *blanquette de veau*, or a *gigot d'agneau*, or even a pot-au-feu, all real French cooking. (The French solution to this has been, inevitably, to create a National Council of Culinary Arts, connected to the Ministry of Culture.)

To an outsider, the real *crise* lies in the middle. That Paris first-night experience seems harder to come by. It is the unforced superiority of the cooking in the ordinary corner bistro—the *prix-fixe ordinaire*—that seems to be passing. This is partly a tribute to the international power of French cooking and to the great catching up that has been going on in the rest of the world for the past quarter century. The new visitor, trying out the trout baked in foil on his first night in Paris, will probably be comparing it with the trout baked in foil back home at, oh, Le Lac de Feu, in Cleveland—or even back home at Chez Alfie, in Leeds, or Matilda Qui Danse, in Adelaide—and the trout back home may just be better: raised wild or caught on the line. Even the cassis sorbet may not be quite as good as the kind he makes at home with his Sorbet-o-matic.

The fear—first unspoken, then whispered, then cautiously enunciated, and now loudly insisted on by certain competitors—is that the muse of cooking has migrated across the ocean to a spot in Berkeley, with occasional trips to New York and, of all places, Great Britain. People in London will even tell you, flatly, that the cooking there now is the best in the world, and they will publish this thought as though it were a statement of fact and as though the steamed hamburger and the stiff fish had been made long ago in another country. Two of the best chefs in the London cooking renaissance said to a reporter not long ago that London, along with Sydney and San Francisco, is one of the capitals of good food and that the food in Paris—"heavy, lazy, lacking in imagination"—is now among the worst in the world.

All this makes a Francophile eating in Paris feel a little like a turn-of-the-century clergyman who has just read Robert Ingersoll: You try to keep the faith, but Doubts keep creeping in. Even the most ardent Paris lover, who once blessed himself at every dinner for having escaped Schrafft's, may now find himself—as he gazes down one more unvarying menu of *boudin noir* and *saumon unilatéral* and *entrecôte bordelaise* and *poulet rôti*, eats one more bland and buttery dish—feeling a slight pang for that Cuban-Vietnamese-California grill on Amsterdam Avenue or wondering whether he might, just possibly, enjoy the New Sardinian Cooking, as featured that week on the cover of *New York*.

I would still rather eat in Paris than anywhere else in the world. The best places in Paris, like the Brasserie Balzar, on the rue des Écoles, don't just feed you well; they make you happy in a way that no other city's restaurants can. (The Balzar is the place that plays Gallant to the more famous Brasserie Lipp's Goofus.) Even in a mediocre Paris restaurant, you are part of the richest commonplace civilization that has ever been created and that extends back visibly to the previous century. In Paris restaurants can actually go into a kind of hibernation for years and awaken in a new generation: Lapérouse, the famous swanky nineteenth-century spot, has, after a long stretch of being overlooked, just come back to life, and is a good place to eat again. Reading Olivier Todd's biography of Camus, you discover that the places where Camus went to dinner in the forties (Aux Charpentiers, Le Petit St. Benoît, Aux Assassins) are places where you can go to dinner tonight. Some of Liebling's joints are still in business too: the Beaux-Arts, the Pierre à la Place Gaillon, the Closerie des Lilas.

These continuities suggest that a strong allegiance to the past acts as a drag on the present. But, after several months of pains-taking, tie-staining research, I think that the real problem lies in the French genius for laying the intellectual foundation for a rev-olution that takes place somewhere else. With movies (Méliès and the Lumière brothers invented the form and then couldn't build the industry), with airplanes, and now even with cooking, France has again and again made the first breakthrough and then got stalled. All the elements of the new cooking, as it exists today in America and in London—the openness to new techniques, the suspicion of the overelaborate, the love of surprising juxtapo-sitions—were invented in Paris long before they emigrated to London and New York and Berkeley. But in France they never coalesced into something entirely new. The Enlightenment took place here, and the Revolution worked out better somewhere else.

|||

The early seventies, when I was first in France, were, I realize now, a kind of Indian summer of French haute cuisine, the last exhalation of a tradition that had been in place for several hun-dred years. The atmosphere of French cooking was everywhere in Paris then: thick smells and posted purple mimeographed menus; the sounds of cutlery on tables and the jowly look of pro-fessional eaters emerging blinking into the light at four o'clock.

The standard, practical account of the superiority of French cooking was that it had been established in the sixteenth cen-tury, when Catherine de' Medici brought Italian cooks, then the best in the world, to Paris. It was not until after the French Rev-olution, though, when the breakup of the great aristocratic houses sent chefs out onto the street looking for someone to feed, that the style of French cooking went public. The most fa-mous and influential figure of this period—the first great chef in European history—was Antonin Carême, who worked, by turns, for Talleyrand, the future George IV, Czar Alexander I, and the

Baroness de Rothschild. He invented "presentation." His cooking looked a lot like architecture, with the dishes fitted into vast, beautiful neoclassical structures.

The unique superiority of French cooking for the next hundred years depended on the invention of the cooking associated with the name Auguste Escoffier. Escoffier's formula for food was in essence the same as Jasper John's formula for dada art: Take something; do something to it; then do something else to it. It was cooking that rested, above all, on the idea of the master sauce: A lump of protein was cooked in a pan, and what was left behind in the pan was "deglazed" with wine or stock, ornamented with butter or cream, and then poured back over the lump of protein. Escoffier was largely the creature of courtiers and aristocratic patrons; the great hoteliers of Europe, particularly César Ritz, sealed in place the master sauce approach that remains the unchallenged basis of haute cuisine.

It was also an article of faith, dating, perhaps, to Alexandre Dumas *père*'s famous *Grand Dictionnaire de Cuisine*, that the cooking of Carême and Escoffier had evolved from a set of provincial folk techniques. At the heart of French food lay the pot-au-feu, the bouillon pot that every peasant wife was supposed to keep on her hearth, and into which, according to legend, she threw whatever she had, to stew for the day's meal. French classic cooking was French provincial cooking gone to town.

|||

I heard another, more weirdly philosophical account of this history from a professor named Eugenio Donato, who was the most passionately intellectual eater I have ever known. Armenian-Italian, reared in Egypt and educated in France, he spoke five languages, each with a nearly opaque Akim Tamiroff accent. ("It could have been worse," he said to me once, expertly removing one mussel with the shell of another as we ate *moules marinières* somewhere on the place de la Sorbonne. "I had a friend whose parents were ardent Esperantists. He spoke five languages, each with an impenetrable Esperanto accent.") Eugenio was a literary critic whom we would now call a poststructuralist, though he called what he did philosophical criticism.

Most of the time he wandered from one American university to another—the Johnny Appleseed or Typhoid Mary of deconstruction, depending on your point of view. He had a deeply tragic personal life, though, and I think that his happiest hours were spent in Paris, eating and thinking and talking. His favorite subject was French food, and his favorite theory was that "French cooking" was foreign to France, not something that had percolated up from the old pot-au-feu but something that had been invented by fanatics at the top, as a series of powerful "metaphors"—ideas about France and Frenchness—that had then moved downward to organize the menus and, retrospectively, colonize the past. "The idea of the French chef precedes French cooking" was how he put it. Cooking for him was a form of writing—Carême and Escoffier had earned their reputations by publishing cookbooks—with literature's ability to make something up and then pretend it had been there all along.

The invention of the French restaurant, Eugenio believed, depended largely on what every assistant professor would now call an "essentialized" idea of France. One proof of this was that if the best French restaurants tended to be in Paris, the most "typical" ones tended to be in New York. Yet the more abstract and self-enclosed haute cuisine became, the more inclined its lovers were to pretend that it was a folk art, risen from the French earth unbidden. For Eugenio, the key date in this masquerade was 1855, when the wines of Médoc were classified into the famous five growths in which they remain today. "The form of metropolitan rationalization being extended to the provincial earth, *in the guise of the reflection of an order locked in the earth itself*," he announced once, bringing his fist down on the tablecloth. He was a big man, who looked uncannily like John Madden, the football coach.

On that occasion we were eating lunch in one of the heavy, dark, smoky Lyons places that were popular in Paris then. (There is always one provincial region singled out for favor in Paris at any moment—*privileged* would have been Eugenio's word. Then it was Burgundy; now it is the southwest. This fact was grist for his thesis that the countryside was made in the city.) The restaurant was, I think, someplace over in the Seventh; it may have been Pantagruel or La Bourgogne. At lunch, in those days, Eugenio would usually begin with twelve escargots in Chablis, then go on to something like a *filet aux moelles*—a filet with bone marrow and Madeira sauce—and end, whenever he could, with a mille-feuille.

The food in those places wasn't so much "rich" as deep, dense. Each *plat* arrived looking mellow and varnished, like an old violin. Each mouthful registered like a fat organ chord in a tall church, hitting you hard and then echoing around the room: There's the bass note (the beef), there's the middle note (the marrow), and there's the treble (the Madeira in the sauce).

It couldn't last. "We have landed in the moment when the metaphors begin to devour themselves, the moment of rhetorical self-annihilation," Eugenio once said cheerfully. This meant that the food had become so rich as to be practically inedible. A recipe from the restaurant Lucas Carton that I found among a collection of menus of the time that Eugenio bequeathed to me suggests the problem. The recipe is for a *timbale des homards*. You take three lobsters, season them with salt and pepper and a little curry, sauté them in a light *mirepoix*—a mixture of chopped onions and carrots—and then simmer them with cognac, port, double cream, and fish stock for twenty minutes. Then you take out the lobsters and, keeping them warm, reduce the cooking liquid and add two egg yolks and 150 grams of sweet butter. Metaphors like that can kill you.

Something had to give, and it did. The "nouvelle cuisine" that replaced the old style has by now been reduced to a set of clichés and become a licensed subject of satire: the tiny portion on the big oval plate; the raspberry-vinegar infusion; the kiwi. This makes it difficult to remember how fundamental a revolution it worked in the way people cooked. At the same moment in the early seventies, a handful of new chefs—Michel Guérard, Paul Bocuse, Alain Senderens—began to question the do-something-to-it-then-do-something-else-to-it basis of the classic cooking. They emphasized, instead, fresh ingredients, simple treatment, an openness to Oriental techniques and spices, and a general reformist air of lightness and airiness.

The new chefs had little places all around Paris, in the outlying arrondissements, where, before, no one would have traveled for a first-rate meal. Michel Guérard was at Le Pot-au-Feu, way out in Asnières; Alain Dutournier, a little later, settled his first restaurant, Au Trou Gascon, in the extremely unfashionable Twelfth. In the sad, sedate Seventh Arrondissement, Alain Senderens opened Archestrate, first in a little space on the rue de l'Exposition, in the shadow of the Eiffel Tower, and then on the rue de Varenne.

From the beginning, the new cooking divided into two styles, into what Eugenio identified as "two rhetorics," a rhetoric of *terroirs* and a rhetoric of *épices*—soil and spice. The rhetoric of the *terroirs* emphasized the allegiance of new cooking to French soil; the rhetoric of the *épices* emphasized its openness to the world beyond the hexagon. The soil boys wanted to return French cooking to its roots in the regions; the spice boys wanted to take it forward to the new regions of *outre-mer*. Even as the new cooking tried to look outward, it had to reassure its audience (and itself) that it was really looking inward.

On the surface the beautiful orderly pattern continues. Alain Senderens is now in Michel Comby's place at Lucas Carton and has replaced the *timbale des homards* cooking with his own style.

Senderens's rue de Varenne Archestrate is now occupied by Alain Passard, the Senderens of his generation, while the original Archestrate is occupied by a talented young chef and his wife, just starting out, who have named the restaurant after their little girl, La Maison de Cosima.

But twenty-five years later the great leap forward seems to have stalled. A large part of the *crise* is economic: A hundred-dollar lunch is a splurge; a four-hundred-dollar lunch a moral dubiety. Worse, because of the expense, the cooking at the top places in Paris is no longer a higher extension of a commonplace civilization. It is just three-star cooking, a thing unto itself, like grand opera in the age of the microphone. Like grand opera, it is something that will soon need a subsidy to survive; the kitchen at Arpège depends on regular infusions of range-struck Americans to fill the space left by the French kids who no longer want to work eighteen-hour days for very little money while they train.

And it is like grand opera in this also: You can get too much of it, easily. It is, truth be told, often a challenge to eat—a happy challenge, and sometimes a welcome one, but a challenge nonetheless. It is just too rich, and there is just too much. The new cooking in France has become a version of the old.

At Lucas Carton you begin with, say, a plate of vegetables so young they seem dewy, beautifully done, but so bathed in butter and transformed that they are no longer particularly vegetal, and then you move on to the new lobster dish that has taken the place of the old one. Where the old lobsters were done in a cowshedful of cream, the new lobsters are done, *épicé* style, with Madagascar vanilla bean. This is delicious, with the natural sugar of the lobster revealing the vanilla as a spice—although, for an American, the custard-colored sauce, dotted with specks of black vanilla, disconcertingly calls to mind melted lunchroom ice cream. For dessert, you might have a roasted pineapple, which is done on the same principles on which Passard's tomatoes are braised: It ends up encrusted in caramel. This is delicious too, though intensely sweet. Lunch at Lucas these days can fairly be called Napoleonic or Empire; the references to the revolutionary principles are there, but finally it's in thrall to the same old aristocratic values.

Lucas is hardly representative, but even at the lesser, less ambitious places the cooking seems stuck in a rut: a chunk of boned protein, a reduced sauce; maybe a fruit complement, to establish its "inventive" bona fides; and a puree. The style has become formulaic: a disk of meat, a disk of complement, a sauce on top. The new cooking seems to have produced less a new freedom than a revived orthodoxy—a new essentialized form of French cooking, which seems less pleasing, and certainly a lot less "modern," than the cooking that evolved at the same time from the French new cooking in other countries. The hold of the master sauté pan, and the master sauce, and the thing-in-the-middle-of-the-plate is still intact.

|||

Thinking it over, I suspect that Eugenio put his finger on the problem with the new cooking in France when it first appeared. "A revolution can sweep clean," he said, "but a reformation points forward and backward at the same time." The new cooking was, as Eugenio said, a reformation, not a revolution; it worked within the same system of Michelin stars and fifteen-man kitchens and wealthy clients that the old cooking did. It didn't make a new audience; it tried to appropriate the old one.

In America—and in England too, where the only thing you wanted to do with the national culinary tradition was lose it—the division between soil and spice wasn't a problem. You could first create the recipes and then put the ingredients in the earth yourself. The American cooks who have followed in Alice Waters's pathmaking footsteps at Chez Panisse, in Berkeley—the generation whom a lot of people think of as the children of M. F. K. Fisher—created a freewheeling, eclectic cosmopolitan cuisine: a risotto preceding a stir-fry leading to a *sabayon*. Then they went out and persuaded the local farmers to grow the things they needed.

In France the soil boys won easily. Some of what they stood for is positive and even inspiring: The *terroirs* movement has a green, organic, earth-conscious element that is very good news. The *marché biologique* every Sunday morning on the boulevard Raspail has become one of the weekly Parisian wonders, full of ugly, honest fruit and rough, tasty country meat. And it is rare for any restaurant in Paris to succeed now without presenting itself as a "regional" spot—a southwest, or Provençal, or Savoyard place. (Even at the exquisite Grand Véfour, at the Palais Royal, the most beautiful restaurant in the world and a cathedral of the cosmopolitan tradition, it is thought necessary to parade around a plate of the cheeses of the chef's native Savoy.)

Yet the insistence on national, or local, tradition—on truth to *terroirs*—can give even to the best new Paris restaurants a predictability that the good new places in London and New York don't share. The French, who invented the tradition of taking things over and then insisting that they were yours all along, are now shy about doing it. The cooking at a French restaurant must now, for the first time, be French. This tendency came to a head last spring, when a group of important French chefs actually issued a manifesto protesting the spread of exotic food combinations and alien spices in French cooking and calling for a return to the *terroirs*.

Peter Hoffman, the owner and chef of the influential Savoy, in New York, is one of those American chefs who went to France in the early eighties, were dazzled, and now find that the light has dimmed. He likes to tell about his most recent dinner at the three-star restaurant L'Ambroisie, on the place des Vosges. "We went to L'Ambroisie and had a classic French dish: hare with blood sauce. It was fabulous, everything you want rabbit with blood to be. But then I got talked into ordering one of the chef's specialties, a mille-feuille of langoustines with curry, and it was infuriating. It was a French dish with powder. It was such an insular approach, as though nobody understood that curry isn't a powder that you apply cosmetically. Nobody had read Madhur Jaffrey, or really understood that curry isn't just a spice you shake but a whole technique of cooking you have to understand."

As the writer Catharine Reynolds points out, the new cooking in America and England alike is really Mediterranean cooking, inspired by Italy, Tunisia, and Greece. It suits the fat-allergic modern palate better than the old butter and cream cooking of the north. France, which has a big window south, ought to be open to its influence yet remains resistant. The real national dish of the French right now—the cheap, available food—is couscous. But North African cooking remains segregated in couscous parlors and has not been brought into the main current. A fossilized metropolitan tradition should have been replaced by a modernized metropolitan tradition, yet what took its place was sentimental nationalism.

It was the invasion of American fast food, as much as anything, that made the French turn back to their own tradition and, for the first time, see it as something in need of self-conscious protection. Looking at America, the French don't see the children of M. F. K. Fisher; they just see the flood tides of McDonald's, which, understandably, strike fear into their hearts. The bistro became an endangered species. To make still one more *blanquette de veau* suddenly became not a habit of commonplace civilization but a form of self-defense.

|||

Waverley Root once divided all Gaul into three fats—lard, olive oil, and butter—and said that they determined the shape of French cooking. That you might be able to cook without putting any fat in the pan at all was an unthinkable notion. The charcoal grill, the brick oven, and all the other nonfat ways of cooking now seem normal everywhere except in France. People who look at cooking more practically than philosophically think that that technical lag is the heart of the problem.

"It's deglaze or die" is how Alexandra Guarnaschelli, an American cook in Paris, puts it. The master sauce approach remains the basis of French cooking, whereas elsewhere it has been overthrown by the grill. The pan and the pot have always been the basic utensils of French cooking—just what was there—in the same way that the grill was the primary element of American vernacular backyard cooking. For Americans, grilled food wasn't new but familiar, and good cooking is made up of familiar things done right. As the excellent American chefs Chris Schlesinger and John Willoughby have pointed out, grilling forced an entirely new approach to saucemaking: With no residue to deglaze, the cook had to think in terms of savory complements rather than subtle echoes. Grilling demanded chutney, fruit mustards, spice mixes. Although the French tradition included these things, they weren't part of the vernacular.

Alex has seen some of the predicament at first hand. She is twenty-seven; she arrived in France five years ago and, after training in Burgundy, became a *commis* at Guy Savoy's two-star place in the Seventeenth Arrondissement. Within a couple of years she had worked her way up to fish chef, and a little while later Savoy appointed her second-in-command at his bistro, La Butte Chaillot. (This is like a young Frenchman arriving in New York, all enthusiastic about baseball, and ending up five years later as the third baseman of the Yankees.)

The other day, over coffee on the avenue Kléber, Alex, who is from New York (she went to Barnard, Mom's an editor at Scribner's, Dad's a professor), said, "I decided I wanted to chop onions, so I tried the CIA"—the Culinary Institute of America, the MIT of American cooking—"but it was like eighteen thousand a year, *tout compris,* so I decided to go to Burgundy and chop. I started learning the French way, which is half beautiful beyond belief and half 'Please shoot me.' It's by the book. Really, there's a book, and you learn it. There's a system for everything, a way to do it. You can't cut the fish that way, because *ça n'est pas bon*. You can't bone a chicken that way, because *that's* not good. 'We do it the way it's always been done in France.' When I first started at Savoy, there was one old stager who, every time I did something, would just frown and shake his head and say, 'It won't do, it won't do.' Finally, I did *exactly* what he did, and he said, 'Good, now always do it exactly the same way.' So I did. You never get a real attempt to innovate, or to use new flavors. You can change an adjective, but the sentence stays the same.

"Whenever we make a classic sauce, everybody gathers around and *argues* about it. Once we got into a two-hour argument about whether you use chervil as well as tarragon in a true béarnaise. There are certain things these days that I will not do. I will not do mayonnaise or béarnaise. Uh-uh. I don't have time for the postgame analysis.

"Of course, there's that tomato at Passard's place," she went on. "But have you seen the way the poor kid has to work to make it?"

Alex's existence helps to explain why the new cooking went deeper in America than it could in France: In America the cooking revolution was above all a middle-class revolution, even an upper-middle-class revolution. A lot of the people who made the cooking revolution in America were doing it as a second career. At the very least they were doing it after a liberal arts degree; David Angelot started slicing carrots at fifteen. The most mocked of all modern American restaurant manners—the waiter who introduces himself by name—is, on reflection, a sign of something very positive. "I'm Henry, and I'll be your waiter tonight" means, really, "You and I belong to the same social class. Tomorrow night I could be sitting there, and you could be standing here."

The French system of education, unrenovated for a long time, locks people in place. Kids emerge with an impressive respect for learning and erudition, and intimidated by it too. For an American, getting a Ph.D. is a preliminary, before you go someplace else and find your real work, like opening a restaurant. Nobody thinks of changing métiers in France because it's just too hard. In America not only the consumers of the new cooking but, more important, the producers and dealers were college-educated. I once met a pair of American academics who had gone off to live with a flock of goats and make goat cheese. They had named the goats Emily, Virginia, Jessamyn, Willa, and Ursula. It was terrific goat cheese too.

|||

Beyond these reasons—the missing grill, the resurgent nationalism, the educational trap—there may be an even deeper reason for the lull in French cooking. A new book, *L'Amateur de Cuisine*, by an unknown author, Jean-Philippe Derenne, which was published last year, offers an anatomy of French cooking—an effort to organize the materials, forms, and manners of the subject in a systematic way. "This cookbook is a book," the author writes on the first page, and then attempts to create a whole taxonomy of cooking based not on folk tradition or cosmopolitan recipes but on an analysis of plants and animals and the chemistry of what happens when you apply different kinds of heat and cold to them before you eat them. He begins his market section with the minerals (a crisp page and a half) and then passes to the plants (more than a hundred pages) and the animals, divided into those of the earth and the sky and those of fresh and salt water. (Even *"Serpents, Sauriens, Lézards, etc."* get their moment in the sun.) He gives a precise biological description of every imaginable thing there is to eat, then presents an exact analysis of every imaginable method of cooking it and shows how all the glories of cuisine rise out of the limitless intersections of these two forces. It is a vast, eleven-hundred-page volume, comprehensive and radiant; it resembles less a cookbook than a medieval almanac, offering a timeless, secure, benevolent universe of food. Its subject isn't cooking. It's *plenty.*

Derenne is a modest and gentle scholar, not a cook or a critic or even a gourmand. He is a doctor, the head of the pulmonary department at a Paris hospital. Over lunch one afternoon at Arpège, Derenne, a small, good-natured man, with the open face and happy appetites of a Benedictine monk, said, "The same week that *L'Amateur de Cuisine* came out, I published another book, called *Acute Respiratory Failure of Chronic Obstructive Pulmonary Disease.*" That was another thousand pages. This, surely, is a record for total weight by one author published in one week.

Derenne wrote the cookbook in seclusion, in the garden of his little house near Fontainebleau, only to find himself, on its publication, a new lion of the French culinary establishment: the man who wrote the book. He gets reverential, *cher maître*–type letters from Paul Bocuse. Passard himself sees him as a friend. Dr. Derenne doesn't know quite what to make of it all.

"My editor said to me, when I gave him the manuscript, 'Why, you've written the first humanist history of food.' I said, 'No, not humanist. It's a religious book, really.' I was inspired by a history of religion by Mircea Eliade, which attempted the same kind of logical organization, rising upward from the types of religious apparition into the possibilities of organized faith. I've done for cooking what that author did for belief: shown an underlying logic without attempting to make it logical."

He went on to talk about a second volume, which he's just started: "It may be called free cuisine, but really it will be about the rejected cuisine. About everything the world throws out. Shells and guts and leaves—the whole world of the rejected. This is religious too, because religion depends on being able to find the holy in the ordinary. It's putting together things banal in themselves which nonetheless become transformed into something transcendent. You know who else has this quality? Duke Ellington—he simply used what he had."

There was something surprising about Derenne's talk, an expansive, open, embracing ardor that a hundred years ago would have seemed more American than French. It seems possible that the different fates of the new cooking in France and America are a sign of a new relation between the two places.

A century ago Americans used to say that what brought them to Europe was its history. At home, there was "no sovereign, no court . . . no aristocracy . . . nor ivied ruins; no cathedrals," as Henry James's famous list has it. What really brought Americans to the Old World, though, was the allure of power: cultural power, political power, military power—imperial power, as it existed in Europe and only there. What fascinated Whistler and James in the Old World was not its age but the extreme self-consciousness that comes with power, the way that power could be seen to shimmer through manners—the way that what you wore or how you stood (or what you ate) spelled out your place in a complicated and potent social hierarchy.

Now that that power has passed into American—or, anyway, English-speaking—hands, the trappings of power that come from extreme self-consciousness are ours too. Even our cooking—especially our cooking—has become involved with power. Where you stand on, say, the spread of McDonald's is a political issue, just as where you stood on the outdoor café was in France a century ago. Even the smaller issues of the palate count. Most American women define their feminism, at least in part, in terms of their attitude toward the kitchen. A century ago the modern form of that self-consciousness was invented in Paris. The limitlessly complicated relation of what you eat and where you eat it to where you stand in the social order is the subject of, for instance, the first two chapters of Maupassant's *Bel-Ami*. But now food and cooking in France have begun to take at least a small half turn back toward their other role, as sources of nourishment, comfort, cohesion. The role of food as anxious social theater, seen at its crudest in the endless worry in Los Angeles and

New York about power tables—where you sit at Spago, what time you leave the Four Seasons—is diminishing in France. We are the worldly, corrupt ones at the table now, and the Europeans, in this regard at least, are the innocents. Even their philosophers eat for pleasure.

‖‖

When the *tomate confite*, which David Angelot had been working on since nine o'clock, came out at last, Derenne tasted it. Then he said, "You see, he demonstrates for us what we knew from the first: that the tomato is a fruit. Would you call that arrogance or modesty?"

Not long after that I finally did what I had dreaded doing, though it would have been the practical thing to do all along, which was to go back to that first restaurant and see what it was like now. I walked back and found both the hotel and the restaurant, though both had changed their names—the hotel belonged now to the Best Western chain—and while in memory I had kept them on the same street, they were in fact a street apart. But the exterior of the restaurant was unmistakable; I found it by getting the Eiffel Tower in exactly the same area of my eye as it had occupied when I was fourteen. It was not far from—I am not making this up—the avenue Marcel-Proust. The restaurant is now called the Tournesol, and the less expensive prix fixe is 114 francs, or about twenty dollars. I ate à la carte. I had a little foie gras, sole meunière, and a cassis sorbet.

The food was even better than I had remembered. This proves either that (a) Proust was wrong, and you can always recapture the pleasures of your youth if you just go back to the places where you had them, or (b) there is more good cooking left in Paris than I knew, or (c) I went to the wrong place. Anyway, there's hope.

Barney in Paris

When people ask why Martha and I, not long after the birth of our first child, left New York for Paris, we can usually think of a lot of plausible-sounding reasons. They vary in tone from the high-mindedly agonized (we couldn't endure the malling of our SoHo neighborhood) to the cloyingly whimsical (we wanted to live within walking distance of the Gérard Mulot bakery, on the rue de Seine). The real reason was Barney. We had seen one after another of our friends' children—charming children of parents who parse Greek texts or write long metafictions set in the eighteenth century—sunk dumbly in front of a television set watching a man in a cheap purple dinosaur suit sing doggerel in an adenoidal voice with a chorus of overregimented eight-year-old ham actors. Just a glimpse was enough to scare a prospective parent to death: the garish Jeff Koons colors, the frantic prancing, the cynically appropriated public domain melodies. And, finally, that anthem of coercive affection—"I love you/you love me/we're a happy family"—sung, so incongruously, to the tune of "This Old Man."

The experienced reader will know of course that Barney stands here for the whole of American kiddie video culture. The experienced reader, though, is wrong. We looked forward to introducing Luke to Bugs and Bullwinkle and Bert and Ernie, and even Steve and Norm on *This Old House*. We just couldn't bear the idea of his watching Barney. The only way, we thought, to be sure that he wouldn't was to pack up everything we had and move to another country.

So, Paris. "We want him to grow up someplace where everything he sees is beautiful," we said, and though we realized that the moment our backs were turned our friends' eyes were rolling, we didn't care. We knew that our attempt to insist on a particular set of pleasures for our kid—to impose a childhood on our child—might be silly or inappropriate or even doomed. We couldn't help it, entirely. The romance of your child's childhood may be the last romance you can give up.

In our first week in our new home on the Left Bank, we were awakened early one morning by loud, oddly fugitive organ music; it sounded like a carousel yet seemed to be moving closer. We opened the long French windows, looked out—and there was an honest-to-God organ grinder coming along the street, "La Ronde" playing as he turned the crank on his hand-painted hurdy-gurdy. I found a ten-franc piece and threw it down to the street; Luke applauded; the organ grinder caught it with one hand and cheerily, nattily, tipped his cap. Things looked good.

That first year we went to a lot of circuses; in Paris there are usually six or seven in residence. We saw the Moreno-Bormann family circus, which is a true family circus: When any performer does anything slightly dangerous, the rest of the family stand around the ring calling out "Careful!" under their breaths and averting their eyes. We also saw the Mongolian National Circus, in a little tent pitched at the Arsenal. It consists of six broad-faced, smiling Mongolians, who do circus tricks appropriate to a nomadic scarcity economy—they eat a *little bit* of fire, walk on *one* broken bottle and save the shards—and finish off with an elaborate, pointless thirty-minute trick using a magician's cabinet that must have been left in Mongolia by an American illusionist sometime around 1860. (A Mongolian girl gets in the cabinet; Mongolian circus members slowly slide the swords through the slots; spend twenty minutes removing the swords from the slots; and then the girl gets out.)

We went to a lot of parks and rode a lot of carousels. In the Luxembourg Gardens is a completely unsupervised playground that's run on lines inspired by the last chapter of *Lord of the Flies*. There is a spinning red platter onto which little children are thrown by bigger ones, who whip it around, with the terrified little ones kept from flying off by sheer centripetal force. There is a weird ski lift–style conveyance that kids cling to with their fingers, dangling ten feet in the air over nothing but hard pavement. There are jungle gyms the kids climb on, to be knocked off the top bars by informal gangs of larger kids. There is not a safety belt, a padded surface, or a liability lawyer anywhere to be found. (Twenty years ago my wife and I, on our first date, saw Truffaut's *Small Change*. We loved the sequence in which a child falls out of a sixth-story window and walks away unhurt. In our early Francophile moments we saw this as charming French fantasy. In fact, it was pure cinema verité. Luke attends a weekly gym class for two-year-olds, along with heartbreakingly exquisite little girls named Amandine and Jolie and Neige. The children are routinely sent leaping from high, splintery boards onto low, uncushioned ones.)

At dusk, however, a uniformed *surveillant* emerges from a windowless shed at the center of the gardens and blows a whistle, and everyone goes home. The child who has his hands around your child's throat lets go, helps him up, dusts off his *tablier*, takes his mother's hand, and trudges toward the gates. The vicious big kids help the terrified small kids off the spinning red platter. The play routine at the gardens explains French history: The restrictive Old Regime, represented by the carousel, leads to the anarchy of the Revolution and the Reign of Terror, represented by the playground; then Napoleon emerges in uniform to blow his whistle and call everybody to order. (Or it could be the occupation, the Fourth Republic, and de Gaulle emerging in uniform.) Between the carousels and the circuses and a wealth of Charlie Chaplin movies, to which Luke developed a deep, sober attachment, we seemed, blessedly, to have skipped right past the *B*'s.

|||

Then, last Christmas, we went back to New York for three days. A friend brought a pile of tapes for a jet-lagged Luke to watch in the bedroom while we had dinner. I should have guessed from the ominous, atypical silence coming from the bedroom that something was off. Scooping up my exhausted little boy at the end of the evening, I noticed that he was looking unusually withdrawn. Then, right there in the backseat of a New York City taxicab, he suddenly looked up and said quietly, "Daddy, I like Barney."

"You like *what?*" I said.

"I like Barney," he said, and he turned over and went to sleep. The next morning we broke down and let him watch the video again—we were pretty jet-lagged too—and that was enough. It was like what they used to tell you about heroin: One taste, and you're hooked for good.

"I want Barney," he would announce early in the morning. He began to *whine* for Barney: "I want Barney, I want Barney." When we got back to Paris (the tapes somehow got into our bags), the need for Barney went right on. It even got worse. We'd be trying to watch one of the long, thoughtful French things that are good for your soul and your French—*Bouillon de Culture* or *Droit d'Auteurs*, or even just the dubbed version of *NYPD Blue* ("Ah, *c'est un boulot difficile, ce travail de policier, Inspecteur Sipowicz*")—and Luke would appear with a Barney tape. We had fled to Paris to escape our appointment with Barney, and Barney had come to meet us there.

Not wanting to be a bad or unduly coercive parent, I thought, Well, he has a right to his pleasures, but I too have a right—indeed a duty—to tell him what I think of them. We began to have a regular daily exchange.

"Daddy, I *like* Barney," he would say with elaborately feigned nonchalance, coming into my office first thing in the morning.

"Well, I don't like Barney," I would say, frankly.

"You like B.J.?" he would ask, tauntingly. B.J. is one of Barney's even more inane and adenoidal sidekicks.

"I love Ernie and Bert," I would say, trying to put a positive spin on my position. "I love the carousel. I love the circus. I love Charlie Chaplin."

"*I* like Barney," he would begin again, and it would go on.

Naturally it occurred to us that the pro-Barney campaign was a resourceful and in many ways courageous and admirable show of independence on the part of a two-and-a-half-year-old who might otherwise have been smothered by his parents' overbearing enthusiasms. We put up minimal Barney resistance. More tapes arrived from America; more tapes got popped in and played.

We tried to be tolerant, but Barney takes his toll: the braying voice, the crude direction, the inane mummery of the dancing, the witlessness of the writing. Our dreamed-of Parisian life was becoming unendurable. One afternoon around four-thirty I wandered into the bedroom, where the television is. My wife was, uncharacteristically, drinking a glass of red wine. On the little screen Barney was leading all the kids in one more rousing chorus of "I love you/you love me." We finished the bottle of Burgundy together. On the screen Barney sang, and our son moved his lips in time.

|||

What puzzled me of course was why. Loving Barney in Paris was partly a way of teasing his parents, but it was not *simply* a way of teasing his parents; it was too deep, too emotional for that. Nor had Barney yet crossed the ocean, so it wasn't any kind of peer pressure from the French kids he played with in class and in the courtyard every day. In Paris, in fact, almost all the childhood icons are those that have been in place for forty years: stuffy, bourgeois Babar; conniving, witty Astérix and Obélix; and imperturbable Lucky Luke, the Franco-American cowboy in perpetual battle with the four Dalton brothers. Although these characters from time to time appear in cartoons, they remain locked in their little worlds of satire and storytelling. There is no Barney in France, and there is no French Barney. Whatever spell was working on my son, it was entirely, residually American.

There are certain insights that can come to an American only when he is abroad, because only there does the endless ribbon of American television become segmented enough so that you can pay attention to its parts, instead of just being overwhelmed by the relentlessness of its presence. In the middle of the winter I happened to see, during some stray roundup of the year's events on CNN International, a clip of another familiar American figure, his arms around his wife and child, swaying and humming as he watched fireworks going off. Suddenly I got it. The nose; the rocking motion; above all, the squinty-eyed, aw-shucks, just-a-big-lug smile: Barney is Bill Clinton for three-year-olds. Or, rather, Bill Clinton is Barney for adults. He serves the same role for jumpy American liberals that Barney does for their children: He reassures without actually instructing. The physical resemblance alone is eerie. There's the odd combination of *hauteur* and *rondeur* (both are very tall without really being imposing), the perpetually swaying body, the unvarying smile, even the disconcerting chubby thighs—everything but the purple skin. Barney and Bill are not amiable authority figures, like the Friendly Giant and Ronald Reagan. They are, instead, representations of pure need: Wanting to be hugged, they hug.

For the first time, I also understood Clinton hating, of the violent irrational kind that, when I left America, was being practiced on the editorial page of the *Times* and in the *New Republic* and had always seemed incomprehensible, directed, as it was, at so anodyne a character. Suddenly I saw that the psychology of the Clinton hater was exactly that of the Barney basher; the objections were not moral but peevishly aesthetic. Like Barney, Bill stripped away our pet illusions by showing just how much we could do without. We had persuaded ourselves that the modern child needed irony, wit, humor, parody to be reached and affected; *Sesame Street* and *Bullwinkle* were our exhibits in this argument. Barney showed that this was not the case. At the same time, we had persuaded ourselves that the modern citizen, similarly wary (he is, after all, merely the *Bullwinkle* viewer grown old), could be recalled to liberalism only through a heightened, self-conscious, soul-searching high-mindedness. Bill showed that *this* was not the case. Both dinosaur and Arkansas governor had discovered that the way to win the hearts of their countrymen was to reduce their occupation to its most primitive form. Where Kermit the Frog, on *Sesame Street,* had sung the principle of brotherhood to children through the poetic metaphor of his own greenness, Barney just grabbed the kids and told them that he loved them and that they loved him too, damn it. Where Mario Cuomo had orated about Lincoln and the immigrants and the metaphor of family, Bill Clinton just held out his arms and watched people leap into them. It turns out that you don't need to be especially witty or wise to entertain children, just as you don't need to believe in anything much to be an extremely effective president. All you need is to know your audience's insecurities and how to keep swaying in time to them forever.

|||

We had kept Barney in quarantine, for the most part, and though Neige and Jolie and Amandine passed through the house, it was mostly to sing lovely French songs—"Pomme de Reinette" and "Frère Jacques"—and play with Luke's puppet theater. Then we decided to hold a party to celebrate the coming of spring, and I went out to Mulot to get a four-part chocolate cake. When I came back to the apartment, half an hour later, the roomful of lively children whom I had left drawling in *haute* French was silent. They were all in the bedroom. I walked in—no cuckolded husband can ever have entered his own bedroom with more dread about what he would find there—and saw the three girls spread out on the bed, their crinolines beautifully plumped, their eyes wide, their mouths agape. Barney was in France, and the kids were loving him. The three perfect French children looked on, hardly able to understand the language, yet utterly transfixed. I held out cake. Nothing doing. Barney was swaying. B.J. was prancing. The kids on the show were mugging like crazy, and everyone was singing.

It was too late. "How do you sing that 'I loove you, you loove me'?" Amandine asked haltingly, in French, when the program ended.

"I love you, you love me," Jolie answered swiftly.

"Happy family," Luke prompted. For the next week the song resounded from the street the way "La Ronde" had, long before.

|||

A couple of weeks later, at breakfast, Luke made an announcement. "Daddy," he said, "I *don't* like Barney."

"You don't like Barney?" I asked, incredulous, delighted.

"No, I *don't* like Barney." He paused. "I like to *watch* Barney." He had stumbled, in a Barneycentric manner, on the essential formula that could be applied to almost every American spectacle: I don't like the O. J. Simpson trial, I like to *watch* the O. J. Simpson trial; I don't like Geraldo Rivera, I like to *watch* Geraldo Rivera. And most basic of all: I don't like television, I like to *watch* television. When he watches Barney now, it's with a look in his eye that I know too well and that I can only call the American look, the look of someone who, though he has seen right through it, still can't take his eyes away—one of us, despite it all.

Lessons from Things,

CHRISTMAS JOURNAL 3

A French school term that I have learned to love is *leçons des choses*, lessons from things. It refers to a whole field of study, which you learn in class, or used to, that traces civilization's progress from stuff to things. The wonderful posters in Deyrolle, which Martha and I love and have collected, were made for *leçons des choses*. They show the passage of coffee from the bean to the porcelain coffeepot, of wine from the vine and soil to the bottle, of sugar from the cane to the *clafoutis*. They always show the precise costume that the beans and grapes and stuff end up in: the château bottling, the painted coffeepot, the label on the jam jar. The Deyrolle posters simultaneously remind you that even the best things always have some stuff leaking out their edges—a bit of the barnyard, a stain of soil—and that even the worst stuff is really OK, because it can all be civilized into things. The *choses*, the things, are what matters.

Of all the *leçons des choses* I have absorbed in Paris, the most important has come from learning to cook. I cooked a bit in New

York, Thanksgiving dinner and a filet mignon or two, and summers by the grill, like every American guy. But here I cook compulsively, obsessively, waking up with a *plat* in mind, balancing it with wine and side dishes throughout the working day ("Do I dare poach a Brussels sprout?"), shopping, anticipating six o'clock, when I can start, waiting for the perfectly happy moment when I begin, as one almost always does, no matter what one is cooking, by chopping onions.

The beautiful part of cooking lies in the repetition, living the same participles, day after day: planning, shopping, chopping, roasting, eating, and then vowing, always, never again to start on something so ambitious again . . . until the dawn rises, with another dream of something else. (Hunger, I find, plays a very small role in it all.) I have learned to make fifty or sixty different dinners: roasted *poulet de Bresse, blanquette de veau à vanille; carré d'agneau; gigot de sept heures.* I can *clafoutis* an apple, poach a pear, peel a chestnut. Big dishes, big food. Much *too* big food, the old cooking. (There is a little culinary bookstore on the rue du Bac that sells menus from the turn of the century. How did people, rich people, middle-class people, eat so much? Our stomachs *must* have shrunk, an argument for the plasticity of appetite, or at least of tummies. Is it fashion, culture, though? Or is it simply central heating; is it that we need fewer calories now than then and eat like West Indians—ginger and lime and rum marinades—because our indoor climate is now West Indian?)

I shop every day, making the rounds: the nice butcher on the rue de Verneuil, the grumpy butcher on the rue du Bac; the expensive excellent vegetable shop on the rue de Grenelle, or the homey mom & pop cheaper vegetable place on the rue de Verneuil. The one good fish place on the rue du Bac, cheese from Barthélemy on the rue de Grenelle (which Luke won't enter, from dislike of the smell, and so he waits outside, picketing). Maybe a bottle of wine at Le Repaire de Bacchus, where we discuss what I'm cooking; dessert from the grumpy ladies at Michel Chemin or the smooth, charming, expensive ladies at

Dalloyau, and then I come home, my hands torn and aching from all the plastic bags biting into them.

Shopping in Paris, even for a simple family dinner, takes a solid hour, since everything has to be picked over, made ready, sorted out. (Of course, there are supermarkets, but real supermarkets—*grands espaces,* large spaces—are not allowed into Paris proper, and, anyway, the local merchants still thrive.) The chicken must have its head cut off, its feet cut off, and then it must be gutted. There is really nothing I enjoy more than watching a good butcher gut a chicken; it is a *leçon des choses* with bloody hands. The butcher incises the gut and then reaches in and pulls out the *whole insides,* a (shocking fact this, to a supermarket-stupid American) long, squalid string of mixed-up stuff, guts and gizzard and liver and heart, and then neatly shifts the disgusting to one side and the palatable to the other. You calm down—oh, look at that, that's nice, that's nasty—although at the moment that he actually pulls out the guts, your North American nice-nasty meter has been swinging wildly from one end of the scale to the other. Guts to one side, liver and heart to the other: *That's* just stuff, but *that's* a potential thing, and what about the neck? Might possibly with a lot of work *become* a thing, but it's discardable as stuff too if you feel that way about it.

The sublime moment of cooking, though, is really the moment when nature becomes culture, stuff becomes things. It is the moment when the red onions have been chopped and the bacon has been sliced into lardons and the chestnuts have been peeled, and they are all *mijoté*ing together in the pot, and then—a specific moment—the colors begin to change, and the smells gather together just at the level of your nose. Everything begins to mottle, bend from raw to cooked. The chestnuts, if you're doing chestnuts, turn a little damp, a little weepy. That's what they do; everything *weeps*.

I suppose there must be a good evolutionary psychologist's reason for the appeal of this transformation, some smart, smutty thing about color change and female rears, but cooking isn't really like sex: appetite and satiation and appetite again. Sex is ravenous rather than reflective. The passage from stuff to things, the moment when the vegetables weep, is a meditative moment and has no point, really, except the purely ephemeral one of seeing it happen. You cook for yourself, or I do anyway. Martha picks through things, New York girl with a New York appetite, and Luke, like an astronaut, would prefer to live on a diet of milk shakes and nutrient pellets. Cooking, for middle-class, end-of-the-century people, is our only direct, not entirely debased line with the hermetic life, with Zen sitting, with just doing things without a thought. No wonder monks make good cheese.

(I tried teaching sublime and beautiful as categories to Luke the other day. He brooded. "Daddy," he said at last, "an example of the sublime: dinosaur bones. An example of the beautiful: Cressida Taylor." Cressida Taylor, I have since learned, is a four-year-old girl with a long blond braid in his class at school with whom he is, understandably, in love, and who is in fact perfectly beautiful. The other day he also came home and said, "That Cressida—she's quite a dish!" I don't know where he gets this slang. The other day I also heard him say, "Oh, brother, what a peach!" about someone or other.)

|||

The absence of stuff may be what makes writing so depressing and cooking so inviting to the writer. (To the yuppie-family-guy writer anyway. It used to be not cooking but its happy, feckless near relation drinking that writers looked forward to at twilight. Perhaps for the same reason; it gives you something to do with your hands at six o'clock other than typing.) Writing isn't the transformation of stuff into things. It is just the transformation of symbols into other symbols, as if one read recipes out loud for dinner, changing the proportions ("I'm adding fifty goddamn grams of butter!") for dramatic effect. You read out the recipe and the audience listens, and pretends to taste, the way Martha does when I force her to listen to jazz records. *Mmm, delicious.* Sometimes, if you change the proportions dramatically enough—nothing but butter! no butter at all!—the people listening gasp, as though they really *could* taste it. (This is the way Burroughs and Bukowski write.) Fortunately they never have to. Writing is a business of saying things about stuff and saying things about things and then pretending that you have cooked one into the other.

This may be why I like this year to take a fundamental *leçon des choses* by going up to Sennelier, the beautiful art supply store on the quai Voltaire, and just buying some stuff that artists use to make things. Ingres paper, or oil pastels, or just a *carnet,* a notebook. How can artists ever make anything ugly at all? you wonder; just a black mark on thick white paper is so beautiful. I feel serene surrounded by paper, having learned that things give lessons enough.

|||

We've gone traveling a lot this year, to Budapest and London many times and to Venice and to Bruges. The weather on CNN, at least, whichever hotel room you find it in (and you find it in them all) always continues cheerful. ("And, hey, would you look here? A big low-pressure area is going to drop snow *all over* the east, from Danzig right out to Ukraine. . . .") I always imagine the businessmen, selling Dunkin' Donuts franchises and Internet stocks from Bucharest to Ulan Bator, checking the weather on CNN every night. Our peculiar American toothless bite is there. (But then I recall a theory Luke and I have learned this year about the *T. rex*: that it didn't actually *bite* at all but just grabbed and tore at its prey, half the time leaving it just wounded, but with enough toxic *T. rex* slime in the wound to infect it fatally. All the *T. rex* had to do was follow the poor sick guy around and watch until he dropped. American capitalism seems to work this way too. Toothless bites, it seems, are the worst bites of all.)

We followed CNN from motel to hotel, Michelin guide to Michelin guide, as we traveled. When I was in New York, all-news radio had the stock exchange highs every day, waiting for the Dow to break a number (eight thousand? ten thousand? It breaks the next one so quickly that we can't recall), the way we waited for a ballplayer to break a record.

Traveling around France, we've been out to the Loire, down to Grenoble and the Savoy, up to Normandy. I begin to get it. France is a big, rich country. It has a lot of people; they have a lot of good things to eat; they don't see why anyone should push them around. France doesn't believe that it was once the big one, as Holland or England does, by virtue of a special mission and an exceptional national character. France believes that it is *naturally* the big one, like China or America. The big one by virtue of its size, its abundance, its obvious cultural hegemony (all cultural hegemonies are believed to be natural by the people at the core of them). It was not so terribly long ago that everybody took this status for granted, and speaking French was like speaking English now: not strictly an accomplishment but a necessity for a cosmopolitan life. It was not so long ago that France was almost *lazily* the big one, as we are now, so to be told, again and again, that not only is it not the big one but not even among the bigger ones riles the French.

|||

Luke decided this year to penetrate farther into the Luxembourg Gardens. He is the Amundsen, the Peary, though I hope not the Scott, of the Luxembourg Gardens. His whole life is devoted to penetrating its mysteries, hoping eventually to get to its core. Someday he will enter the surveillants' shed, where the policemen sit and warm their coffee and watch for park infractions, and it will be time to go home. Or else he will spend the rest of his life as a Paris policeman; he will become Pierre! On the carousel he is now up and mounted on a horse, with the leather rope tight around his waist, eyes fixed straight ahead, hands clutching the pole, still too unsure for the stick and rings, but looking at them, hard.

This year he penetrated into the inner temple of the gardens. He went to a puppet show. It was a huge move, much meditated on and discussed in advance.

"Daddy, I think I want to go to the puppet show," he said sometime this spring, and then, having chosen *Les Trois Petits Cochons,* The Three Little Pigs, as his first show, we debated for a week, before the fateful Saturday matinee arose, what it was going to be like. He would jump into bed at seven in the morning with a new theory. "I think they'll dance like this," he said worriedly one morning, putting his hands on his waist and oscillating his torso back and forth mechanically. Then he stopped and looked even more worried. What if they *did* dance like that, God help us?

"I think there will be a wolf in it," he said on another morning, "and he will look like this," and then he grimaced, horribly. (I realized that he had become a precise replica of the young Marcel getting worked up about seeing Berma for the first time. It is a French moment, though not exactly the one we had in mind, puppets as pigs rather than Sarah in Racine, still . . .)

Saturday came around at last, and we lined up at the entrance to the puppet theater, just to the left of the playground, where we have gone so many afternoons. The owner–proprietor–producer–chief puppeteer is named Francis-Claude Desarthis, and he walks up and down the gardens with a bell before each show begins, ringing hard—not ringing to be fetching but ringing to fetch. As so often in Paris, it is hard to know if the puppet theater is making a mint—it charges twenty-four francs a ticket, about five dollars, and on weekends always seem full up—or hanging on by its nails.

Desthartis's father started the theater back in the thirties. His framed picture is still in place on the facade of the theater, looking plaintively at a puppet. Many of the shows seem to have been left untouched since then. The performance of *Les Trois Petits Co-chons*, for instance, uses, with slight variations, many of the devices, not to mention the music, of the Disney version of the story from the thirties. There are French touches, though. The *catastrophe*, or climax, occurs when the wolf pretends to be a minor official come to read the water meter. The pigs have to let him into the one remaining house; the French little pigs *have* to open the door to administration, even when it has bright white teeth and an immense jaw and sixty white papier-mâché teeth. Fortunately the day is saved, first by a series of electric shocks administered by the smart pig to the wolf by way of a rigged water meter and then by a snapping crocodile that arrives wrapped in a package (who sent him isn't clear, at least not to me). Finally, before the hunter arrives, the day is really saved by a black American boxer (Joe Louis?) with gleaming white teeth and thick lips and a terrific, wolf-devastating right uppercut.

There are dances—various animal puppets leaping up and down in time—at regular intervals, even when some necessary question of the play has yet to be resolved. The line to the seventeenth-century theater—for Molière too is full of arbitrary dances—is real. The puppet shows are real puppet shows. They use puppets, the kind you hold with your hand from beneath. They're big puppets, with overlarge, papier-mâché heads and long arms, but no legs.

The no-legness of the puppets puzzles and discourages Luke. Far from seeming to him an invisible artistic convention, I think that he believes it to be a notable, disturbing piece of amputation. He thinks not Well, their legs are represented by sheets of fabric but, rather, Their legs have been cut off, and they have been forced to perform in a theater! In every show the hero is always Guignol, a kind of Puck or Trickster puppet, with a long Chinese braid. It is alarming to see his face, since it is obviously modeled on that of M. Desarthis himself—or, even scarier, on that of his father, who, from his portrait on the side of the building, seems to have had more or less the same features. They have passed themselves, it seems, into Guignol, who is, interestingly, amoral. Guignol takes the splinters out of the paws of wounded tigers ("*Le pauvre*," he soothes) but is in business for himself, and mocks and bedevils the well-meaning admirals and librarians and magistrates he always seem to encounter. (Many of these, interestingly enough, have British accents.)

So far we have seen *Les Trésors du Sultan* (first a mixup on a ship and then a second act on a desert island, including, oddly, a tiger with a thorn in its paw and that noisy, impressively snapping crocodile. Also highly Semitic caricatures of the pirates and the sultan), *Minochet* (a cat in a Paris garret), *Le Cirque en Folie* (the Mad Circus, many animals, including, again oddly enough, a tiger and a crocodile), *Le Rossignol et l'Empereur de Chine* (adapted, the sign says honorably, from the *comte* of Hans Christian Andersen, although, interestingly, a tiger and a crocodile have been added), and, of course, those pigs.

As in any vast dramatic corpus, the puppet plays are of varying styles, ranging from the classic heigh-ho heartiness of *Pigs* and *Trésors* (as they are known to scholars) to the darker, more static style of *Minochet* and *Le Vieux Château*—the problem puppet shows, as they are known. (*Le Vieux Château* begins with a long, endless sequence in a scholar's library, and *Minochet* with an act, half Céline and half Beckett, about the poor cat, Minochet, trying to have her little supper while a mad butcher searches for her to turn her into cat sausage.) All of course are in French, using recorded voices that must have also been registered sometime in the late thirties—you can practically see the Pathé rooster on the side of the box that the records are kept in—and since the language is idiomatic and jokey, it is often hard for me to follow. Luke, whose French, despite his going to a French school, is in and out—as Hemingway's friends said about him, you never know if he knows a lot or a little—kneels up on the seat beside me and demands translations. ("What's he saying?" "That they're going to kidnap the princess . . . no, now he's saying something else" . . . etc.)

That first performance, though, the epochal *Pigs*, was so over-whelming that he couldn't sleep, and so we tried a usually reli-able soporific: walking him down to the Seine in his *poussette* to watch the boats from the ponts des Arts. Usually, almost always, he falls asleep on the walk back. This night, though—a wonder-ful May night, chestnuts in blossom, a month later than the song advertises—he couldn't sleep, and his troubled, obsessive mind kept returning to the puppet show, to the struggle 'twixt damna-tion and impassioned *papier-mâché*.

We wandered through the Sixth, taking what I still think is the most beautiful walk in the world: up the rue de Seine and then right through the little, unprepossessing-looking arch—a hole punched in a wall—that gives no promise at all that it opens right onto the esplanade of the greatest of grand siècle buildings, the Institut de France, Mazarin's great curved library topped by its perfect dome. Passing through the tiny, *poussette*-wide arch onto the curved esplanade is like walking backstage through a flat and onto a great set.

There are no guards, no guardrails—nothing between you and the great building. It's all just there, and you can push a child's *poussette* back and forth in front of the institute entrance and even lean on the door to rest, though it is the center of French civilization. It is one of those odd Parisian absences that are as strange as the pervasive presences elsewhere. (There are enough policemen in the Luxembourg Gardens for each to be assigned one child each, but not a single guard anywhere here.)

Luke all the while was keeping up a running, troubled com-mentary on *Les Trois Petits Cochons*. "Why there were two wolves?" he would spring up, sleepy, from his *poussette*, to de-mand. (Actually there was just one, but he would appear, with sinister effect, on either side of the proscenium.) "Why he wants to eat the pigs?" "Why that man knock him?" "Why that croco-dile bite?" Why why, why . . . the question the pigs ask the wolf, that the wolf asks the hunter, that the hunter asks God—and the answer, as it comes at midnight, after all the other, patient parental answers ("Well, you see, wolves generally like to eat pigs, though that's just in the story." "Well, hunters, a long time ago, would go hunting for wolves with guns when they were a danger to people"), the final, exhausted midnight-in-the-lamplight answer, wheeling the *poussette* down the quai Voltaire, is the only answer there is, the Bible's answer to Job: because that's the way the puppet master chose to do it, because that's the way the guy who works the puppets likes to see it done.

|||

Wednesday afternoons, Luke and I take our local bus, the 63, which runs down the boulevard Saint-Germain toward his school and the Seventh Arrondissement, back up toward the Jardin des Plantes and the Fifth, to visit the dinosaur museum. Luke has been following a course in Picasso and dinosaurs in his *maternelle*. I had already taken him round the Picasso museum, which Luke liked, and the dinosaurs were an even bigger hit. He talks knowingly, familiarly, of the brachiosaurus and pterodactyl. I have told him that dinosaurs were defeated by an alliance of daddies, that *only* daddies can defeat dinosaurs. Look around, I ask, are there dinosaurs? (No.) Are there daddies? (Yes.) Well, then . . . He sees the flaw in this argument more quickly than I expected. Daddies came long after dinosaurs; daddies claimed the terrain of power only after dinosaurs had already abandoned it. That's the way the dinosaurs tell it, I say. Long discussions. Long pause. Finally: "Here's one dinosaur you can *never* defeat [dramatic pause] . . . *T. rex!*" He needs an undefeatable dinosaur, a dinosaur beyond the reach of a dad.

The entrance to the paleontology museum at the Jardin des Plantes is graced by a statue of Lamarck, with the engraving "The Father of Evolution," in giant letters, on its pedestal. Darwin, on the other hand, is nowhere in sight.

There is nothing more exasperating than French monuments to unheroic local heroes. In the Luxembourg Gardens, where I run many mornings, there are statues of the great writers of France, genuinely towering and Olympian figures—real all-stars, the greats. Baudelaire scowls at the southern end of the gardens; Delacroix is greeted by angels at the other end. I salute them both every morning, while jogging by Verlaine and Sainte-Beuve. In the midst of them all there is a statue to a man whose name I, at least, have never heard, a guy named Branly, whose pedestal proclaims him to be the father of the wireless communication, radiotelegraph, and television. I am skeptical of this claim. It is a few feet away from the small, just larger than life-size Statue of Liberty, made by Bartholdi for fund-raising back when. This Liberty looks, well, sexy, free.

At last we get to the big Hall of Evolution, and Darwin sneaks in there—sideways. He gets a plaque. The Hall is filled with stuffed animals, giraffes and elephants, from another time, all apparently done by the artisans of Deyrolle but now placed in modernized half-light, the same kind of light you see in the fish restaurants of the Seventh Arrondissement. Recessed lighting says modern in France the way that a pastel arch says postmodern in New York.

The boy, however, wants to see his dinosaurs, so we go down in the gardens to the old Hall of Paleontology, off by itself down by the entrance to the gardens. It is two floors of pure bones—all bones, wall-to-wall bones, more bones than I have ever seen. At the entrance, a few feet from the Lamarck memorial, there is a statue by Frémiet of the Eternal Struggle. It shows a great ape—a species unknown to nature, with the ears of an elephant, the face of a magazine executive, and the grin of a Santa Monica maître d'—who, clutching his (her?) infant, has just wrapped his hands around the throat of a beautiful human youth. The youth, before being killed by the ape, managed to plant his ax in the ape's side, where it has left a hideous and gaping wound, perfectly cut out in stone. It is lurid, preposterous, and loud, the most improbable memorial, and this by the guy who made the golden and boring St. Joan on the rue de Rivoli. It defeats my dusty and out-of-date attempts at iconographic analysis, despite Luke's constant questions: Why the ape, why the man . . . ? Does it represent the triumph of Lamarckian evolution? Then the man with the culture (i.e., the ax) should be triumphing over the ape. It can't represent the domination of the ape-in-man over the beauty-in-man. Is it the Triumph of the Monkey in Us? Or is it simply (simply!) a lurid show piece? Eugenio would have pointed out that the "trope" or conceit of the ape-on-the-loose is a rich nineteenth-century Parisian one, ranging from "The Murders in the Rue Morgue" to this. Man and Ape in Evolutionary Metaphor . . . these days you could probably put it out front of the Concorde and redub it "France and America."

The dinosaurs are upstairs. They are enormous and articulated to look big. Of course, this is easy: They *are* big. But they are made to look even bigger, perhaps by contrast with the delicate beaux arts architecture. They *loom*. There is a single mold of a *T. rex* head, which turns out to be a copy taken from the New York *T. rex*. Just as the famous mechanical nightingales of Byzantium that Yeats admired so were, as you discover when you read Byzantine history, the *same damn bird*, brought out century after century to impress out-of-town visitors, until the paint was peeling off the thing, so the *T. rex* that has scared several generations of schoolchildren in the two cities is the same damn lizard, dead so many million years.

In the new New York hall, where we took Luke last Christmas, the dinosaurs look wise and cunning, balanced forward on their middle feet, delicate little hands trembling like base stealers. They have fabricated fiberglass skins too, in gleaming, subtle, elegantly understated two-tone, Armani colors. Here, in Paris, in the old museum, they are still upright and looming and stolid. There is even a brontosaurus, still called that, though I think I read that there never *were* brontosauruses, that they were a false association of two different animals.

The force—I suppose I have to say the image—of the dinosaur, as it was understood by the nineteenth century, comes through here, terrifyingly. It is like reading Conan Doyle's "Lost World." The giant Irish elk (a mammal and, anyway, not that amazing—just a big moose) shares pride of place here with the big lizards, as he does in Doyle's story. The reason, I suspect, is that it wasn't so much the distant, scary past that drew the nineteenth century, but the simple specter of giganticism, bigness itself. They wanted their dinosaurs to loom over them, as their tycoons did. In the "Lost World" of Conan Doyle, in fact, the dinosaurs are constantly being called Gothic. They were interested in big, whereas we are interested in mean. (Was this because bigness was their problem—mass armies, mass society, massiveness—whereas meanness is ours—small wars, horrible murders?) The difference between the old Parisian and the new New York dinosaurs is the difference between an industrial dinosaur, big and dumb and looming, and the postindustrial dinosaur, swift and smart and a scavenger. We make our monsters according to the armature of our fears. They wanted what loomed over them to be huge, stolid, immovable, and a little slow, like J. P. Morgan or Mr. Frick. We want them now to be smart, fast, mean, ugly, and wearing expensive suits, like Barry Diller or Rupert Murdoch.

|||

A little while later I visited the new Bibliothèque Nationale, the big—the unbelievably vertigo-inspiringly enormous—library, out at the other end of the quai in the Thirteenth. It seems to have been designed by a committee made up of Michel Foucault, Jacques Tati, and the production designer of *The Man from U.N.C.L.E.* The whole thing is set up, way up, on a wooden platform the size of six or seven football fields, high up off the street. There is an unbelievably steep stairs, leading up to this plateau, which is like nothing so much as one of those stepped pyramids where the Aztecs plucked the hearts out of their sacrificial victims. Then there are four glass skyscrapers, each one set at one of the corners of the platform, and all very handsome, in a kind of early-sixties, post–Lever House, Skidmore, Owings & Merrill way. The vast space has been planked with teak boards, to make it "warmer," but this just makes it more slippery. They have had to put down cheap-looking runners on a sticky backing, to keep people from breaking legs. (Apparently there were quite a few victims early on.)

The vast, windswept plaza, with the four towers at its corners, is *so* vast that it creates what one would have thought would be a perfectly predictable wind tunnel effect. This not only means that you walk with your head down against the gusts, even in the middle of July, but also means that all the bushes and shrubbery that were meant to "humanize" the wooden plaza had to be put inside vertical cages of mesh, which in turn are placed between white bunkers. Left out on their own, the shrubs would just die in the wind. It looks like a bad conceptual art installation about the domination of nature by man. (This is the Foucaultian part.) A stray piece of foliage peeks out forlornly from some of the enclosures, like Hans's fingers from the witch's cage. Looking across the platform toward the tiny and impossibly steep steps, you cannot see the stairs at all; it simply looks like a platform from which one could leap, suicidally, gratefully.

Downstairs you wait at the *accueil* for your card. This is done with the usual French functionary hospitality: Who are you, what do you want, what makes you think, etc.? Finally, after an hour, you may get a card. First you visit the desk of one severely disciplinary young lady, who takes your coordinates and enters them into the single-overseeing computer system that was intended as the glory of the place. You are now sent to another young woman, who reenters and corrects all the information the first girl entered, and then asks if you are ready for your picture. (This is the Jacques Tati part.) You nod and rise, looking for the photo booth. She shakes her head gravely and tells you just to sit back. A camera, mounted to your right and above, swivels, moves down on its track, and gawks at you, musing in and out. Don't move; your hostess has just become Annie Leibovitz, she is the photographer. She clicks her mouse forward onto the next screen of her computer, and there you are: The photo system is computerized too. She waits, thoughtfully for the moment of maximum exhaustion, and snaps your picture. You can, if you crane your head a bit, see a thousand images of yourself on the screen, being entered into the system.

When you at last have your card, you begin your descent into the vast underground caverns, the *sous-sol*, where the reading rooms are. (The books are, famously, all up in the towers.) First you go to a kind of master computer terminal and enter your request for a seat. The computer lets you know that there is no room for you in *L, M,* and disdainfully awards you your number, the new you: N-51. You repeat your name to yourself.

You insert your card into a turnstile; it takes its time and then lets you pass into a tiny space with a spiked metal floor, which leads in turn toward two immense two-story-high brushed metal doors. There is no signage or any indication of where you are going—because where you are going is into *another* turnstile, *another* spiked metal floor, and *another* pair of vast metal doors. Windows and sunlight have been left far behind. Once you are through those, you get on an escalator for a *ten*-story descent into the basement; there are concrete pillars around the escalators, winsomely decorated with iron-mesh hangings, that in the context look like chintz.

When you come to the end of the escalator, there are two more turnstiles and two more windowless metal doors to pass through. Now you are into the entrance to the reading rooms, and you see that the reading rooms are built around a grass court, which opens to the sky, high, high above. In the glassed-in court is a bizarre amenity, a garden—no, a small forest of immense trees, pines and evergreens mostly, all planted close together in tight rows, in the shallow green center block of grass. Their grass base is surrounded by a margin of concrete. The trees are so shallowly rooted, though—or else, according to other people, the wind sweeping down from above is so strong—that they have all had to be chained to the concrete floor. Each one has at least two guy wires leading down to stakes in the ground, crisscrossing diagonal lines of black and steel cable. The bushes above in cages, the trees below in chains.

Step up three or four shallow steps from the glass wall enclosing the trees and wires—it is absolutely forbidden, by the way, for anyone to pass through the seamless glass walls and into the garden—and you are in the main reading room: dark, gloomy, and at once terrifyingly vast without being compensatingly magnificent. It is just one huge horizontal space, broken by discreet letter indicators telling you that you have passed from N to M and onward. Searching, at last you find your seat, N-51, which is simply a single space at a vast table with several hundred such spots marked. You feel more like an ant than an archivist.

Then you search, among consoles set off near the walls, for an empty, operating computer terminal on which to make your book requests. Most of the terminals are out of order, and when you insert your identity card, they sigh and say that they are initializing. After fifteen minutes you give up and walk up and down the great hall, looking for a terminal that works. When you find one, you can penetrate the catalog fairly quickly; then you claim the page and demand the book; the computer registers that you have made the demand and tells you to go sit back down. The entire library is, in principle, served by, or subject to, the same vast, single computer system, which knows who you are, where you are, what you're doing, and what you want, can track you from visit to visit, and anticipate your interests, etc. This of course means in practice that any tiny bug in one part of the system destroys the entire operation of the library. The latest bugs are posted on photocopied sheets Scotch-taped to the terminals: Please, don't ask to "resee" your list, they say, just ask to "revise" it, etc.

Now comes the part that transcends ordinary functionary fiendishness to touch the high, misty edge of French bureaucratic-sadistic genius. The keyboard on the computer terminals is almost, *but not exactly*, an ordinary keyboard. It *looks* like an ordinary QWERTY keyboard—it doesn't just have some entirely new, Pierre Boulez–inspired keyboard, so that you're warned in advance to watch your step, or finger—but *three characters* have been moved. *Q* is exchanged with *A*, and the comma with the period, and, I think, the *E* with the *O*. This means that if you are a touch, or just a plain, mildly experienced, typist, you feel exactly as if you were having a stroke, since you have to interrupt the flow of typing each time you make a tiny error, and pretty soon you are so scared that you stop trying to maintain your normal speed and begin to hunt and peck.

On the desks there is a single red light that is supposed to illuminate when your books arrive, but these lights have never been known to work. Or, rather, they have been *occasionally* known to work. So you have to get up regularly and check your computer terminal again, to see what's up. The light may be off because the books haven't arrived yet, and it may be off because it's not working. This means that if you go to the main desk, thirty yards away, to check, and the books aren't there, everyone will be annoyed at you for taking up a place in the line. There is usually at least an hourlong wait for books and a sharp limit (eight, right now) on how many you can take out. Guess wrong, and you've wasted a day. There is no cafeteria, only an appalling, gloomy little café near the subterranean entrance, with a view of the gagged and bound trees straining toward the invisible sky. Americans working there have taken to sitting on the steps that run down toward the atrium, where there is at least some light, though of course, it is also extremely hot; given the underground location and the abundance of plate glass, you are always either freezing or baking. But clerks come to shush them. "After the shock of the first few days, you get used to it," someone says.

It is not cheap-looking, God knows, very much not. It is in the style of Totalitarian Luxe, which was the Mitterrand trademark. The materials are rich: brushed steel, mesh curtains, thick carpet. The trees alone, their purchase and upkeep, must have run into the millions of dollars. The floor on the concourse is made of teak. You see the production values but worry about the production. It is the largest and most depressing of all the monuments of pompous official French culture that have been produced in France since the war, the administration's ultimate revenge on the individual. All that French wit, all that charm, all that gaiety, all that somber pessimism, even all that intelligent despair sunk deep into the earth like a missile installation, with bad sandwiches and a chained and bound garden. I ordered a book by Blondin and a picture book on Trenet, just to recall that there was something gayer in Paris, up there above, where the light was.

When I left at last and saw, on the quai, with the cars rushing by, a typically French beauty poster—this one for Lancaster sun cream: a perfect girl's bottom, bare and in full color, five times normal scale, with a gold sheen in the summer light—I was pathetically grateful for the sight of something humanly beautiful, curved and soft to the eye. French civilization is all the more a miracle, given the obstacles the French put in its way.

|||

The curious thing about all of Mitterrand's *grands projets*—the Bastille Opéra, the pyramid of the Louvre, above all, this library—is that though they are big, they don't *feel* big. They don't feel big the way the dinosaur museum feels big, the way the Parisian monuments of the last century still do, even when those old monuments are actually smaller than the new ones. The new *grands projets* don't feel big so much as claustrophobic and confusing and stifling—emotionally trivial, small. The *grands projets* of the last century were either the biggest of their kind or else a kind unto themselves. The Eiffel Tower maintains its aura of height partly because it really *is* tall and big and partly because there is still nothing like it anywhere else. (The radio masts and post office towers and skyscrapers that have been built since and that in some ways resemble it really don't, since its form is uniquely feminine—not phallus into sky, but skirt into bodice into long throat.) The pyramid of the Louvre, though, looks like a shopping center, a mall, because that kind of Plexiglas and aluminum architecture has been done so much bigger elsewhere.

There is here a fundamental lesson from a thing, a *leçons des choses*. Architecture at its most successful passes from stuff (bricks and mortar and metal) through things (buildings) all the way to *thats,* single unforgettable objects, instantly recognizable, the thumbprints of the world. Their closed, permanent, pyramid-like *thatness* is its glory. Paris has perhaps more *thats*—the tower, the Louvre, the arch, the palace—than any city in the world, a greater concentration of distinctive monuments. Yet despite its best efforts, the *grands projets* fail to achieve the requisite *thatness.* They fail because of their comparative smallness, of course, when compared with other things in our mental library, but also because they lack something else, a kind of confidence in the things they enclose. The last thing the new Opéra makes you think of is music; the last thing the new library makes you think of is books. The paleontology museum *is* at least a semi-*that,* so filled with stuff that has been dignified into things, animal dust made hard and significant, that it becomes a *that* by virtue of the immensity of the thingness it encloses. The new library, the Bibliothèque National, isn't even a thing, much less a *that.* It evokes, after you have experienced it, merely a huh? and, like all failed monuments, in the end resolves in memory merely into a vast and barren and echoing Why?

|||

I realized this year that the appeal of jazz in France, and the reason for its holding a place so much higher in the French estimation than in America, where it remains a cult enthusiasm, is the exact equivalent of the American appreciation of impressionism (which held, and to a degree—look at the way the pictures are shown at the Musée d'Orsay!—still holds a much higher place in the American estimation than in the French one).

Jazz, like impressionism, gives dignity to comfort. Resting in an apparently artless myth of bourgeois pleasure—Gershwin and Kern melodies play the same role for the great jazzmen that the outdoor cafés in Argenteuil played for Renoir and Monet—jazz, like high impressionism, reaffirms the simple, physical basis of powerful emotion and removes it to a plane of personal expression that we recognize as art; it gives us a license to take pleasure in what really provides our pleasures. You play "All the Things You Are" and you are playing the beautiful tune, and you are playing more than the beautiful tune, in the same way that Manet is painting just the asparagus and more than the asparagus without venturing into asparagus symbols or the grand manner of the asparagus. But the tune is there, even if the more pretentious kind of jazz critic doesn't like to admit it, just as the asparagus is there, even if the more pretentious kind of art critic doesn't like to admit it. A Bill Evans playing "Someday My Prince Will Come," like Manet painting a lemon, is a stuff into things—into more than things, all the way into *thats*.

In every period, every century, there is one art form or another that is able to combine simple affirmation of physical pleasure with a quality of plaintive longing, and this becomes the international art form of the time. Living abroad convinces you that just as French painting was the event of the nineteenth century and Italian painting of the fifteenth—the one universal language—American popular music is the cultural event of our time. It is the one common language, the source of the deepest emotions and the most ordinary ones too. The taxi driver hums the riff from "Hotel California," and the singer Johnny Hallyday, simply by impersonating Elvis, in some decent sense inhabits Elvis (just as Childe Hassam, impersonating Monet, at some decent level inhabited him too). Every epoch has an art form into which all the energies and faiths and beliefs and creative unselfconsciousness flows. What makes them matter is their ability not to be big but *to be small meaningfully,* to be little largely, to be grandly, or intensely, diminutive.

|||

The best lesson I have learned from a thing this year, perhaps in all my time in Paris, occurred on another afternoon this spring. I was sitting on the bench under the metal and glass porte-cochere at the playground at the Luxembourg Gardens, watching Luke climb up the sliding board, the "toboggan," the wrong way—glancing warily over his shoulder for the surveillant to whistle him down—when I looked down at the plastic-cupped *café crème* that I had bought at the little entrance shed a few moments before. About to unwrap the sugar cube, I saw that the little paper wrapping had a picture of the poet Mallarmé on it—an odd, Benday-dot, unintentionally Lichtenstein-like portrait of him—while on the two other faces of the sugar cube there were quotes from his poems ("*Et finisse l'écho par les célestes soirs, Extase des regards scintillements des nimbes!*") and a brief, summary life ("LIBERTÉ SANS MESURE: STÉPHANE MALLARMÉ, POÈTE 1842–1898"). The fourth face just had the name of the sugar company, Begin Say. The sugarcane had not only become a sugar cube, like the one in the Deyrolle poster, but been wrapped in a picture of a poet. I saved it to keep on my desk in my writing room and for once drank my coffee unsweetened. A lesson from a thing, and thrown in for the price of the coffee too.

The
Rookie

I don't really remember how we first thought of the Rookie. I think it may have been right after I saw Luke, who had just turned three, playing with a soccer ball in the Luxembourg Gardens. It wasn't just the kicking that scared me but a kind of nonchalant bend-of-the-body European thing he did as he rose to meet the ball with his head. Next, he would be wearing those terrible shorts and bouncing the ball from foot to foot, improving his "skills." He had been born in New York, but he had no memory of it. Paris is the only home he knows. (Or, as he explained to a friend, in the third person he occasionally favors, like Bo Jackson or General de Gaulle, "He was born in New York, but then he moved to Paris and had a happy life.")

"You want to have a catch?" I said, and he looked at me blankly.

That night at bedtime I said, "Hey, I'll tell you about the Rookie." It was eight o'clock, but it was bright outside. Paris is a

northern city, on a latitude with Newfoundland, as New York is a
Mediterranean one, on a latitude with Naples, and so the light
here in the hours between seven and nine at night is like the
light in the hours between five and seven in New York. The sun
is still out, but the sounds have become less purposeful—you
hear smaller noises, high heels on the pavement—and though it
is a pleasant time to lie in bed, it is not an easy time for a small
boy to go to sleep.

I had been drawing storytelling duty for a while and had made
increasingly frantic efforts to find a hit. A story about a little boy
who turned into a fish in Venice hadn't gone anywhere, and a remake of *The Hobbit* had done no box office at all. This story,
though, rolled out easily. Every dad has one good bedtime story
buried in him, and desperation will bring it out.

The Rookie (I said) was a small boy in Anywhere, U.S.A., in
the spring of 1908. Out walking with his mom one day, he discovered that he had an uncanny gift for throwing stones at
things. He picked one up and threw it so hard that it knocked a
robin off its perch a mile away, and then, after his mama chided
him, he threw another one, just as far but so softly that it snug-
gled into the nest beside the bird without breaking an egg. His
parents, a little sadly but with a sense of obligation, immediately
sent him off on the train to New York, to try out for the New York
Giants and their great manager, John J. McGraw. All he took
with him was a suitcase that his mother had packed for him,
filled with things, including his bottle, that she thought might be
useful in case of an emergency. (At that point the contents of the
suitcase were unparticularized, but they eventually included a
complete dictionary of the animal languages, a saxophone, a design for the first car radio, compressed early rocket ship refueling
pills, a map of Paris, a window defogger, a time machine, a Sherlock Holmes deerstalker, a map of a secret route to the South
Pole, and reindeer medicine for Santa's team.)

He got out at Grand Central, took a cab all the way uptown to the Polo Grounds—his mother had told him to take taxis in New York—and asked to see John J. McGraw. McGraw, staccato and impatient, was at first skeptical, but he finally agreed to watch while the kid threw, because he was so polite and the letter from his parents was so insistent and because, well, you never know. He called Big Six, the great Christy Mathewson, out of the dugout to watch, and Chief Meyers, the great American Indian catcher, to get behind the plate. The Chief came out, with a weary, crippled, long-suffering gait, and squatted. (I thought of the Chief as a creased veteran, though the real Chief was still in his twenties and not yet even a Giant.) The little guy walked to the mound, tugged at his cap—not a baseball cap, the cap of his knickers suit—and let fly.

Everybody was impressed, to put it mildly. "Hey, Mr. McGraw!" cried the Chief. "I ain't never seen speed like that, and ain't he got movement on it too!"

"Well," Matty said mildly, peering at the tiny, doughty figure on the mound, "when you think about it, he's more or less got to have that upward movement on his fastball, don't he?" (My ideas of credible 1908 ballplayer dialogue were heavily influenced by Ring Lardner.)

McGraw shrugged, since tryouts were one thing and baseball was another, but in the end he decided to give the kid a start that Sunday in a big benefit exhibition that the Giants were playing at the Polo Grounds against the Detroit Tigers.

I stopped. Outside we could hear the steady stop-and-start rhythmic passage of the sanitation workers. Impossibly chic, in grass green uniforms with a white stripe running down the side, the men of the *Paris Propre* come down our street every night to collect the garbage. The garbage is put out by *gardiens* in city-issued green plastic canisters, and the garbage men place the canisters on little elevators, one on each side of the rear of the truck. The containers are lifted, turned upside down, shaken out, and returned trembling to the ground. Then the truck proceeds, at a stately, serene, implacable pace; a cabdriver who gets caught behind one on a little street lets out a moan, like a man who has just been bayoneted.

At this point I decided I'd made a decent start and was getting ready to say good night. "Go on," he said, muffled but sharp, from under his covers. An order.

In the benefit exhibition that Sunday (I went on at last), the big bathtub-shaped stadium, with its strange supporting Y beams, was packed with fans, come to see the three-year-old phenom. The Rookie took the mound, throwing smoke, and it looked as though it might be a first, a perfect perfect game, twenty-seven men up, twenty-seven Ks, until, in the sixth, he had to face the Terrible Ty Cobb. (I realized that I had a problem here since Cobb should have been batting cleanup from the start; I explained that he had been late suiting up, because he insisted on extorting extra payment from the Tigers' management for playing in a charity exhibition, even though everybody else was playing for free. Cobb was just like that, I explained: terrible.) The crowd quieted as the confrontation neared. Cobb came to the plate, sneering and drawling.

"Hey, baby," he called out, taunting the Rookie. "Looks to me like you're nothin' but a *baby*." (Luke's whole body stiffened. If there was a worse insult, he hadn't heard it; Jackie Robinson, in his first year with the Brooklyn Dodgers, had never been called a name so vile.) Shaken, the Rookie lost a bit off his heater. It was still blazing, though, and Cobb just got a piece of it, dribbling it toward first; he took off, and the Rookie, who knew his assignments, dutifully scampered over to cover. Cobb came in hard, hard as he could, his spikes sharpened to razor tips, and stamped down on the Rookie's three-year-old foot. The Rookie dropped the ball. Safe! Stinking rotten way to get on base, but safe all the same. Shaking off a couple of tears, the Rookie went back to the mound. "Hey, I reckon you're a crybaby. Hey, everybody, look at the crybaby! Looks to me like you're nothin' but a *cry*baby" came the taunting Georgia drawl from first, and the Rookie pitched out of trouble. But the pain lingered, and in the top of the ninth, the Giants having pushed over one run on a hit-and-run executed by the Chief, he made a few mistakes, walked a couple of batters—hey, he was *three*—and left himself with the bases loaded and the Georgia Peach due up again. The crowd was going crazy, and now the taunting began again, worse than ever. ("Hey, baby! Hey, crybaby! Whyn't ya cry some more, crybaby?")

The Rookie knew what he had to do. In the dugout he had taken his old bottle from the suitcase his mother had packed for him when he went off to join the Giants, just in case, and stowed it under his cap. Now he dripped a couple of drops of milk onto the seams of the baseball, the Rookie's soon-to-be-notorious bottleball. It was before they brought in the rule against foreign substances on the ball, I explained. The Rookie was playing fair. ("Hey, when are you guys going to sleep?" Luke's mother's voice came from the other room. "Soon," I called back abruptly. The lights of the traffic on the boulevard Saint-Germain came in through the windows, but I didn't even draw the curtains.)

The Rookie stretched and threw, and the bottleball dipped and twisted and dipped and twisted again, curving all the way out to the third-base line and then cruising halfway toward first before finally slipping in, softly and cleanly, right across the plate, a strike at the knees. Cobb had time to take a really good cut—he had *all day*—but the pitch had him so fooled that he didn't just whiff, he twisted himself in knots while he whiffed: real knots, his whole body pulled around like a wet washrag, hands ending up back of his butt. (Luke chuckled deeply at that.) "Steer-rike-uh three," cried the umpire. The bleachers of the Polo Grounds went nuts.

The Rookie trotted off the field. "Who's the baby *now*, Mr. Cobb?" he asked, with quiet dignity, on his way back to the dugout.

My kid sat up, shot up in bed, like a mechanical doll, as

though he had a spring hinge right at his waist. Christy Mathewson (I went on) didn't say anything—that wasn't his way—but he went over as the Rookie came into the dugout, took off the Rookie's cap, and mussed up his hair. Outside, the crowd wouldn't leave. They chanted, "Rookie! Rookie!"

Now the only sound from Luke's pillow was of short, constant breathing. I had the uncanny knowledge of a kind of silent excitement, the certainty—I have witnessed it once or twice on opening night in a theater, though I had certainly never created it before myself—that what we had here was a hit. The Terrible Ty Cobb had called him a baby, and he had thrown the bottle-ball, and *then* who was the baby?

That night (I said) the Rookie was offered a contract with the Giants (doubtless a mean, exploitative contract, but I left that out), and the team got on the overnight sleeper to St. Louis, heading out to steamy Sportsman's Park. (I knew that the Browns, not the Cardinals, played there, but I liked the way it sounded.) The Chief tucked the Rookie into his berth and, before he went off to play pinochle with the guys, asked him, gruffly, "You OK, Rookie?" "I'm OK, Chief," the Rookie said, and then he listened to the sounds of the train tracks clacking and the whistle blowing and the other ballplayers in the next car, laughing and playing cards, before he fell deep asleep, somewhere outside Columbus.

"I'm OK, Chief," Luke repeated, and he did something he had never done before, or at least not in my presence: Without negotiation or hesitation, without tears or arguments or requests to come and sleep in the big bed, he rolled right over and fell asleep.

From then on we had a story about the Rookie—Luke called it the Rookie story—every night. The characters firmed up pretty quickly. The Rookie was an earnest, resourceful, somewhat high-strung little hero. The Chief was blustery and honest, wanting nothing more than to settle in with his copy of the *Police Gazette* and have a peaceful afternoon at McSorley's. The Rookie's triumph over Ty Cobb, though, had bad consequences. Cobb developed a bitter, unappeasable Tom DeLay–type enmity toward the Rookie and set himself the task of doing anything he could to destroy his career. John J. McGraw, thumbtack sharp and demanding, and Christy Mathewson, handsome and deep-voiced and friendly, though a little remote—on a couple of occasions, when the Chief left town to go on a scouting trip to Cincinnati, he was the Rookie's baby-sitter—filled out the dramatis personae.

After a couple of months I went down to the cellar of our building and got out the few baseball reference books I had brought to Paris and never unpacked. (This cellar is an honest-to-God *cave*, a stone cellar with little arches where you could keep wine. I kept meaning to bring the wine down, but I never remembered to do it, and instead the books were there, moldering away.) The 1908 National League pennant race, which I had plucked out of the air and dim memories of *The Glory of Their Times,* turned out to be even more interesting than I'd thought. It was a three-way race—Cubs, Giants, Pirates—that included Merkle's boner and the season-capping rematch it produced, and in a sense, it made baseball in America. I discovered that 1908 had been a kind of watershed year, a time when baseball had, for the last time, an air of improvisation about it, with, as someone said of those days, "stupid guys, smart guys, tough guys, mild guys, crazy guys, college men, slickers from the city, and hicks from the country." If a three-year-old with a major-league fastball *had* ever existed, 1908 would have been the right season for him to play, and he probably would have been roomed with an American Indian catcher.

I even found a wonderful photograph of the Polo Grounds in that magical year, and we hung it over Luke's bed. It shows a hundred or so fans lining up on Coogan's Bluff, overlooking the ballpark—too poor or, more likely, too cheap to buy tickets, since you can see that there are still a few seats left in center—backs turned and heads bowed as they stare down at the field. Every single one of the men (there are no women) is wearing a derby; the kids are wearing cloth caps. One kid and an elderly gent have got up on a barrel, and five men in suits and hats are standing, precarious but dignified, on a plank that slopes down from it. You can't really see a thing going on in the park—not a baseline, not a ballplayer, not a glimpse of a dugout or a bullpen, nothing except the outfield grass down below, a perfect and absolute blank. It's as good as a Magritte: the solemnly dressed businessmen, backs turned, gazing out at the bare and uneventful field. Of course Luke didn't have to be told whom they were looking at down there, and why; we both could see it plain as day. They were watching the Rookie, pitching his way out of another pinch.

Yet I began to wonder: What picture did he summon up when, night after night, he heard the words *Polo Grounds, full count, all the way to the backstop*? Not an inexact picture; no picture at all. He had never been to a baseball game, never seen a bat or a glove, never been inside a ballpark or even watched a ball game on television. He spent his days in parks where kids played soccer on dusty gravel, and you put a toe in the grass on pain of being whistled down by the surveillant, watching from his shed. No one Luke knew played baseball, no one talked about it; the words and situations were pure language, pure abstract lore. The clichés I rolled out—"He had all day," "steamy Sportsman's Park," "no foreign substances on the old pill"—what did he think, what did he see when he heard them? I knew that he wanted to hear the words as much as I needed to say them— he zipped through dessert to get to bed every night—but what did the words mean to him?

I had spent my adult life believing that storytelling depends on the credibility of its details, and now, finally, I had made up a story that someone liked, and the details had no credibility at all, no existence except as sounds. You are supposed to use a word, I had always been taught, to point at a thing and hope that the thing will somehow end up pointing at a symbol: a feeling, a state of mind. When I lived in New York, I had on occasion even brought this faith to writing students. (Not that they cared. The fetching female ones listened gravely and then came up after class to ask if I had Gary Fisketjohn's phone number.) But now I said "Polo Grounds" or "full count" and the words called up in my son a powerful reaction. What of that second range, where the words were supposed to become things, even just images in his head?

There is, I believe now, a force in stories, words in motion, that either drives them forward past things into feelings or doesn't. Sometimes the words fly right over the fence and all the way out to the feelings. Make them do it one time out of three in private, and you've got a reputation as someone who can play a little, a dad who can tell a decent bedtime story. Do it three times out of three in public, and you're Mark McGwire or Dickens.

And I needed the words too, just as words. After four years in Paris I found that though I missed American sports a lot less than I had thought I would, I missed the lore of American sports keenly. I didn't really miss sports; I missed the sports pages. I didn't miss the things—sometimes the baseball season was twenty or twenty-five games old before I knew it had started—but I missed the words that went with the things. My passion for baseball, which at one point in my life was pretty intense, is now almost gone. My team, the Montreal Expos, is on the verge of going out of business; when I visit New York, I no longer know, or can even guess, which player is wearing which cap.

I still care about the words, though. One day, shopping for dinner along the rue du Bac and waiting in one of the interminable lines that are created by the individual care of French service—a line that is briskly, infuriatingly violated by the same arrogant dyed-blond woman in a fur coat and with a great jaw—I thought, Nobody in this line but me knows what an RBI is, or who Gene Mauch was, or what Jarry Park used to look like, or what a twinight doubleheader is. And I felt yearningly, unappeasably homesick. (This was not a rational emotion, since I have lived for years with a woman who doesn't know what an RBI is either.)

The things an American who is abroad for a very long time misses—or at least the things I missed—I was discovering, weren't the things you were supposed to miss. We are supposed to come to Europe for leisure, sunshine, a more civilized pace, for slowness of various kinds. America we are supposed to miss for its speed, its friendliness, for the independence of its people and the individualism of their lives. Yet these were not the things I missed, and when I speak to Americans who have lived abroad for a long time, those are not the things they seem to miss either. I didn't miss crosstown traffic, New York taxicabs, talk radio or talk television, or the constant, appalling flow of opinion that spills out like dirty floodwater. (Paris is an argumentative but not an opinionated city; it is the ideal of every French newspaper columnist to have premises so inarguable that the opinions can more or less look after themselves while he goes to lunch.)

I didn't miss American "independence" either. If anything, I missed its opposite, American obsequiousness, that yearning, beseeching tone of a salesman trying to sell something that you never hear in statist Europe. (The French, I think somebody said, have every vice *except* obsequiousness.) Buying shoes for my son, I missed the shoe salesmen of my childhood, my own uncles among them, their glasses held together with tape, their voices keening as they got down on their knees to tie the laces and make the sale. "Now the youngster can wear this shoe as a sports shoe or a dress shoe. Yeah, you got plenty of room there at the toe, young fellow—stand up. Now show your mom these shoes. Walk around." Quieter: "I have it in burgundy, in brown, in blue . . ." A French shoe salesman, indignant at his position, laces the child's shoes in silent anger and rises to his feet pretty much shaking his fist in your face.

I found, to my surprise, that what I missed and longed for was the comforting loneliness of life in New York, a certain kind of scuffed-up soulfulness. In Paris no relationship, even one with a postman or a dry cleaner, is abstract or anonymous; human relations are carved out in a perpetual present tense. There's an intricacy of debits and credits. Things have histories. The little, quickly forgiven bumps of New York social life—the missed phone calls, the suddenly canceled lunches, the early exit from the dinner party, which are, if anything, signs of status, of "busyness"—are sources of long grievances, permanent estrangements, endless reexplanations. It isn't possible just to remove yourself from a friendship in Paris for a month or two, as you can in New York. ("What have you been doing?" "Working." "Oh.") Even the most apparently professional relationships get overloaded. The dry cleaner is recovering from cancer, and her visits to pick up the clothes are scheduled around her treatments, with enough time to talk about them; the man who puts up shelves is a jazz guitarist, and an extra hour must be budgeted in to trade licks and discuss Jim Hall. On your way down the street in the early morning to run with all the other Americans in the Luxembourg Gardens—only Americans and French riot police go running; the Americans you know by their music festival sweatshirts, the French police by their flattop cuts and thoughtful, coiled power—you hear footsteps coming after you, and you worry that you have violated some ordinance, stepped on some forbidden grass. It is the fishmonger. "The wild salmon went well?" he demands anxiously. You find a café where you feel at home—and then become reluctant to go there, since it will involve such a wearing round of handshakes and "How is Madame?"

New York is devoted to the cult of busyness, but like all cults, it has at its heart the worship of a single, unforgiving idol, the office. After the idol has been served, life can be pretty formless. The things Americans miss tend to involve that kind of formlessness, small, casual, and solitary pleasures. A psychoanalyst misses walking up Lafayette Street in her tracksuit, sipping coffee from a Styrofoam cup with the little plastic piece that pops up. My wife, having been sent the carrot cake that she missed from New York, discovered that what she really missed was standing up at the counter and eating carrot cake in the company of strangers at the Bon Vivant coffee shop. I thought I missed reading Phil Mushnick in the sports pages of the *Post*; when I read him on-line, I discovered that what I really missed was reading Phil Mushnick on the number 6 uptown train on a Monday morning around ten.

It was, in a way, the invisibility of the men up on Coogan's Bluff in 1908 that drew me to them. The consensual anonymity of men in crowds is what we are escaping when we leave, and then it is what we miss. You can be alone in Paris a lot, but it is hard to be lonely; there is always another pair of eyes, not unfriendly, appraising you. (The French husband of an American friend will not meet her in the park in his tennis shorts. He does not know who will see him, but he is sure that he will, in some way, be seen.) You are a subject, not an object, and if this is part of the narrow, centuries-old happiness of life in Paris, it is also one of the things that narrow that happiness. Walk into Central Park to watch the sea lions, and you disappear from the world for a little while. In the Luxembourg Gardens, or at the menagerie in the Jardin des Plantes, you are always conscious of the long *allées* leading you back the way you came; of the surveillants' shed at the center of the park, where the two uniformed men sit with their hot plate, warming up coffee and watching the world; of the lion looking back at you. We go to cities to be invisible, or to be invisible and visible by turns, and it is hard to be invisible in Paris. The light at night is too strong. Gershwin got this right at least: The car horns and the syncopations in *An American in Paris* are all French. What that American misses is the blues.

|||

After about a year of telling the Rookie story, I went to New York to give a talk, and I turned the trip into a literary mission, a sort of Rookie collecting expedition. I wanted to bring home tangible evidence of something that, as a matter of fact, had never taken place there. I bought a baseball encyclopedia and a box of books on the Cobb era and borrowed a Ken Burns video. A vintage Giants cap, child size, which I thought would be the hardest thing to find, turned out to be absurdly easy; the past is so neatly packaged now that I just walked into a memorabilia store on Lexington Avenue and found a replica cap, no problem.

When I got home, I put on the video, from the PBS *Baseball* series, which I had never seen, and we watched all those flickering, overfrantic little ghost figures racing around. One by one the faces and bodies and actions that you couldn't see in the photo above Luke's bed were being filled in. There was Ty Cobb, looking appropriately evil; there was John J. McGraw. There was pitching and batting (I realized, from Luke's comments, that he had them the wrong way around). There was baserunning.

There was Christy Mathewson, and then a picture of Matty, handsome and assured as ever, slowly dissolving into a picture of a small, serious boy with blond bangs, wearing a baseball cap and a perfectly sober expression, going into a pitching windup. I still have no idea who he actually was (it's not Christy Mathewson's kid; I've found a picture of him, and he had darker hair), but of course Luke knew, perfectly well.

"There he is," he said. "Rewind it." We watched Matty and the Rookie appear again, and then he told me to turn it off. He was uncharacteristically silent for the rest of the afternoon, but before dinner I heard him talking to his mother in the bath. "He had his hands up like this," he was saying chattily. "I don't know why."

Sometime that month I began to think that it was time to round off the Rookie story, give it a suitably grand ending, turn the legend into a myth; I would find another story. I was having a hard time thinking of new plots, and anyway, it had been two years.

It was, at last, the seventh game of the 1908 World Series.

The Rookie had started three for the Giants, Matty the others. (Of course we had made the Giants, not the Cubs, grab the gonfalon on the final day.) It was the bottom of the ninth, the score tied one to one on homers by the Chief and Sam Crawford. Cobb was up. He dragged a bunt and headed for first, and this time he didn't just spike the Rookie; he actually slid into first base, razor-clad feet up. Hit hard, the Rookie held on to the ball. But the umpire ruled that the ball had rolled foul down the first-base line. The Rookie was bleeding, fed up, homesick, crowded by a ringer like Gizmo McGee, a Tiger midget pretending to be a four-year-old, and he had endured a full season (in two years) of cruel torment at the hands of this terrible man. So he did an awful thing: He loaded up and threw his best fastball right at Ty Cobb's head, threw so hard that Cobb's head came right off, popped up high, before settling back down, with a surprised look, on his shoulders.

Umpire Bill Klem checked out Cobb—he was OK; the Rookie knew what he was doing—and then looked at the Rookie. "You're outta here, Rookie," he said, giving him the longest, slowest, saddest thumbing heave-ho that the major leagues have ever seen. "There's just no throwing at people in baseball." The crowd sat silent, disbelieving. The Rookie, head bowed, walked off the field.

And (I said) he kept walking. The Chief and Matty and Mr. McGraw were waiting for him in the dugout, but he walked away from them, didn't even stop to take off his uniform in the center field clubhouse, just kept walking, right out of the Polo Grounds, day after day, week after week, until he was back in Anywhere, U.S.A., still in his uniform. His mother didn't ask any questions. She hugged him, helped him out of his uniform (she hung it in the closet), and asked him if he wanted something to eat, and the next day he went back to school. His legend grew, but he never picked up a ball again.

Luke sat up. "He did not go home to his mother," he said

clearly. I felt horrible, as evil as Ty Cobb. I saw in his eyes what seemed to me not anger, exactly, but something more like doubt, religious doubt as it is described in nineteenth-century novels. What if the Rookie hadn't risen again? What if the story had been only a story? What if someone was obviously manipulating it for a moral purpose? He had the relics and the photos, but like a true believer, he knew that it was all just talk if the Rookie didn't rise again.

"He did not go home to his mother," he said again, and as quickly as I could, in a panic, I turned it around. Of course not, I said. He went home for that day, to relax. The next day a delegation from both leagues was in his front yard, insisting that he come back to the Giants. "Baseball can't survive without you, kid," said Ban Johnson, president of the American League. Even Cobb himself, bandaged and sheepish, was there. Finally the Rookie agreed to come back—"But no more dirty tricks," he said—and they played an eighth game (as they'd done once before), which he won.

"You told the story wrong," he said finally. (And the next day he said to his mother, "Daddy told the Rookie story wrong.") So the story goes on, only now it is much more under the child's control. The Rookie soon entered a Gothic phase, as the little boy began to demand scary Rookie stories ("With a real witch. Not Ty Cobb dressed up like a witch. Not the Chief dressed up like a witch. A real witch") and, more recently, a decadent phase. The current story, for instance, involves Sherlock Holmes, the genie from *Aladdin,* a *T. rex,* and the Pirate King from *Pirates of Penzance.* Having been, if only momentarily, betrayed by the story, he was doing what the literary critics would call "contesting the narrative." The story belongs to him now.

My Rookie never really played ball again, no matter how many stories I tell, any more than Sherlock Holmes really came back alive from the Reichenbach Falls, no matter how many stories Conan Doyle wrote about him afterward. I think the Rookie just went home to Anywhere, U.S.A., and back to school like all the other kids.

Luke and I tried playing a little catch this spring in the Luxembourg Gardens but gave up after about five minutes. For a present, around that time, he asked us to make him his own *carte d'identité,* marked with a *métier de journaliste*—a press pass from the government—so that he could pretend to cut through red tape. We made him an impressive-looking fake government document, with a black-and-white photo and lots of cryptic, official-looking stamps. At bedtime now before the Rookie story starts, he likes to act out a French bureaucratic drama: I play a functionary guarding an entrance to something or other who scowls at him until he haughtily flashes his *carte,* and then I let him pass with many apologetic, ah-monsieur-I-did-not-recognize grimaces and shrugs, while his mother acts out the role of irate bystander, fuming in line as the privileged functionary serenely passes by. I suppose it is about time we took him home.

I don't think about the Rookie as much as I used to, but when the bombs began to fall in Serbia I began thinking about that other Serbian conflagration, in 1914, and everything it had led to, and I realized with a start that by making the Rookie three years old in 1908, I was leaving him, unprotected, to the century's horrors. Then I did a quick calculation and realized that he would have been far too young for the First War, and just too old for the Second. The Rookie was lucky that way, I think.

A Machine to
Draw the
World

The World Cup,
and After

The World Cup soccer tournament got off to a strange, promising start with a pageant that closed down Paris—a seventeenth-century-style allegorical masque, with music and dance and speech, which featured four sixty-five-foot-high inflatable giants that walked across the city from four Parisian monuments (the Opéra, the Eiffel Tower, the Arc de Triomphe, and the pont Neuf) to the place de la Concorde. The giants were steel-framed latex-covered figures—dolls, really—with fork-lift trucks for feet, and hydraulic hinged arms and hips and shoulders, and even moving eyelids. They turned their heads, and shifted their gaze, and raised their arms in wonder as they slowly shuffled along the Paris streets. Each one was a different color and represented a racial type. There was Romeo, the European; Pablo, the Amerindian; Ho, the Asian; and Moussa, the African (he had purple skin). It took four hours for them to get from their starting points to the place, where they bowed to one another, and the whole spectacle was broadcast live on television, while Juliette Binoche breathed over the loudspeakers on the streets and to the audience at home. ("The giants confront each other, but do they see a stranger or themselves?" etc.) The theme of the masque seemed to be the Self and the Other; the giants, never having seen one another before—or anything else, apparently—wake in the middle of Paris, to find their Selfness in the Others. Apart from that, the commentators on French television were hard put to find something to say as the big guys inched their way along the boulevards toward this revelation and at one point were reduced to noting that the technology that had produced the hydraulic giants had military applications, leaving you with the comforting knowledge that if NATO is ever in need of a crack synchronized team of huge, slow-moving inflatable dolls, the French will be the ones to call. (One sees them cornering a particularly sluggish war criminal in a Montenegrin mountain hideaway with a very large door.)

The vague internationalist symbolism—not to speak of the snail-like pace—seemed the right allegory for the tournament. The Coupe du Monde, which includes thirty-two nations, began on Wednesday, June 10, and continues through Sunday, July 12. I set myself the task of watching it all, wanting to figure out what exactly it is that the world loves in a game that so many American sports fans will sit through only under compulsion.

I understand why people play it. When I was a teenager, I lived in London for a while, and I spent most of my time playing soccer, or at least the middle-class Kensington Gardens version of it. I even learned how to talk the game. It was the opposite of trash talking—tidy talking, I suppose you'd have to call it. If you did something good, it was brilliant; something less than brilliant was useless; if all of you were useless together, you were rubbish; and if a person did something brilliant that nonetheless became useless, everyone cried, "Oh, unlucky!" By the end of my time in London, I wasn't brilliant at the game, but I wasn't useless either. I suppose this was all faithful to the game's English-school-playing-field origins. "Thoughtful ball," a commentator on the BBC would say about a good pass. In the papers you'll read things like "The signs of decline in the still-clever but jaded Teddy Sheringham sadly became too patent to ignore." "For all his apparent world-weariness, Beckham is still young." "[Anderton] has been stubborn to the point almost of self-destruction, however, and it cannot happen again this week." This isn't sportswriting. It's end-of-term reports.

As I began watching the cup games, though, I had a hard time making a case for soccer as spectacle. I found myself torn between a cosmopolitan desire to love a game the world loves and an American suspicion that they wouldn't love it if they had a choice. The trouble wasn't the low scores, although the ribbon of late sports news often sounded like one of those condensed, hopeless, rising-and-falling monologues about marriage in Beckett: "Nil-nil. One-one. Two-one. One-one. One-nil. Nil-nil." The trouble was what the scores represent. The game has achieved a kind of tactical stasis. Things start off briskly and then fritter away into desultory shin kicking, like a *Wall Street Journal* editorial. In soccer the defense has too big an edge to keep the contest interesting, like basketball before the coming of the twenty-four-second clock or the western front before the invention of the tank.

All sports take turns being dominated by their defense or their offense, and fully evolved defensive tactics will in the end beat offensive ones, because it is always easier to break a sequence than to build one up. Eventually the defensive edge will be so enormous that to stay in business as a spectacle, a sport has to change its rules, openly or surreptitiously. The big recent change in basketball, for instance, which took place somewhere between the Julius Erving and Michael Jordan eras, was a silent modification of the rule against traveling, so that now, it seems, a player can take about as many steps as he needs—a fact that only Rabbit Angstrom has officially noted. American football changes its rules every few years to allow quarterbacks to survive and prosper. Even baseball has tinkered with the mound and the depth of the fences. Soccer players, though, have come to accept the scarcity economy—all those nil-nil draws—and just live with it, like Eskimos. The defense has such an advantage that the national sides don't need their offensive stars. In this cup two of the most inspired forwards in Europe—David Ginola, of France and Tottenham Hotspur, and Paul Gascoigne, of England and whatever pub is open—didn't even make their national teams.

Since a defensive system keeps players from getting a decent chance to score, the idea is to get an indecent one: to draw a foul so that the referee awards a penalty, which is essentially a free goal. This creates an enormous disproportion between the foul and the reward. In the first game that Italy played, against Chile, for instance, the great Roberto Baggio saved the Italians' *pancetta* by smoking the ball onto the hand of a surprised Chilean defender, who couldn't pull back in time. "Hand ball" was ruled, which, near the goal, meant an automatic penalty and a nearly automatic goal. The other, more customary method of getting a penalty is to walk into the "area" with the ball, get breathed on hard, and then immediately collapse, like a man shot by a sniper, arms and legs splayed out, while you twist in agony and beg for morphine, and your teammates smite their foreheads at the tragic waste of a young life. The referee buys this more often than you might think. Afterward the postgame did-he-fall-or-was-he-pushed argument can go on for hours.

European defenders of the game tend to put on haughty, half-amused looks when the sport is criticized and assume that the problem lies with the American doing the criticizing, who is assumed to love action for its own sake. When you point out that ice hockey, the greatest of all games, shares with soccer the basic idea of putting something into a net behind a goalkeeper and has the added bonus of actually doing it, they giggle: "Oh, dear. In ice hockey you can't see the ball, or whatever you call it. You can't follow it. Besides, they fight all the time." It does no good when you try to explain that you can always see the puck, and anyway, better to fight like heroes than to spend all your time on the sidelines bickering about who touched the ball last before it went out of bounds, the way soccer players do, even though—as a Tom Stoppard character once pointed out—there is absolutely no doubt on the part of those two players about who touched the ball last.

European soccer apologists tend to overanalyze the triumphs of their heroes. In Brazil's game against Scotland, Ronaldo, the Brazilians' star, took the ball, faked right, and then spun around to his left, leaving a defender fooled while he rushed forward into the gap. Then he let go a weak shot, and it was over. A nice move—but exactly the same move that Emmitt Smith makes three times a game with three steroid-enraged three-hundred-pound linemen draped on his back (and then Emmitt goes in to score) or that Mario Lemieux made three or four times a period after receiving radiation therapy for Hodgkin's lymphoma and having three Saskatchewan farm boys whacking at his ankles with huge clubs (and then Mario would go in to score). In the papers, though, that moment became a golden event. Rob Hughes, the estimable soccer writer for the *International Herald Tribune,* treated the three seconds of actual activity as though it were the whole of the Peloponnesian War, or a seduction by Casanova. "Receiving the ball from Cafu on the right, Ronaldo lured Colin Hendry, Scotland's biggest and most worldly defender, to him. 'Come closer, Big Colin, come to me,' the Brazilian seemed to say. And Hendry bought the invitation. Tighter and tighter he came until, suddenly, Ronaldo swiveled 180 degrees. . . ."

Soccer writers seemed as starved for entertainment as art critics; anything vaguely enjoyable gets promoted to the level of genius. In the old days, at the Kitchen, it was the rule that three recognizable notes sung in succession by Laurie Anderson heralded a new, generous lyricism. Ronaldo's magic was like a performance artist's lyricism: It existed but was apparent only against a background of numbing boredom.

In the first ten days I watched, by my count, sixteen games, including odd, hallucinatory matchups out of some fractured game of Risk: Denmark against Saudi Arabia (1–0); Croatia against Japan (1–0); Nigeria against Bulgaria (1–0). There were a few players who stood out from the general run of bowlegged men in shorts. There were Englishmen (I root for England, from residual Kensington Gardens chauvinism): the pained, gifted O. J. Simpson look-alike Paul Ince; a speedy, tiny boy with a shining morning face named Michael Owen, only eighteen and just off the Liverpool bench. The French players were dogged, unelectric, powerful, and, as many people pointed out, mostly not ethnically French, with lots of "exotic" names: Zidane, Djorkaeff, Karembeu. Though their countrymen long for the dash and élan of David Ginola and the vanished Eric Cantona, they see the functionary logic of this harder-working, intelligent side. There were the Argentines and the Germans, who never seem quite as glamorous as, say, the Brazilians and the Dutch, but who have a brutal purposefulness. Between them they have won four of the last six cups. And there were moments of wonder, when a previously unknown—and probably soon to be unknown again—ballplayer would shock himself and his team-mates with a single stunning moment. A young Cameroonian named Pierre Njanka, with no major-league experience, made his way through the entire Austrian team, his eyes wide as he ducked and swerved, stumbling forward, out of control, hardly believing what he was accomplishing, and then scored. He may spend the rest of his life defined by that run.

But such moments were mostly drowned in tedium and then by something worse. By the time the English players arrived on the scene, on Monday, June 15, everything was already ruined. Hooligans had invaded Marseilles, where England was opening against Tunisia, and not merely got drunk and beat up shop-keepers but overran a beach where Tunisian families were pic-nicking (there is a big Tunisian community in the South of France) and beat up kids and moms there. Everyone had known that they were coming. One source said that the authorities had done their best to keep out the hardboiled Category C hooligans, but some of them had managed to sneak in—a rare case of England's having a deep bench.

Though headlines about English hooligans sweep the world, they don't do justice to the terror involved. "Lager louts" and "hooligans" sound vaguely quaint, but these guys are cruel, violent, and twisted by inarticulate hatred in a way that terrifies the French and makes them wild partisans of the Scottish team. The persistence of English hooliganism—the Englishness of hooliganism—can maybe be explained by the possibility that at some half-conscious level a lot of English people are proud of their thugs and approve of their behavior. This approval consists of a toxic combination of sentimental left-wing anti-Thatcherism (a kind of *Trainspotting* pride that at least the thugs aren't businessmen) coupled with a romantic right-wing chauvinism (it's an English tradition to go to the Continent and hit foreigners). In the Marseilles attacks most of the thugs turned out not to be poor kids, or unemployed kids; they couldn't have afforded the passage over. The thugs were, apparently, mostly postal workers (what is it about mail?), and they were not going to be damaged in the eyes of their mates for having gone over to France to beat people up, or for being sent back from France for having beat people up.

|||

Despite the reports of violence from provincial fronts, Paris itself has been relatively blasé about the cup. The streets are peaceful, the mood is calm, the atmosphere pastoral. The boulevard Saint-Germain has never been so quiet. The morning after the giants' march, for instance, with Scotland and Brazil about to begin at the Stade de France, the only evidence I saw of anything unusual was the appearance of two Scotsmen in kilts waiting for a taxi on the rue du Bac. Expecting to hear a war cry ("Ay, we'll leave them samba-dancin' laddies guid and bloody"), I tentatively wished them good luck. "We'll need it!" one said feelingly, and the other chimed in, "It's simply a privilege to be playing Brazil." They turned out to be lawyers from Hong Kong—Scottish lawyers from Hong Kong, but lawyers. They talked about the Brazilian esprit, and then got in their cab and, in perfect French, ordered the driver to go to the Stade de France.

I saw Italy beat Cameroon, 3–0, from the back of a bar in Venice. Watching soccer in Italy, you have the feeling that you have wandered into a family drama more complex and intense than you can understand. Each player—Vieri, Di Biagio—was greeted with a combination of hoots, cheers, and tears so personal and heartfelt that it was almost embarrassing for an outsider to witness. With Italy into the eighth-finals (eighth-finals!), the papers, from left to right, were bursting with pride. ITALIA PADRONE! read one headline. "Italy Rules." The curious thing was that Italy played one of the dullest defensive games of all—the famous "blue chain." But this didn't seem to bother anyone. Whatever people were watching for, it wasn't for fun.

Just afterward I spoke on the phone to an English friend, a big World Cupper.

"How are you getting on with the cup?" he asked.

"It's a bit—well, don't you think it's a bit lacking in entertainment?" I said weakly.

There was a pause. "Why would you expect it to be entertaining?" he asked, reprovingly.

Perhaps that was a clue. I came back to Paris resolved not to be entertained. I watched a double-overtime confrontation between an overmatched Paraguay and an overpressed France. The Paraguayans, who looked worn out from stress, essentially surrendered the idea of scoring and kept dropping back—kicking the ball out, heading it out, willing it out, again and again. It was obvious that their desperate, gallant strategy was to force a nil-nil draw, over 120 minutes, and then "go to penalties," the shoot-out at goal where anything can happen and anyone can win. The nil-nil draw wasn't a "result" they would settle for; it was everything they dreamed of achieving. When the game finally ended, as Laurent Blanc (a traditionally French-sounding name) stumbled a ball into the Paraguayan net, what was most memorable was the subdued triumph. The French celebrated, but they did not exult; the Paraguayans cried—really cried—but they did not despair. They did not seem ruined or emptied out, as American losers do. They seemed relieved. The tears looked like tears of bitter accomplishment. We knew we were going to lose, the faces and the back pats said, but, hey, didn't we hold it off for a while? ("*Héroïque, héroïque,*" murmured the French commentator.)

The next morning I slipped in a tape I'd made of the fifth game of the NBA finals, for purposes of comparison. It was a French broadcast, and the commentators announced that the game was a test of truth—*une épreuve de vérité*—for the Utah Jazz. To my surprise, I was, after a week of starvation, used to the austerity of soccer scoring. All those basketball points seemed a little loud, a little cheap. Points coming in from left, from right, cheap points, inspired points, stupid points—goals everywhere you looked, more goals than you knew what to do with, democratic goals, all leveled and equal. It was too much, like eating whipped cream straight. And why had I never before noticed the absurd, choppy, broken rhythm of deliberate fouls and time-outs in the last two minutes of the game?

A few nights later England-Argentina—to see who would go to the quarterfinals. The match started off with two typically exasperating soccer events. After only five minutes David Seaman, the English goalkeeper, lunged for the ball, and an onrushing Argentine stumbled over him. Penalty and, inevitably, a goal. Then young Owen, who, with his brush cut, looks as if he ought to be wearing a blazer and beanie, got tripped. He acted out the death scene from *Camille* and drew a penalty himself, which was knocked in by Alan Shearer, England's captain. A few minutes later Owen raced half the length of the field—really sprinting, huffing—mesmerizing an Argentine defenseman, who kept moving back, back, defeated in his own mind, and then he sent it in: 2–1, England! With fifteen seconds left in the half, Argentina got the ball, executed a jagged, pinball-quick exchange of passes and, shockingly, the ball was bouncing in the net, and the game was tied.

At the start of the second half, David Beckham, the blond midfielder who was at the time engaged to Posh Spice, was expelled from the game, leaving England, like the Spices, a performer short. Though England scored on a corner, the goal was ruled out by the referee for a meaningless, barely visible (but undeniably real) elbow. Nothing happened in thirty minutes of overtime, and the game went into the self-parody of soccer: a series of penalty kicks. With England needing only one more to tie, David Batty, of Newcastle, stepped up and, rushing his shot, fired it right into the diving goaltender. The Argentine side rushed out into the pitch, weeping with joy and exhaustion.

The game had been marked by everything that can exasperate an American fan: the dominance of defense, the disproportion between foul and consequence, the absurd penalty shoot-out, the playacting. (In England they will be arguing did-he-fall-or-was-he-pushed about the first Argentine penalty for years.) But it had been as draining as any contest I'd ever seen.

Soccer was not meant to be enjoyed. It was meant to be experienced. The World Cup is a festival of fate: man accepting his hard circumstances, the near certainty of his failure. There is, after all, something familiar about a contest in which nobody wins and nobody pots a goal. Nil-nil is the score of life. This may be where the difficulty lies for Americans, who still look for Eden out there on the ballfield. But soccer is not meant to be an escape from life. It *is* life, in all its injustice and tedium: We seek unfair advantage, celebrate tiny moments of pleasure as though they were final victories, score goals for the wrong side. (In the first three nights of the World Cup, three of the seventeen goals were "own" goals: A player would head the ball away and watch it backspin past his own goalkeeper, his face a rapidly changing mask of decision, satisfaction, worry, disbelief, and despair.) A bad play or call in baseball—Merkle's boner or Denkinger's call—hurts, but usually there's a saving air of humor. "We're due," "It's our turn," "Wait till next year" are the cheers of American sport. We are optimists and look to sports to amplify our optimism.

In soccer tomorrow is a long way off, even in ordinary circumstances, and four years in these special ones. By then everything will be different; there are no second chances in the World Cup. It is a human contest on a nearly geologic time scale. Grievances, injustices rankle for years, decades, forever. But along with that comes, appealingly, a sense of proportion. Accepting the eventual certainty of defeat in turn liberates you to take real joy in any small victory, that one good kick. If American sports are played in paradise, soccer takes place after the fall. Even its squabbles have their echoes: Did he fall or was he pushed? It's the oldest question.

Finally, on a stray, leaking cable channel, I got to see highlights of Detroit and Washington in the Stanley Cup final. I turned it on with joy and then found, to my shock, that . . . I couldn't see the puck! It was too small, way too small—a tiny black spot on a vast white surface, with huge men in bright-colored sweaters hulking over it. When a goal was scored (and goals do get scored), I knew it only by the subsequent celebration. I squinted at the set and called in Martha, a purebred Canadian, and asked if she could follow the puck. "I could never follow the puck," she told me.

Had I been corrupted by the Old World's game or enlightened by it? Another of the old, unanswerable questions. All I knew was that I was looking forward to the next big match, between France and Italy. Anything might happen, or nothing at all.

|||

Although France didn't win the World Cup until just before midnight on Sunday, the celebrations in Paris started hours before the game began. By two o'clock in the afternoon the beeping of horns along the Seine had become a din, and the kids with their faces painted red-white-and-blue, heads poking up through the sunroofs of Peugeots racing along the quays, had become a menace. Win or lose, the *crise* was already over.

Cars are cars all over the world, of course, and horns are horns, and a victory celebration in Paris doesn't sound much different from a victory celebration in New York or, for that matter, from a traffic tieup outside the Holland Tunnel. Even the theme song of the French victory was not the "Marseillaise" but Queen's "We Are the Champions."

Anyway, the whole point of the celebration was that it wasn't a champagne occasion. It was bottled water and cheap booze and a lot of beer. What made it memorable was that, for once, the carnival atmosphere of the Latin Quarter and the Marais spilled over into official French culture, and kept right on spilling. (By Tuesday morning, it had even spilled over into the garden of the Élysée, where a visibly blanching President Chirac greeted the players to a chorus of "We Are the Champions," sung, in best Freddie Mercury English, by the crowd thronging the team.)

At one-thirty in the morning after the victory, you could take the world's most beautiful walk—beginning at the Institut de France and moving across the pont des Arts and around the cour Carrée of the Louvre and then to the Tuileries and the Champs-Élysées—and feel as if, in the presence of so many happy people, the grand siècle itself had gone a little lopsided and blissed out. Misrule ruled. A man wrapped in a tricolor was relieving himself against the front wall of the Institut de France—discreetly, with maximum esprit de corps, but, still, relieving himself. Someone was selling beer out of a cooler, violating about twelve hundred French laws in the act, and someone else had one of those pinball arcade love-o-meters set up. (Everybody's hand was hot; even an American writer saw his score shoot past "Casanova" and all the way up to "*Chaud Lapin*"—"Hot Rabbit!") Kids were singing; men were grabbing politely at girls, presumably with a memory of 1944, when the girls were said to have grabbed back. This time they didn't, but it didn't matter.

Many people had talked a lot about the ethnic mix of the French team, which was composed of players of Algerian, Basque, and Ghanaian descent, among others, but the players themselves seemed a lot less self-conscious about this than journalists did. French identity is not that hard to achieve; if you speak French, you feel French. What is hard for an immigrant or an outsider in France to achieve is French institutional acceptance, a place in the crowded, ancient French iconography. The faces you saw on the World Cup team—the faces of Zidane and Djorkaeff and Karembeu—are already part of French society. They just hadn't been integrated before into the French self-image, and now they were.

It's natural for people to hope that the victory of a multiracial team might be the beginning of the end of Le Pen and the racist National Front, but it probably won't be. The ability of sports to solve social problems is limited—the Dream Team didn't change black income levels—and anyway, Le Pen blandly claimed the victory for himself. It was a reassertion of French glory, he said, and who is more glorious about France than he? The logic of nationalism always flows downhill, toward the gutter.

The real victory on Sunday night was a victory for disorder, an unexpected blessing, bonking the head of an unprepared population. On that long, beautiful walk, there's a moment when you arrive at the gate of the Tuileries and, for the first time, see the expanse of the Champs-Élysées. On Sunday you expected to see what you always see: a line of red car lights going up the right side of the champs and a line of white lights running down the left—two perfect, side-by-side mile-long lines of red and white, framed by the Arc de Triomphe. On Sunday night, for the first time that anyone could remember, the two neat columns of light were gone. The champs, a chaos of people and cars, was a blur of indistinct movement, the lights and colors a smear of milky pink. For once Paris was all mixed up.

The Balzar
Wars

The Balzar, on the rue des Écoles, in the Fifth Arrondissement of Paris, happens to be the best restaurant in the world. It is the best restaurant in the world not because it has the best food—though the food is (or used to be) excellent—and not because it is "hot," or even particularly fashionable, but because of a hundred small things that make it a uniquely soulful and happy place.

The Balzar is a brasserie, which means that it is Alsatian in origin, serves beer, and stays open late. Over the years it has added a full dinner menu, so that it has become indistinguishable from a restaurant. For more than a hundred years the Balzar has been a family business, and each of the families has managed to keep it constant without making it stale. It's a one-story, one-room spot, small by brasserie standards—with only ninety or so covers—and has a glass front that looks out onto the street; you can see with one eye people boarding the number 63 bus in the twilight, and with the other a pretty little park dedicated to Montaigne, with plane trees and pink-flowering chestnuts.

The Balzar is a democratic place. You are greeted at the door with a handshake and a quick squint of crinkled, harried warmth, by the two maîtres d'hôtel—one always in a tuxedo, the other in a suit—and are shown to your table with a few pensive words about families, children, and the weather. There's not a trace of unctuousness or forced familiarity, no appraisal of your wallet, your last review, or your weekend gross. There are long banquettes covered with dark brown leather along the walls, and a T-shaped banquette in the middle of the room. On the tables are white linen and glasses and silver. The light—from eight round globe lamps, high above—is warm and bright, gay without being harsh. The *carte* is a long printed card, with the dishes listed on the front and the wines on the back, and it never changes. There are leeks and tomato salad and herring for starters—foie gras if you're in an expansive mood—and then the same five or so *plats*: *steak au poivre*, roast chicken, grilled sole or salmon, calf's liver, *gigot* with white and green beans. The wine list is short, and usually the best thing on it is the Réserve Balzar, a pleasant red Bordeaux. The only sauces are the sauce au poivre on the steak and a béarnaise for the grilled salmon. The *pommes frites* are fine, the *crème caramel* is good, the profiteroles the best in Paris.

It is the waiters—or *serveurs*, as they're called—who give the Balzar its soul. A team of the same ten men has been in place for decades: They are courteous, warmhearted, ironic (able to warn a client off a dubious *plat* with an eyebrow), and mildly lubricious. (They have been known to evaluate, sotto voce, the size and shape of a woman's rear even as they pull out the table to make way for it.) They work hard. By tradition at the Balzar, the *plats* arrive beautifully arranged on an oval platter and then are carefully transferred by the waiter to a round plate. This doubles the work but creates an effect. Whenever I am feeling blue, I like to go to the Balzar and watch a waiter gravely transfer a *steak au poivre* and its accompaniments from an oval platter to a plate, item by item. It reaffirms my faith in the sanity of superfluous civilization.

The other famous Left Bank brasserie, the Lipp, is known as a canteen for the men of power in the Fifth Republic, but when Lionel Jospin, the virtuous Socialist who is trying to transform French politics, was running for president three years ago, he made an event of being photographed, for *Paris Match*, having dinner at the Balzar. Everyone got the point.

On a Sunday night in April, Martha and I, with Luke, were sitting at a table in the back, just finishing one in a long line of good dinners and were once again refining our long-term plan to be buried at the Balzar—or, more precisely, to have the urns containing our ashes placed on the dessert counter just above the mille-feuilles and the lemon tart, and on either side of the flowers. The plaques, we decided, should read "A Faithful Client" or, better, should repeat the words of those inscriptions you see all over Paris: "Here, fallen for France . . ."

Just then Jean-Claude, the maître d' in the tuxedo, came over to our table. His gravelly *sud-ouest* voice was pitched low, and to my amazement, his eyes were glistening. "I'd like to introduce you to someone who'll be working with us," he said graciously, and he summoned a melancholy-faced, lantern-jawed man, buttoned up in a good suit, whom I had idly noticed standing by the door earlier in the evening. "This is M. Delouche," he said. I shook hands with M. Delouche and raised my eyebrows at Jean-Claude.

"The Balzar has been sold," he said. "M. Delouche is here representing the new management." He walked away quickly, and M. Delouche followed.

I grabbed our waiter as he came by the table. "The restaurant has been sold?" I said. "To whom was it sold?"

"To the Flo Group," he answered, in a strangled voice.

The Flo Group! I felt as I imagined I would feel if I had been stabbed: first surprise, then nothing, then pain. The Flo Group is the creation of an Alsatian waiter turned restaurant tycoon named Jean-Paul Bucher, and in Paris it is often referred to as the *rouleau compresseur Flo,* the Flo steamroller. It is for many people the symbol of the forces of restaurant consolidation, globalization, standardization, and even Disneyfication; Flo runs five restaurants at Disneyland Paris. Over the past thirty years Bucher has bought up some of the oldest and most famous brasseries and bistros in Paris, while also running a chain of lesser Flos, a catering business, and a chain of cheap restaurants called Hippopotamus. Some of the Flo Group restaurants—Julien, Le Boeuf sur le Toit—are actually pretty good. But even the good places have a processed, overwrought quality, and the food at one is pretty much like the food at the others. They lack all the things that the Balzar possesses so effortlessly: distinctiveness, eccentricity, and a sense of continuity.

A few moments later one of the waiters, whom I had known for a long time, and whom I'll call Thierry, came up to me and suggested, under his breath, that we meet for coffee the next day. When we met, Thierry told me the history of the Balzar, seen from below. He was in mufti, wearing jeans and a jean jacket, a standard uniform for off-duty waiters, like blue windbreakers on off-duty New York cops. The Balzar had never been a perfectly happy place, he maintained, and the *syndicat,* the union, had suffered a good deal even under the old owners. Nonetheless the *garçons* loved the work, because they liked the clients and the clients liked them. (I noticed that he referred to the waiters by the usually forbidden, old-fashioned word *garçons,* or boys, and that he also referred to their métier as *restauration,* or restaurant work. The two words together gave their profession blue-collar integrity.) He outlined their fears. The Flo people, he said, might close the Balzar "for restoration" and disperse the waiters to other Flo restaurants, all over Paris, never to be reassembled. "They express a savoir-faire that dates from 1968," he said. "Ours dates from 1894." It was said that the Flo people had arranged to have American tour groups brought to the Balzar; it was also said that they were standardizing the kitchen produce, bringing it in line with the rest of the Flo Group. More immediately, the *garçons* were appalled because the new man, M. Delouche, had been put "on the service," drawing his salary from their tips—the

15 percent service charge that is added to all French restaurant bills. (Thierry explained to me that the service charge was real and sacrosanct; before Flo took over, one of the *garçons* collected it at the end of every evening and put it in a drawer, to which each of them had a key. Now they have to wait five weeks for the same money.) It also turned out that the suit-tuxedo distinction among the greeters was a deeply significant code: A maître d' in a suit was aligned with the owner, one in a tuxedo with the staff.

Within a week or so a group of Balzar regulars, mostly editors and publishers and professors—the Balzar is around the corner from the Sorbonne—arranged to meet at the apartment of one of the staunchest clients, on the quai Anatole-France, to think about what we could do. It was a beautiful day, but ominous reports were coming in from all sides. Someone had had a doubtful sole; someone else had noticed that *oeufs crevettes,* hard-boiled eggs with shrimp, had been sneaked onto the menu. (No, no, someone else said, reassuringly, the *oeufs crevettes* were there twenty years ago; it was really a restoration.) More seriously, it was said that the waiters were being forced to rush checks to the table. It is a Balzar tradition that you can nurse even a cup of coffee and a plate of cold cuts for as long as you like. Now, it was said, after seventy minutes the waiters were forced to put the check on the table. This was—well, there was no other word for it—so American. You see this in California, someone said; he had eaten once in Santa Monica, and the young woman slapped the bill on the table after an hour and a half. (I could only imagine the waitress, on her way to her tai chi or acting class, dying on the vine while a couple of Frenchmen sat polishing off a bottle and solving the world's problems.) More horror stories were told; a keen-eyed regular claimed to have spotted a Flo Group camion parked outside the Balzar at six o'clock one morning, bringing in Flo produce.

It was obvious that something had to be done, but what? One person suggested a boycott; another person a sit-in; someone else a campaign of letter writing. We had a left, a right, and a center even before we had a party. Finally a leader emerged, a handsome, round-faced young publisher named Lorenzo Valentin. He had an excellent plan: Why not invite all the regulars we could find to reserve tables on the same night, occupy the restaurant, make a scene, and demand that Bucher meet with us? Fine, someone else said, but added that if we did it, we had to be sure not to leave the waiters, on whose behalf we were acting, "in an ambiguous position." If we sat in, occupied the restaurant, and didn't order anything, they would be the ones to suffer. Therefore we also had to order and eat dinner. Good, one woman said, but we had to be sure to hold on to the tables for the entire evening. "Eat, but eat slowly" would be our motto. Why not order foie gras on toast, she suggested; that could be spread very slowly. She mimed just how to do it, like a veteran of many a foie gras slow-down on the barricades. We all watched her studiously.

During the next two weeks, as I helped organize the occupation, I felt exhilarated, though I recognized in my exhilaration a certain hypocrisy. Like every American in France, I had spent a fair amount of time being exasperated by the French because of their inability to accept change, their refusal to accept the inevitable logic of the market, and their tendency to blame Americans for everything. As I raged against the changes at the Balzar, I began to hear people repeating to me the same tiresome and sensible logic that I had been preaching so long myself: that nothing stays the same; change must be welcomed; one must choose to live in the world as it is or live in a museum whose walls increasingly recede inward. . . . It was all true, and when it came to the Balzar, I didn't care. I would like to say that the difference was that my concern was now attached to particular people—to Thierry and Jean-Claude and the rest. But that would be giving myself too much credit for disinterestedness. The difference was not that it was happening to the Balzar. The difference was that it was happening to me. I was being asked to give up the continuity of a thousand small associations and pleasures—the night we went after we signed the lease, the night we went, still jet-lagged, after a summer away—and I didn't see why I should.

"Can't repeat the past?" says Gatsby. "Why of course you can!" And every American schoolchild is taught that in this belief lies Gatsby's tragedy. But why should the thought be so absurd? Can't repeat the past? We do it every day. We build a life, or try to, of pleasures and duties that will become routine, so that every day will be the same day, or nearly so, "the day of our life," Randall Jarrell called it. There seemed to me nothing stranger about my wanting to eat forever at an unchanged Balzar than about my wanting to stay married to the same wife or be father of the same kid. ("M. Bucher has now bought your family, and will be adding a new child to the staff on the same terms. Change is good. Here, try Ralphie for a while. He comes from the centralized nursery and only speaks German, but you'll soon find that . . .") On the day of my life, I eat dinner at the Balzar—the Balzar as it is and was, and not some improved, Flo Group version. I realize that one of the tricks of capitalism is to lure you into a misleadingly unreciprocated love with a cash register, but what impressed me about my friends in the Balzar war was that they weren't prepared to treat their attachment to the Balzar as somehow less real than the cash register's attachment to it.

June 25 was picked as the day for our occupation of the Balzar. We carefully arranged to stagger our phone calls to reserve tables for that Thursday night, to avoid tipping our hand. When my turn came, I was so nervous that I had to dial twice, and then, in a high-pitched quaver, I reserved my table. (*"Oui, madame,"* said an obviously bemused maître d'.) On the night I arrived with a couple of friends. The tables filled up with regulars, gaily overacting the part of ordinary diners: Oh, how *sympa,* you're here too, we said to each other, exchanging meaty, significant winks. We ordered apéritifs and made nervous conversation. Finally, at nine o'clock, the last regular sat down, and, with two taps on a glass, Lorenzo Valentin rose. The revolution was under way.

"We are here tonight," he said, "to demonstrate our sympathy with the waiters, clients, and tradition of the Balzar." Valentin stepped away from his table and addressed Bucher's man, M. Delouche, directly. Delouche clasped his hands behind his back and thrust out his chin, both obsequious and defiant. When I saw him like that, bearing the brunt of a sudden wave of disapproval—and, surely, thinking, I'm the working stiff here, these people are rich *gauchistes*, easy for them—I have to admit that a small whitecap of sympathy for him rose in my mind.

"This is not a personal assault on anyone," Lorenzo declared. "We have gathered here tonight as, shall we say, an opportunity to discuss the issue at the heart of our concerns about the recent purchase of the Balzar by the Flo Group. Our question is: Is this merely a place to eat or is it something more, and if it is something more, what is it? Our organization, Les Amis du Balzar, is here to safeguard the quality and, what's more, to defend the spirit and the staff of a place that we believe offers a respite from time itself." This was grandly said, and he got a big hand.

M. Delouche attempted to defend his position, but his voice was mostly inaudible. All you could make out was "logic," "safeguard," "continuity."

"But what about the staff?" Lorenzo demanded. "What of their continuity?"

"*Les serveurs! Les serveurs!*" The cry went up from around the room as we pounded the tables and hit cutlery against glasses. The waiters, their eyes fixed studiously on the floor or on the tables, continued to serve.

"Why can't this place be different from other places bought by Flo?" another protester said, rising to his feet. "We all know what Flo does. How many people here are former clients of La Coupole?"

"*Anciens! Anciens!*" we chanted in unison, pounding the tables some more, meaning that we used to go to La Coupole and didn't anymore.

We were building up to an impressive pitch of indignation,

but at that point the waiters began to serve the dinners that we had ordered while we were waiting to begin our protest, and this weakened the revolutionary spirit a little. There was, I sensed, a flaw in our strategy: If you take over a restaurant as an act of protest and then order dinner at the restaurant, what you have actually done is gone to the restaurant and had dinner, since a restaurant is, by definition, always occupied, by its diners. Having come to say that you just won't take it anymore, you have to add sheepishly that you *will* take it, *au point* and with béarnaise sauce. It was as if at the Boston Tea Party the patriots had boarded the ship, bought up all the boxes of tea, and then brewed them.

Nonetheless we carried on. We loudly criticized the fish; we angrily demanded a meeting with Bucher; we rose and offered memories of the Balzar, and vowed that we would fight for the Balzar yet to be.

We were hoping for a little *médiatisation,* and we got it. Pieces about the protest appeared in the magazine *Marianne* and in *Le Figaro*. Then, unfortunately, Jean-Pierre Quélin, the food critic of *Le Monde,* who is a kind of Jonathan Yardley of French restaurant writing, weighed in, announcing that the food at the Balzar had always been terrible—but that he had eaten there since the Flo Group took over, and now it was even worse, so to hell with everybody. Lorenzo thought that this might actually be a useful article for our cause: By defining the Balzar radical fringe, Quélin was allowing us to occupy the rational center.

To the surprise of my American self, Bucher sent back word that he would be delighted to meet with our association, to have breakfast with what amounted to our Directorate at the Balzar itself. At nine on a Saturday morning we assembled at the Café Sorbon, across the street and then trooped over to meet the enemy. Bucher turned out to be a simple round Alsatian, wearing an open shirt, and he spoke with the guttural accent of Alsace. We all shook hands—he had a couple of his PR people sitting behind him at a second table—and then Lorenzo Valentin, with quiet dignity, began his speech.

"We are here," he said, "as representatives of our association, to argue that your regime is not compatible with the spirit of the Balzar. This is not meant to be offensive to you—"

"Not at all," Bucher said politely.

"But without denying your right of property, we claim for ourselves a kind of right of usage." And from that premise Valentin carefully outlined our thesis that what mattered was the esprit of the Balzar and that the esprit of the Flo Group was, on the evidence, not compatible with that esprit we were defending. We asked him to keep the Balzar an autonomous brasserie, outside the Flo Group proper, and to make no changes in the staff, in the decor, or in the spirit of the place. After stating these demands, Lorenzo looked at him squarely.

I don't think any of us were prepared for what happened next. Bucher looked us over, up and down the table. "No problem," he said, a friendly, gap-toothed smile creasing his face. "No problem. Tell me, my friends, why would I want to change something that is working so well right now, something that works so effectively? I bought the Balzar because it's the crown jewel of Parisian brasseries. I bought the Balzar because I love it. What motive would I have to want it to be different? I'm here because if I weren't, McDonald's would be—and that would be too bad. I sincerely think that we are defending the same thing."

Our committee exchanged glances. Lorenzo pressed his point. "It's not just the cuisine," he said. "It's something more. A certain relaxation, the feeling of time suspended, the spirit of a place. You see, five hundred and fifty people have already joined Les Amis du Balzar."

Bucher nodded emphatically. "I know. You are to be congratulated," he said. "What an accomplishment!" After some more conversation about the cooking—he had brought out the *chef de cuisine*, who was understandably upset about the piece in *Le*

Monde—he said, "I am sixty years old. I give you a guarantee that I will keep the Balzar as it is. This wasn't a good buy for me. My accountants advised against it. My analysts advised against it. My heart and my soul told me to do it, and they're with you. A restaurant this small—it makes no sense for my chain. A hundred covers. It makes no sense for me except as the jewel in the crown of my Parisian brasseries, whose quality and values I'm going to defend."

We mumbled something and, after more handshaking, withdrew to the sidewalk. We had not anticipated the strategic advantage to Bucher of total, enthusiastic assent. We wanted to save the *steak au poivre* on the oval plate and the waiter serving it, but you couldn't argue with the man when he pointed to the steak, the plate, and the waiter and said nothing's changed. (Thierry, when he heard of our breakfast with Bucher, said, "It is the old technique of the kings of France: Treat your worst enemy like your best friend.")

I did not doubt that Bucher was being perfectly sincere, as far as it went, and that in his case as-far-as-it-went went as far it could. The Balzar would stay the same until it changed. The waiters seem encouraged by our actions. When I go to the Balzar now, Thierry, bringing a coupe champagne, slips by and, under his breath, makes a toast: "À *la santé de l'association*—to the health of the association!" We repeat the toast, under our breaths. It is like being in the resistance. (But when M. Delouche comes over, we shake his hand too. Perhaps that is also like being in the resistance.)

Les Amis du Balzar has sent an eloquent new letter to Bucher, written by Lorenzo Valentin, and describing the *objet de nos préoccupations*: that no dish will come from a centralized kitchen and that there will be real autonomy for the staff, and real autonomy in the management. My Parisian self is prepared to defend the Balzar to the end, whatever it takes. My American self suspects that the Balzar will stay the same, and then it will change, and that we will love it as long as we can.

Alice
in Paris

Not long ago, in the brown dawn light of the western Paris suburbs, three Americans could be seen taking a mildly illicit walk through the Rungis wholesale food market. The three Americans—the California chef Alice Waters, the vegetable scholar Antoine Jacobsohn, and I—all had something on their minds, and all were in a heightened emotional state that had its origins in something more than the very early hour and the very chilly weather.

Alice Waters was in a heightened emotional state because, as many of her friends believe, she is always in a heightened emotional state, particularly when she is in the presence of fresh produce. Alice, who was wearing a wool cloche, is a small, intense, pale, pretty, fiftyish woman, with a quiet, satisfied smile and a shining, virtuous light in her eye, the kind of American woman who a century ago would have been storming through saloons with a hatchet and is now steaming fresh green beans, but with similar motives. Her vision is rooted in the romantic Berkeley politics that she practiced before starting her restaurant, Chez Panisse, with a ten-thousand-dollar loan twenty-seven years ago. She believes in concentric circles of social responsibility, with the reformed carrot in the backyard garden insensibly improving the family around the dinner table, the reformed family around the dinner table insensibly improving the small neighborhood merchants they shop with, the reformed neighborhood merchants improving their city, and so right on, ever upward and outward, but with the reformed carrot always there, the unmoved (though crisply cooked) mover in the center.

Earlier this year Alice was invited to open a restaurant at the Louvre, by Mme. Hélène David-Weill, the *très grande dame* who is the director of the Musée des Arts Décoratifs there. An enthusiastic article in the *Times* gave the impression that this was a fait accompli, or nearly so. In fact in September it still existed essentially only as an enthusiasm in the eye of Alice Waters, Mme. David-Weill, and Richard Overstreet, an American painter who lives in Berkeley and Paris and has been the go-between since the beginning. (Francis Ford Coppola was the first person to suggest Alice to Mme. David-Weill.) Alice had come to Paris to move the project along, and Richard had brought her together with Antoine as a possible "principal forager," on the lines of a principal dancer, for it. Rungis was the setting for their long-awaited meeting.

Antoine Jacobsohn was in a heightened emotional state because he is in a heightened emotional state whenever he visits the Rungis market. Twenty-nine years ago Rungis replaced the great Les Halles complex, which had dominated central Paris from the fifteenth century until after the Second World War and which Zola called, in a novel he devoted to it, "The Belly of Paris." For Antoine, Les Halles was not just the belly of Paris but its heart, and for him the replacement of Les Halles by Rungis is the primordial sin of modern France—the destruction of Penn Station, Ebbets Field, and B. Altman's combined.

"When the market moved out of Les Halles," Antoine was saying, as he led our little party—it was illicit because, strictly speaking, you need a permit to shop at Rungis—"it effectively changed the relationship between pleasure and play and work in all of Paris. For centuries, because the market was at once a center for restaurants and for ordinary people, a whole culture grew up around it. Shopping and eating, the restaurant and the market, the stroller and the shopper, the artisan and the bourgeois— all were kept in an organic arrangement. And because many of the goods couldn't be kept overnight, it meant that what was left at the end of every day was given to the poor. But for trivial reasons—traffic and hygiene—they made the decision to move the market to Rungis, and left a hole in the heart of Paris. There was no place allotted here for the small artisan, for the small grower, or for the organic market."

He shook his head in disbelief. Antoine was raised in North Plainfield, New Jersey, by a French mother; he has a research fellowship at the Museum of Vegetable Culture, in the Paris suburb of La Courneuve, a degree in agricultural sciences from Cornell, and a perfect, crisp, contrary French mind trapped in an American body and voice box. Antoine has been known to give his friends an idealized poster of the twenty-four cultivated radishes—some lost, some extant—of the Île-de-France, and he has written beautifully, not to say longingly, of the lost monstrous spinach of Viroflay and the flat onions of Vertus.

We had been joined by Sally Clarke, of Clarke's restaurant, in London, who is one of Alice's many spiritual godchildren. The two chefs seemed torn between delight and surprise—delight in the freshness and green beauty of the vegetables, surprise at the lack of variety.

"I'm going to show you the space left for the local growers," Antoine went on. We walked through the aisles of the vast, chilly airplane hangars of vegetables: bins of *girolles,* crates of shiny eggplants. It all looked wonderful but remarkably standardized, explaining the standardization of what the average Paris green-grocer sells.

"Imagine," Antoine said. "So many radishes gone; the artichokes of Paris, almost gone; the turnips of Vaugirard, gone. There's a variety of beans that one reads about all the time in nineteenth-century texts. But gone! We've kept some seedlings of the plants in the museum, and they could be revived."

"We'll plant them in the Tuileries," Alice said softly, but with determination. One of her dreams for the restaurant is to raise a vegetable garden right outside the door.

Antoine walked along, greeting old friends and growers. "This man has excellent tomatoes," he now whispered to Alice.

"Does he grow organically?" she asked urgently. In recent years Alice has become a fanatic of organic growing.

Antoine, who had been telling Alice how the French sense of *terroir*—of the taste and traditions of a local region—was more important to authentic produce in France than the precise rules of organic growing, asked the grower. The man shrugged and then explained his situation. "He says he's giving up the business, in any case, as it happens, since it's becoming hopeless," Antoine said to Alice. (He failed to add that every French merchant, in every field, will always tell you that it's hopeless, he's going to give up the business; when French weapons salesmen go to China to sell missiles, they probably shrug when the Chinese start to bargain and say, Well, it doesn't matter, we're giving up the business anyway, it's a hopeless métier.)

Alice gave the grower a steady, encouraging look. "We just have to get the suppliers to adapt," she said. "That's what we did at Chez Panisse. You have to let them know there's the demand. You have to bring them along with you." In the early-morning light you could sense Alice Waters's eyes radiating the spiritual intensity that for so long has startled and impressed her friends and admirers and has set her apart from other chefs, making her a kind of materfamilias to a generation of chefs ranging from Sally Clarke to Michel Courtalhac, in Paris. (He keeps a photograph of

Alice in the window of his restaurant.) Aubert de Villaine, who is the codirector of the Domaine de la Romanée-Conti, the greatest wine estate in France, speaks of her in hushed tones, less as a superior hashslinger than as a kind of cross between Emily Dickinson and La Pucelle. "There's something crystalline about her, an extraordinary purity of spirit," he said not long ago. "She's one of *les vigiles en haut,* the watchman in the crow's nest, seeing far ahead. The thing I most admire about Alice is the sense that the sensual is not really sensual if it is not, *au fond,* spiritual."

Antoine nodded at another merchant across the way. "Now, this man grows excellent asparagus," he whispered. "It's interesting. Two hundred, a hundred and fifty years ago it was always green asparagus; now the demand is for white asparagus."

He went up to the grower and said, in French, "Why is it that no one any longer grows green asparagus? When was it that people went over to white asparagus?" The man gave him an incredulous look and then said, in the beautiful clear French of the Île-de-France, "You know, I would say that what you've just stated is the exact contrary of the truth." It was a perfect Parisian tone of voice—not disputatious, just suggesting a love of the shared pursuit of the truth, which, unfortunately, happens not to be in your possession right now.

Antoine made the right response. He raised his eyebrows in polite wonder while smiling only on the left side of his face, an expression that means, How greatly I respect the vigor of your opinions, however much they may call to mind the ravings of a lunatic. "What do you mean?" he demanded.

"Well, it is my experience that everyone grows green asparagus now. It's all you see for decorative *plats,* that touch of green. In the magazines, for instance, among the fashionable chefs, it's all you see, green asparagus. It has a much greater decorative effect. It's obvious."

"Ah, yes, for decorative effect," Antoine agreed calmly. Everybody won.

As they were speaking, I was poking a pile of *girolles* nearby, and wondering if I had made a mistake in not planning to serve some kind of autumnal mushroom plate for dinner the next night. I was in a heightened emotional state because I had offered to cook dinner for Alice Waters, and I had spent most of the summer worrying about what I would cook and how it would taste. I had decided to try and sneak in a little serious shopping while I was observing Alice and Antoine. I had also decided to go out later that day and buy a new set of dinner plates. I had come to both of these decisions more or less in the spirit of a man who, having in an insane moment invited Michael Jordan over to play a little one-on-one, decides that he might as well use the occasion to put down a new coat of asphalt on the driveway.

I had made up my mind to do a lamb braised for seven hours—a *gigot de sept heures*, as it's known—which would be cooked in the Provençal style, with eggplant and tomatoes. But to be in Rungis at dawn with two such devoted *terroiristes* as Alice and Antoine, for whom cooking is meaningful only if it is an expression of the place where the things are being cooked, made me feel a little guilty. I was going to have to get the tomatoes out of a can, and though the canned tomato is absolutely typical of my own *terroir,* I somehow felt that they would disapprove.

Nearby Alice had found *frisée* and watercress and was looking at them raptly—not with the greed of a hungry man seeing dinner but with the admiration of William Bennett looking at a long marriage. "There's nothing so beautiful as French watercress," she said. "I can recall walking down the rue Mouffetard in 1965, my first year in Paris. I was a girl from New Jersey who'd grown up on frozen food, and to see the baskets and baskets of greens, so many shades of green and red!

"I walked up and down the street, my eyes unbelieving," she went on. "I had never tasted an oyster. I went through Normandy, eating eighteen at a time, and drinking apple cider, and it was so wonderful that I was just carried away, and I would fall asleep by the roadside. When I got back to Berkeley, I thought of opening a creperie, and I tried to import some of the cider and found out that there was alcohol in it. That was why I kept passing out! I thought it was just the oysters and the apple juice and France." She was lost for a moment.

"You know," Antoine said, coming over, "there used to be asparagus grown in Argenteuil, just down the river from Paris—great asparagus. And they used to have figs in Argenteuil too. The white figs of Argenteuil, they were called in the nineteenth century. The trees were bent over with weights, so that the branches could be buried in the ground, to protect them all through the winter. Yet we think of figs as a southern fruit."

"Oh, we have to have them," Alice said, her eyes moist with emotion. "The white figs of Argenteuil! We'll grow them again. It can be done, you know." We had been wandering through the airplane hangars and were standing among towers of carrots and leeks, mountains of *haricots verts*. She looked upward and, Pucelle-like, seemed to be seeing before her—in a vision, as though they were already tangible, edible—the white figs of Argenteuil: an improbable Berkeley Joan, imagining her France restored to glory.

I had been thinking about various menus ever since I'd had the idea of cooking dinner for Alice, and for a while I'd thought I might do a four-hour braised leg of lamb that I had found the recipe for in the Sunday magazine of the *London Independent*. Unfortunately I had lost the issue of the magazine. I had the phone number of the editor, but I thought that it was unprofessional journalistic practice, in this day and age, to call up a fellow scandalmongering cynic and ask him if he would mind thumbing through his back issues for a recipe.

Then, this summer, I came upon a copy of a twenty-five-year-old recipe book written by the wonderful (and blind) food writer Roy Andries de Groot. The book was called *The Auberge of the Flowering Hearth*. Half cookbook, half *Lost Horizon* remake, it

tells about a little inn—the Auberge of the Flowering Hearth—
that the author discovered in the French Alps, while he was on
an assignment to write something on how the monks down there
make Chartreuse. The menu called for mussel soup, poached
pears, and a *gigot de mouton de sept heures*—the same slow-
cooked lamb that I had lost the recipe for but, in this case, given
the whole, classic nine yards, or seven hours. Sounded great and
was in the right spirit for the occasion, part of the history of the
American love of French cooking.

Then I had another inspiration. As Alice Waters would have
wanted, my childhood had been a series of intense family dinners, evening after evening, with their own set of "social protocols," and one of the most cherished of these family dinnertime
protocols was known as Getting Someone Else to Do the Work.
I decided to call Susan Herrmann Loomis, who lives in Normandy, and ask her to come to Paris to help me cook. Susan is
the author of books on French and American country cooking
and has a CIA-worthy gift for going into deep cover in a strange
region and coming out with all its secrets. She cheerfully agreed
to help, and after much discussion—she felt that the mussels
would be too similar in color to the *gigot*, a feat of previsualiza-
tion that increased my respect for the things a professional cook
knows that an amateur doesn't—we decided that we would cook
together. We scoured markets and arrived at a menu: steamed
autumn vegetables with *aioli*, or garlic mayonnaise; the seven-
hour lamb with eggplant and tomatoes; and an apple tart with
rosemary. I went out and got the best bottle of Chartreuse I
could find, to keep it honest to de Groot's memory.

While we prepared, Alice continued her tour of Paris. The
idea of a restaurant turned out to have been something of an af-
terthought at the Musée des Arts Décoratifs, which is an annex
of the Louvre, out on the rue de Rivoli. For many years, it had
been a sleepy, unattended institution, filled with old clocks and
settees. Mme. David-Weill's reign devoted a recent exhibition to

the Tati stores, a kind of French Woolworth's, and has promised in general to be much more swinging. Still, the space that had been put aside for eating, though it looked out from the back of the museum onto the Tuileries gardens, lacked some of the amenities of modern restaurants. "It's all those kinds of basic things," Alice explained after she had seen it. "Where do the employees wash their hands? Where are the umbrellas for the rainy days? It's only ninety covers, which is even fewer than Chez Panisse." She went on, diplomatically, "It's really more of a tea-room size than anything else. I worry that the space is too small to express what we'd like to express."

In a kind of mission statement, she has described the restaurant as she imagines it: "A platform, an exhibit, a classroom, a conservatory, a laboratory, and a garden. It must be, in a phrase, an art installation in the form of a restaurant, expressing the sensuousness of food and putting people in touch with the pleasures of eating and with the connection between those pleasures and sustainable agriculture. . . . All the elements of the collaboration, from the menu to the decor, will clearly demonstrate where the food comes from and how it was grown. The emphasis is going to be on the food, the kind that makes eating a soul-nourishing experience. Amid the grandeur of the Louvre, the restaurant must feel human, reflecting the spirit of the farm, the *terroir*, and the market, and it must express the humanity of the artisans, cooks, and servers who work there."

Yet Alice seemed unperturbed by the difficulties; she has the sublime California confidence that all physical problems are susceptible to a little intense spiritual pressure. "I'm not worried," she said. "If we can solve the space problem, everything else will fall into place. I don't really want it to be an extension of Chez Panisse in Paris. There will be a vegetable garden, but more important will be establishing a relation to a whole network of suppliers. I'm going to work with Eiko Ishioka, the great Japanese designer, who will do an inspired job. And now I've found my forager, in Antoine. This restaurant could be the next step. It could be a statement about diversity on so many levels. It could be the next part of an effort to keep people from perceiving life in the unified way that the mass culture demands." (When she's asked if her daughter, Fanny, has ever gone to a McDonald's, she answers, carefully, "She may have. During a soccer match or something. But I've told her that while she's free to do it if she wants to, I would rather not get involved in that kind of activity.")

Alice is acutely aware that there are people who see something hypocritical or unreal about a woman who presides over an expensive restaurant preaching against commercial culture. This is silly, of course—if there's going to be a faith, somebody's got to live in the Vatican—but it is also false on its own terms. She has scrupulously kept Chez Panisse out of mass merchandising of any kind. There are no Chez Panisse frozen foods, no Chez Panisse canned sauces, no Chez Panisse pasta. There are only cookbooks and a line of granola. Alice Waters is in every way the anti–Wolfgang Puck. (People who know insist that the restaurant still makes remarkably little money for such a famous place.) In a speech she made recently to teachers involved with the "garden in every school" project, in California, she pointed out that "all too many kids—both rich and poor—are disconnected from civilized and humane ways of living their lives," and then added the Berkeley Basic Truth: "The sensual pleasure of eating beautiful food from the garden brings with it the moral satisfaction of doing the right thing for the planet and for yourself."

Most people feel that Alice is the figure par excellence of the great Berkeley Transformation, in which the wise children ate the revolution before it had a chance to eat them. Kermit Lynch, the wine importer, who has done more than anyone else to bring the organic revolution to French winemaking (and has been called a "hopeless romantic" for his efforts), is a product of the same history. "Alice and I both started our businesses around the same time," he recollected recently. "She started cooking for an underground newspaper in San Francisco, and I was working for the *Berkeley Barb*—and there we were. Who could have imagined that we'd end up this way? It was very political what she was doing then, and it still is." Alice herself traces the crucial moment for the creation of Chez Panisse to the defeat of Robert Scheer, now a well-known journalist in Los Angeles, whose congressional campaign she had worked for in 1966. "I was so crushed, and I thought, I'm just going to start my own world," she says.

It may be this reconciliation of utopian politics and aristo-cratic cooking, more than anything else, that has divided the cooking cultures of France and America. The *soixante-huitards* were as disappointed in France as they were in America, but they drove their political disappointment into more political disap-pointment. The culture that the French radicals were counter-ing, after all, was already epicurean; there was no cultural space to be found in expanding it. The counterculture in America had just the opposite situation—it was Nixon who ate cottage cheese with ketchup—and anyway, the counterculture in America liked pleasure; its anthem was "Feed Your Head," not "Clear Your Head."

Over time, an obsession with sex and drugs slid imperceptibly into an obsession with children and food. This obsessiveness is what separates Alice Waters from all the other "Anglo-Saxon" restaurateurs who have arrived in Paris recently to open restau-rants. (Sir Terence Conran, the London food lord, has just re-made an old cabaret on the rue Mazarine, for instance, bringing the new English style to Paris.) For Alice, the idea of making the millennial restaurant in France is a way of closing a romantic cir-cle. Like de Groot, she sees France as the cradle of organic cul-ture in every sense: "The restaurant I imagine is a way of repaying that debt to France, of Americans taking the best of ourselves, instead of the worst of ourselves, to help recall the

French to their own best traditions, a way that my generation can repay the debt we owe to France."

|||

On the day of our dinner Kenneth Starr's report had just appeared, and all afternoon friends from New York were calling me about it. Susan Loomis and I ran back and forth from the study to the kitchen, doing a lot of "Can you believe what he's saying?" (and also a fair amount of "Can you believe what they were doing?"). I was trying to adjust the heat on the lamb when the phone rang, from Luke's school. Once again, as he often had since the term began, he had refused to take a nap, and the school wanted me to bring him home. I sighed, forgot about the report, checked the lamb, left Susan in the kitchen, and raced off to pick him up. (I thought ruefully that you could bet a million dollars that if he were in a school in New York, there would be a Nap-Averse Support Group, a special room for the dormitively challenged, and a precedent-setting lawsuit launched by the attorney father of an earlier child, guaranteeing the right of every child to refuse a nap. But this was Paris: strictly no nap, no school.) I hesitated about leaving the lamb in the oven untended, but then decided, well, seven hours. . . . Throughout the afternoon, instead of feeling, as I had hoped, like Roy de Groot luxuriating in the Alps, I felt a lot like Ray Liotta spinning in the last reel of *Goodfellas*, when he's cooking veal for his crippled brother, and the police helicopter is circling overhead, and he and the mule who's carrying the cocaine have to go and get her lucky hat.

How was the lamb? The evening went well, though all through dinner the Starr report was being faxed to us by a friend; pages—four hundred of them—kept churning out of the machine, just a room away. You couldn't help hearing them as they arrived, and every now and then I would go in and peek at the latest revelation. There was an odd symmetry: on the one hand, at our dinner table the high priestess of the American generation that has come to believe that only through refined sensual pleasure can you re-create an ideal America; on the other, page after page of legal detail documenting the existence of those who believe that talking about ideals while pursuing sensations is just what makes this generation such a bunch of louses. It was a kind of two-course meal of radical hedonism and extreme puritanism, both as American as, well, apple pie.

But how was the lamb? Alice spoke freely about the problems that the space at the Louvre represented. Listening between the sentences, you could deduce that if she had not lost heart, she had, at least, a larger sense of how vast and difficult a project it promised to be. Susan Loomis's *aioli* was fabulous. People talked, as they do everywhere, about Clinton and Monica.

But *How was the lamb?* The wine was excellent. The *tarte aux pommes* was fine.

And the lamb? Well. The lamb had a strong resemblance to a third baseman's mitt—if I had Antoine Jacobsohn's gift for precision, I would compare it to Buddy Bell's glove, circa 1978—with interesting hints of Naugahyde, kapok, and old suede bomber jacket. There were plenty of white beans, though, and some sauce, so everyone pushed it around politely on the plate. I think I know now what went wrong: after three years of a French oven, I realized that it was easy to forget that American cookbooks were still written, so to speak, in Fahrenheit. De Groot's two hundred degrees were almost half as hot as the two hundred degrees of my Celsius oven.

I also saw that Alice Waters didn't notice. If you are playing tennis with Martina Hingis, she does not notice when your backhand is off, because she does not notice when your backhand is on. What you have is not what she would call a backhand. At least I was able to explain to the company that the lamb came from Roy de Groot's book, and I talked about what a haunting image it gave of a now-vanished French cooking culture: the iron pots on the hearth, the shy Provençale lady in the kitchen, the daily bounty from the farms and the hunters. Alice got that look in her eye. "I love that book," she said. "And I went on an expedition to the Alps just to find the auberge."

Did that perfect auberge really exist? I asked.

"Well, no, not really. Not exactly," she said, in a tone that sounded like "not at all." "I mean, yes, it didn't, not like that." She thought for a moment. "Of course, it existed for him. It still exists for us, in the minds of the people around this table. Maybe that's where the ideal restaurant always will be."

|||

Postscript: After Alice Waters left Paris, *Le Figaro* published an interview with her in which she gently reviewed her concerns about the Rungis market. THE MARKETS IN PARIS ARE SHOCKING! was the headline on the piece, whose effect, from a PR point of view, was like that of a Japanese baseball manager who, after a trip to Yankee Stadium, is quoted in a headline saying, "You call that a ballpark?" Alice Waters is learning that the real France is an inscrutable, hypersensitive place.

I have come to suspect that what is called a seven-hour lamb was really meant to be seven-hour mutton. I am aware of course that there may be other, better recipes for this dish and other, more careful cooks who have prepared it. (The four-hour lamb was great.) But it is also my suspicion that like so many vanishing things in French cooking, the seven-hour recipe was actually made for harder sheep in tougher times. In the late-modern world, where we get all the pleasure we can as soon as we can get it and on any terms we can, and none of us wants to take a nap, for fear of missing some pleasure we might otherwise have had— in a world like that, as I say, there may just be no place left for the seven-hour *gigot*.

A Machine to Draw
the World,

CHRISTMAS JOURNAL 4

In April the knock we had been fearing came on the door. The owners of our apartment were coming back from Tokyo. The Asian banking crisis had sent them back to Paris a year early, History leaping its track to knock Experience cold. It came as a shock. Three months and we would have to leave, be gone from 16 rue du Pré-aux-Clercs.

The phone call came, exasperatingly, in the French manner, the way the apartment had come: your whole life thrown upside down in an aside. "Oh, the owners are coming home and will need the apartment in July," the real estate woman said; no apology or even a "sorry for the inconvenience." We stayed up all night debating, in the way you do with big news: avoiding, digressing, suddenly feeling sick in the pit of the stomach at the thought of leaving. When we lost the apartment, we thought of going home early, and so we asked ourselves what were the things we loved in Paris, really loved, not just officially appreciated or chose to be amused at? Well, the places our child went. The Luxembourg Gardens at three in the afternoon. The Guignols, and Luke saying, "I'm so excited" before the curtain went up.

The curious thing was that with the loss of Paris threatening, we became more Parisian. The same thing, I had noted, had happened in our last few months in New York. The city, which had become increasingly difficult, suddenly seemed like a playground—people eating outside, in T-shirts and shorts and sneakers in the Italian restaurants in SoHo; the open-all-nightness of New York; the sweet funkiness—registered as it hadn't in years. When we left the loft for the last time, without trouble, with tears, the music box on Luke Auden's stroller played "Manhattan."

Now after the knock on the door, it happened to Paris. I began to cook Parisianly. I bought the chef's cookbook from Le Grand Véfour and began to make the buttery, three- and four-part dishes that I had been exasperated by before: *suprêmes de volaille,* with mint, that sort of thing. I even made soufflés again. We put Trenet back on the CD player; strangely the clarity of his French had improved enormously over three years, so that now one could understand the meaning of nearly everything he sang. Or maybe it was just a better record player.

Is this simply the unique perversity of the human heart that wants (and wants and wants) what it doesn't have—Italian food in Paris, American jazz in Saint-Germain—and, only when it is about to lose it, returns to the things that drew it to the desire in the first place? Or was there a kind of peace in it too? We would now never be Parisians or integrate; we might not even stay in town more than another eight weeks. Loss, like distance, gives permission for romance. In a better-ordered Verona, Romeo and Juliet would have grown up to be just another couple at dinner.

Finally we went for a long walk, down to see the boats, by the river, and thought, No, we're not ready to leave yet, haven't yet found a good-bye. So we moved. To a bigger, actually nicer apartment. A slight, permanent overhang of depression lifted; the new place was so bright, and it was connected to the street, the life of the city. One by one our stuff came over, three blocks from one apartment to the other.

In every move, I've noticed, there is always *something*—a roll of Christmas wrapping paper, a boxful of hangers from the dry cleaners, a metal extender whose use no one can recall—that is left over in the apartment you're leaving, which you step around in curiosity and then, on the last trip, take with you. In this case it was an antenna that belonged with something—a shortwave radio? a portable television?—which we could no longer recall, a plastic dagger, with a "Kings and Knights" sticker on it, and a hardcover of Nabokov's *Pnin,* which came from nowhere and I could never remember reading in Paris. Leaving 16 rue du Pré-aux-Clercs for the last time, I opened *Pnin* at random, to a bit about a boy's imaginary father, a king: " 'Abdication! One third of the alphabet!' coldly quipped the King, with the trace of an accent. 'The answer is no. I prefer the unknown quantity of Exile.' "

|||

Just after the move, for my birthday, Luke and Martha gave me a wonderful toy, *La Machine à Dessiner le Monde,* a machine to draw the world. Really, all it is is a camera lucida, but nicely done in plastic, with a viewing stand on top. You put a piece of vellum on it, and if the light's bright enough, and it has to be very bright, it projects the thing you're looking at right onto the paper. All you have to do is trace it.

All! For just tracing turns out to be the hardest thing of all. All the clichés and exasperating French abstractions about the insuperable difficulties of realism turn out to be plain truth when you have your machine to draw the world pointed out the window at the plane trees on the boulevard Saint-Germain, your pencil poised, and then you try to decide where to make the first mark. The world *moves* so much—shimmers and shakes like a nautch dancer, more than you can ever know when you're in it rather than looking at it. You bless any leaf that holds still long enough for you to get it. Hold still, you tell the tree, the light leaping up and down on the balustrade, as though you were talking to a small child as you try to get on its galoshes. Just *hold still.* Where you finally make the mark is mostly a question of when you finally get fed up.

Tracing becomes a deep, knotty problem, a thing to solve, and I am completely absorbed in it. I take the Machine to Draw the World to the Palais Royal or the Luxembourg Gardens and just watch the screen, pencil poised, at the translation of Paris into this single flat layer of translucent, lucid shimmer. I no longer try to circus it, or mourn it, or even learn from it, since just drawing it is enough. What you really need from the world in order to draw it is a lot of light and for everything to just stand still.

|||

Martha and I went for our Christmas lunch together at Le Grand Véfour. The Palais Royal in December: undecorated *sapins* line the arcades, and Monet smokiness hangs over the gardens. Christian David, the maître d', is suave and perfect and has been *utterly* worn out, in the five years we have lunched there twice a year, by the experience of having kids. One of his kids, Antoine, has swallowed a peanut, and he has spent six nights in a hospital; the other is having trouble at school, so David has, beneath a crackle of suave, the hollow, thousand-yard stare of the Parent.

He insisted that next time, next spring we bring Luke Auden, and I told Luke (or Luca, as he now likes to be known) about the invitation when we got home. "Is it Chinese food?" Luke asked, eyes alight with faint hope. "Or regular Paris food?" Regular Paris food, I told him. His eyes became doleful. He loves Chinese food.

One of our accomplishments of the year has been to invent Chinese takeout in Paris. There is a Chinese restaurant in the *rez-de-chaussée* of our new building, Le Coq d'Or or something, and we asked them if we could sometimes simply call them up and have them prepare the food in the kitchen and then let us come down and pick it up. They looked at us dubiously: We would call in advance and have prepared food awaiting us? Yes, we said. They could even, if it were convenient, have someone run upstairs with it; we would be glad to give this messenger a little something extra for his trouble. We now have this system worked out, and it is regarded as very piquant and original.

We were so proud that we tried to extend it to the Mexican place around the corner. This was a new place that had just opened on the little street around the corner called, of all odd things, Spicy Dinners. There is a new, depressingly Japanese–Third World–style enthusiasm in Paris for "American"-style names. Some, like Buffalo Grill, are ordinary enough. Others are alarming: Speed Rabbit Pizza, for instance, a chain that is beginning to blanket the city, with a very up-to-date image of a racing hare. I don't think that you can actually get a rabbit pizza from them, a *pizza au lapin*, but they think it looks streamlined, late century, thrillingly global. A speedy rabbit, delivering speedy food. Anyway, Spicy Dinners really did have spicy dinners, and I miss them terribly, spicy dinners. It serves Mexican food basically, though with various West Indian accents. The owner seems to be East Indian, though. We proposed that we try the same system of calling up and coming over to take out, and the owner, after a few unconvinced looks, said fine, that would be good. Around six o'clock we called in our order—burritos and chili and enchiladas—and, eyes alight with expectation (man, at last some spicy food), went around a few minutes later. He had prepared all the dinner on normal plates—big, restauranty white china plates—and had it waiting for us. It was Parisian takeout; he trusted us with his plates. I held out my arms, and he carefully put one heavy plate after another in them, placing a second plate upside down on the first, to keep everything warm, so that I had six plates and three dinners all in my hands. I felt like a circus juggler. Luke delicately guided me home and, since I didn't have the use of my hands, had to punch out the code and push open the big courtyard door himself, while I balanced the plates and spicy food as best I could, with visions of crashing china and spilled burritos all over the boulevard. It was quite a weight. "Please bring back the plates," he had called out as we left the premises. But we ran them through the dishwasher that night, and then Nisha put them away, and we forgot all about them. A month later, when we remembered, the little spicy restaurant had gone out of business. We feel very guilty about the whole thing.

|||

Earlier in December Luke fell terribly sick—far sicker than I ever hope to see him again. We packed him off to his pediatrician, our wonderful Dr. Pierre Bitoun, who looks exactly like a kinder Groucho Marx. When we called him, he picked up the phone himself, as he always does, and said to get him over. Dr. Bitoun looked worried as hell and told us to get him to a surgeon right away. I picked Luke up in my arms, and we ran to the surgical hospital, where the gentle, grave-eyed surgeon, just emerging from an operation, examined him, said that he didn't have appendicitis but that he was very sick and that we ought to get him over to the Necker Hospital for an emergency workup. The Necker is the central children's hospital in Paris. We raced over, without an introduction, into the packed emergency ward, showed our *carnet de santé,* the pediatrician's record of inoculations and so forth. The girl at the desk barely glanced at it, and within an hour Luke had had a sonogram, an X ray, a barium enema, and various other tests and got examined by three doctors. Two and a half hours later we were back home with a diagnosis. (It turned out that Luke had salmonella poisoning.) It was only after we had left the hospital that we realized that not only had we not paid a penny but that no one had asked us to show our insurance, fill out a form, or do any of the other standard, humiliating things that happen to our American friends with sick children. Nor had any of the procedures had to be run by the profit-and-loss manager of an HMO. This is socialized medicine, of course, which the insurance companies have patriotically kept Americans from suffering under. There are times, as one reads about the uninsured and the armed and the executed, when French anti-Americanism begins to look extremely rational.

|||

The Christmas windows are weird in Paris this year. Every year, in Paris as everywhere else, the American imperium of shopping opportunities continues to rage, unbanked. Yet the windows are weird, a fin de siècle note of disquiet seeping in. The Bon Marché, which usually has hordes of industrious elves and bears dancing at the end of invisible wires, this year has its windows filled with life-size human figures mechanically enacting a story of incest, bestiality, murder, and fashion narcissism. They play out an updated version of Charles Perrault's story "Peau d'Ane," in which a king in mourning for his queen threatens to force himself on his own daughter and is outwitted only by the princess's decision first to distract him with a series of over-wrought holiday dresses and then by the killing of the royal don-key, whose dripping skin . . . well, it's a long story, and a strange one, and what connection it has with Christmas—or what the Parisian children, pressed toward the animated windows in their duffel coats, careful scarves bunched like packages around their throats, think of it all—is hard to imagine.

Luke and I went Christmas shopping after he recovered. He desperately believes in Santa—we have sold it hard, I don't know why—and has been trying to arrange his Christmas list to fit the dimensions of Santa's sack, which he studies in illustration. "You know what is the problem?" he says as he turns from the Bon Marché toy catalog to his Thomas Nast pictures of Santa. "I don't think that a big race set is a good idea; it won't fit." He loves the Christmas windows and a Louis Armstrong song called "Zat You, Santa Claus?"

After nearly four years in Paris he has developed a compli-cated, defensive sense of his own apartness, rather like his dad's.

He recognizes that his parents, his father particularly, speaks with an Accent, and this brings onto him exactly the shame that my grandfather must have felt when his Yiddish-speaking father arrived to talk to *his* teachers at a Philadelphia public school. I try to have solid, parental discussions with his teachers, but as I do, I realize, uneasily, that in his eyes I am the *alter kocker*, the comic immigrant.

"Zo, how the boy does?" he hears me saying in effect. "He is good boy, no? He is feeling out the homeworks, isn't he?" I can see his small frame shudder, just perceptibly, at his father's words. I had thought to bring him the suavity of the French gamin, and instead I have brought onto him the shame of the immigrant child.

I sense too that he is in a larger confusion: What's French, what's American, where am I? His French vocabulary is very large, but he doesn't like to use it, or show it, except in extremis. (He always seems to know the answer to the question, in even the most rapid and complicated French, "Would you like a little treat/candy/pastry?") A family is a civilization, and a language is a culture, and he is left with a sense of being doubly islanded. Watching the children at the gardens, he turns to me. "*All* children in New York speak English?" he demands. Yes, I tell him, and he imagines the unthinkable: a world of English speakers, where English is the public, not the private, language.

When we go out to eat—at the Balzar or at a nice French-American place called the Café Parisien—we play the game of Imaginary Restaurants, making up places we would like to open. (My best so far is a Franco-American inn specializing in game, called Les Fauves.) He has invented a restaurant that will be called the Toy Store Restaurant, and will serve an eclectic menu, French and American: baked chicken—fresh from the oven, hamburgers—fresh from the oven! And something everyone likes (dramatic pause): fruit salad! He has intuited his way toward a New York coffee shop.

But: "No French people," he says decisively.

"No French people!" I say, with genuine shock; increasing his French-bashing was not the reason we came here.

"No," he says. "I'm the owner, and it would be too nervous." He sees himself as the next Toots Shor, and wants to feel relaxed, ready to put an arm around his clients and pound their backs, without worrying if he remembers the word, which language he is speaking.

In other, unconscious ways he is thoroughly French and will, I fear, be lost in New York when we go back. He ate a hamburger for the first time on July 4. He took three bites, pushed it away, had some ice cream, his normal routine, but the next morning he said, "I liked the hamburger"—decisively—"but I did not like that sauce you served with it."

"What sauce?" I said, puzzled. I hadn't made a sauce.

"That *red* sauce," he said, disdainfully, with exactly the expression I have seen on the face of Jean-Pierre Quélin, the food critic of *Le Monde*, when he gets a corked glass of wine. "I did not like that *red* sauce." He means, of course, the Heinz ketchup, bought at La Grande Épicerie, in the American specialties section.

|||

When he went back to New York, his one trip, to interview at a New York nursery school, where you have to go a year and a half before you enter, he was asked what he liked to eat for breakfast, and he said, "Croissants and *confiture*." Everybody laughed, thought it was cute, though he was being serious as hell. It is, perhaps, a truth of expatriate children that rather than grow up with two civilizations, they grow up with less than one, unable somehow to plug in the civilization at home with the big one around. They grow up, we have noticed with other kids, achingly polite, and watchful and skilled, "adult," and guarded.

His one island of calm and certainty remains the Luxembourg

Gardens. He is master there, and he has his itinerary nearly perfectly arranged: first the playground, then the carousel, then the ponies, if there's time, and then a crepe from the crepe man. He rides the horses now, upright, and I feel sure that any day now he will ask for a stick.

Nothing stops the wheel, though, and now even the puppet shows have been revolutionized: Las Vegasized, Americanized, globalized. At God knows what expense, and rolling dice of a size I can only imagine, this Christmas M. Desarthis discarded the reliable run of *Cochons* and *Trésors* and launched an entirely new kind of spectacular called *La Valise Enchantée,* complete with an original recorded score, with drums and organs, and black backgrounds and animated fluorescent fish and squirrels. In terms of his little park theater this is a ratchet up of enormous dimensions—and all very well done by a staff of four new puppeteers, though with the slight tang of the lounge act.

I can only imagine that M. Desarthis, in the French manner, decided that he was slipping behind the times and thought of this as a way to modernize. It couldn't be a bigger hit with Luca, who plays the cassette we bought of the show and has committed it to memory, racing over the French word he doesn't know with suave Sid Caesar inventions: *"Quand il était très petit, sa maman s'amusait . . . hunsta whoosta weestsa. . . ."* I like the new show, but I am worried about what is going to happen to the *Cochons*.

On Christmas Eve we saw a department-store Santa at Hédiard, shopping for champagne. We stood in line behind him; Luke was not a bit shaken. When we got home, he said to his mother: "We saw Santa at Hédiard. I think he was just getting a little cheap wine for his elves."

|||

The *lycéens*, the high school students, are on strike this Christmas, and we see them march by the windows of our new apartment along the boulevard Raspail. Like the protesters in Lewis Carroll's *Sylvie and Bruno* who march with the banner "Less

Bread! More Taxes!" the *lycéens* are, officially, striking for more classes and harder teachers. But their strike has nearly universal support: The government is for it; the opposition is for it; the press is for it.

What is startling and instructive to an outsider is how earnest the French *lycéens* look as they march; they have a worn-out, exhausted, genuinely oppressed look that is miles away from the overfed, ironic complacency that American kids of the same age have. This is the consequence of the school system. The *lycéens'* normal, nonstriking day begins at eight-thirty in the morning and often runs to six o'clock in the evening and, for all the reforms that have been attempted in the last twenty years, is still conducted in an atmosphere of rote-learning, reflexive authoritarianism. (You see even ten- and eleven-year-olds emerging from school at the end of the day pale as veal, clutching for a *pain aux raisins,* starved for a little pleasure.)

|||

Outside the Galeries Lafayette are stationed official city guards in uniform and a store surveillant, telling everyone how to get up to the windows and which way to walk once you're there, directing traffic, with no appeal. Everyone meekly obeys. The authoritarian impulses shapes everything, even the traffic by the windows.

|||

The weird thing is that by taking tracing on as an ambition, I've become more in tune with the fundamental French temperament. The will toward contemplative observation is the keynote of French sensibility and tied, in ways both beautiful and horrible, to French indifference. My favorite French writers when I arrived were, dutifully, Proust and Camus and Stendhal, who generalize, brilliantly; now my favorites are Colette, Antoine Blondin, and Maupassant, who above all look, who are part of the great French Machine to Draw the World.

The greatness of Colette and Maupassant, who is the real father of modern writing, have leaked out back home (though I think Maupassant is still known as the father of the trick ending), but I think Blondin is just about completely unknown in America. He was a French newspaperman and essayist, thriving in the 1950s and 1960s, who wrote novels and reportage and essays for the French papers. He is most famous for writing a kind of all-purpose column in the French sports daily *L'Équipe*.

Blondin is a wonderful, easy writer, and what I admire most about him is the fluency, the particularizations of his language. Everything seeks a joke, but nothing misses a point. He captures tiny moments of reality: a rainy day in the stadium where someone is listening to the radio of the rugby game below, and the crackling broadcast is more real than the game it is describing, which takes you back outside the stadium, is more real than the game it describes. His most emphatic aphorism was simple: "The only duty of the writer is not to have one."

|||

Against the official French culture of the academy, the French empirical tradition has to keep itself alive in the oddest corners, like Blondin in *L'Équipe*. Manet's lemons and asparagus are its best emblems. It produces an atmosphere of *calm*. The calm of Manet's flowers, the calm of Colette's dialogue, the precious, life-enhancing calm of the Palais Royal at three in the afternoon, the last coffee on the table, the light slanting in, French calm. Has anyone ever thought how incongruous and touching the use of that word is in the Baudelaire poem, the Matisse title? "Luxe, Calme and Volupté"? Luxury, Calm and Voluptuousness. *Calm* and Voluptuousness? Not hot and voluptuous or funky and voluptuous? We have grown accustomed to it by familiarity, but really, *Calm*—it is as if one put some other flat, bourgeois word in there: Luxury: nice and voluptuous? Luxury: comfy and voluptuous. And yet it works. It is the essence of the French vision. *Everybody calm down.* (Luke Auden about the excitable little boy in his class: "He was nervous, but Sonia calmed him up.") Matisse, Manet, calm us up.

|||

In France private life still turns on the closed seventeenth-century model of *ce pays ici,* this little country here. The crucial unit of social life in France is the Cohort, rather than the social Class, as in England, or the Clan, as in Italy (or the Company, as back home in America). These Parisian cohorts—loosely defined working alliances of people in politics and art and literature, who draw together in youth for one purpose or another and then remain linked, if only in mutual hatred, for life—get drawn from a lot of different social classes and clans and therefore need neutral places to inhabit. This has produced the unique Parisian commonplace civilization of parks and cafés and salons, which give the illusion of democratic entry.

It is *only* an illusion, though. What looks like a café is really a kind of club, and you can no more really enter it than you can enter White's or Boodle's in St. James's just by walking in there. The cohorts of Paris—the impressionist group is a perfect example of the kind—look open but remain essentially closed to anyone not in at their formation. Pressed beyond a polite point, they clam up as firmly as an Italian family.

John Singer Sargent's relations with the impressionists are a perfect example of how this works. Throughout the 1870s he stood right on the friendly edges of the impressionist cohort, knocking politely on the door again and again. They looked him over, but they never let him in. All that's left to the outsider is the beautiful surface. The two favorite sites of Sargent—the Luxembourg Gardens and the Winter Circus—strike a guilty chord; parks and circuses are open and seem to offer the illusion of assimilation. You end up by walking around and around the Luxembourg Gardens. French life just goes on, with its enormous insular indifference. Americans and Frenchmen always agree that they share *something,* something deeper than anything they share with any other people—the love of happiness, perhaps, or of social pleasures. Really it is this insularity that they share, as they discover sadly in the end. Americans welcome everyone with open arms and forced smiles, and in the end the immigrant-expatriates discover that that's the problem; the next man off the next boat is just as welcome too. Paris is open to anyone, but what is open isn't entirely Paris. It is another, simulacra Paris, which wraps around the real one and is there to be looked at, to be seen. About all you can do is paint it, and Sargent did that about as well as it could be done for about as long as it could be done. It was a great subject, but never Home, and Americans want home.

|||

More comfort: Food here is comfort, not theater. Last night we had our good friends B. and R. over, and we had champagne (Drappier '90) and then lemon tart from Ladurée, where Luke and I stood in line for half an hour. It's a beautiful Proustian store on the rue Royale with a pale green wooden front, old wooden tables, and absolutely no line discipline. We get *bûches* from Ladurée too. Tonight, Christmas night: a brined turkey, Brussels sprouts with *crème fraîche,* chestnut stuffing, and those *bûches de Noël.* As always in Paris, each thing has a thing associated with it, a story: The turkey was ordered, argued over (take two small ones, I don't want two small ones, etc.).

|||

I was, if anything, a slightly too complacent universalist when I arrived in Paris and have become a far too melancholic particu-larist as we get ready to leave, someone who believes in the spirit of places, although he always expects to be outside them, and can pay them only the compliment of eternal comparison.

Luke, once this winter, brought home the school goldfish, Swimmy, for the weekend. He got up on a chair to stare at his bowl and said hello. No answer. Then he recalled what kind of goldfish it was. "*Ça va*, Swimmy?" he said at last, "*ça va?*" speaking the goldfish's language to the goldfish.

It is better to speak to the goldfish in their own language, and better still just to jump into the bowl and become a goldfish yourself, or try to. Without that immersion you feel a constant temptation to compare them with the nongoldfish you know back home, to say what they are like, to engage in the constant stilted game of comparison. In the end it is better just to say what goldfish do than to say what they are like, goldfish, like Parisians, in the end not being "like" anything, but just busy *being,* like everything else. Yet the attempt to say what the goldfish are like—they're swimming, they're gold, oh, how they shine—is in its way the sincerest tribute to their glitter.

|||

Once again, and reliably, the Christmas lights got themselves tangled, and this time, since the ceilings in the new apartment are higher, and the tree we bought taller, I had to go out and get even more new ones. Hundreds and hundreds of dollars have now been spent by this family on French Christmas tree lights, which will have absolutely no use when we go home. I had to get on a really high ladder this year to toss them onto the tree and felt like something between Will Rogers and one of those people on the old Don Ameche circus show. Luke followed me up the ladder, "helping," and I could sense in him this year not so much admiration as sheer impatience, an almost unbeatable Oedipal urge. I can do that as well as the next guy, as well as you can.

Our Parisian friends Agnès and Richard came over this year for the tree trimming and laughed as they saw me lassoing the tree. "No, no," Agnès explained, "the idea is to hold them up in two strands and drape them on like an apron, and then they tie in the back."

"I can't believe he never thought of that," Martha said.

The real Christmas story is not about Jesus and/or Mary, or the Wise Men, but about poor Joseph, sound asleep under the stable, glad that this first time, at least, everyone is busy, and no one is counting on him to put up the lights.

|||

All I can do is trace something, flip open the red plastic lid of the machine to draw little bits of Paris. Luke's school, for instance, is on the rue Saint-Dominique. You take the 69 bus to get there, and it goes down the rue du Bac, and then along the rue de Grenelle, narrow and twisting, with the high walls and plastered fronts of other schools for older children and government buildings alongside, broken now and then by a lace curtain front on a bistro where no one ever seems to go. Often, the 69 can't make the turn onto the rue de Grenelle because someone has parked on the sidewalk, half on the street. Then the bus driver just stops, blows his horn, and folds his arms. We'll wait it out, like a war. In a rush, a *high*, the bus breaks out after three minutes into the esplanade des Invalides, the huge, flat, officially forbidden lawn—though, on a Wednesday afternoon, I once did see two brave and determined Americans playing Frisbee there (you could tell they were Americans because they looked thirty and were dressed like six-year-olds). The golden covered dome of the church stands straight up behind, not looming but preening, and the Invalides itself sits below, an old military hospital with the two horses incised on its front, combining splendor with the odd barrackslike solidity, the bureaucratic confidence of the architecture of the grand siècle.

The bus whizzes across, witness to this old beauty too many times, and pushes along to the real heart of the Seventh, and Grenelle warms up. The rue Cler, which breaks off it, is one of the nicest shopping and *marché* streets in Paris, and it acts as a heart for the neighborhood, warming even the chilly great avenues of Tour Maubourg and Rapp. They are lined with chestnuts and planes, and there is more art nouveau architecture there than perhaps anywhere else in Paris save the Sixteenth.

Luke's school is a block up, on the rue Saint-Dominique; Grenelle is one of those sandwiched streets, between the truly busy Saint-Dominique and the rue Cler, where there are two lingerie stores to a block (how can women *wear* so much underwear?). Luke's school has an archway for an entrance and is set back in a deep courtyard, with geraniums and ivy tumbling over the courtyard walls. On warm days the single classroom window is open, and you see the (overregimented) kindergarten children, already in their rows. Since we still feel that eight-thirty to four-thirty is just too long a day for a four-year-old, we have arranged for me to pick up Luke every day at three.

I catch Luke's eye, and we wave. He is breaking out, free, and sometimes we have an omelet and a grenadine in the café down the street, where Luke likes to pull the lace curtains and the old lady who is always there has an old black cocker. Then, by now four o'clock, violet twilight falling, watching that sky that looks as though it were ready to snow though it never does, we get the bus back home. Going home, it goes down Saint-Dominique, gently, formally, perfectly curving across the Left Bank, rather than snaking, as Grenelle does. Saint-Dominique is lined with wonderful shops: butchers with fat-wrapped *noisettes d'agneau* and bakers with various-sized *tartes Tatins*, all caramel-colored, and children's clothing stores, their windows filled with violet coats for small girls. They believe in blitz advertising in Paris; usually all the poster columns and the sides of all the buses are covered with the same image of the same single thing: Julia Roberts's teeth; or a girl, seen from shoulder to knee in black and white, perfectly lit, sculpted lit, lingerie, snapping her garters; or Johnny Hallyday's face on a new issue of *Paris Match*. Once there were a thousand images of a woman behind a gold yellow champagne glass, *Le Moment Taittinger*. That time I remember that I looked up the rue Jean Nicot and could see lights twinkling, like fireflies, right across the Seine, filling the trees. I went to investigate another day and found out that they were just lights strung in the trees to draw tourists to the *bateaux-mouches*.

The hardest thing to convey is how lovely it all is and how that loveliness seems all you need. The ghosts that haunted you in New York or Pittsburgh will haunt you anywhere you go, because they're your ghosts and the house they haunt is you. But they become disconcerted, shaken confused for half a minute, and in that moment on a December at four o'clock when you're walking from the bus stop to the rue Saint-Dominique and the lights are twinkling across the river—only twinkling in the *bateaux-mouches,* luring the tourists, but still . . . —you feel as if you've escaped your ghosts if only because, being you, they're transfixed looking at the lights in the trees on the other bank, too, which they haven't seen before, either.

It's true that you can't run away from yourself. But we were right: you can run away.

|||

I brined the turkey for Christmas dinner in a big white pasta pot that Martha and I bought years ago on lower Broadway. I put it out on our tiny terrace overlooking the boulevard Saint-Germain, covered with foil—all night long a shiny white ceramic and silver foil American beacon on the boulevard.

|||

And a Christmas surprise! We're going to have another kid, a small French child! The big Machine to Draw the World, which traces from two objects at once and makes something of the superimposition, is drawing a new one, down in Martha's belly. Stow the elegies, pal; we *can't* leave, not quite yet.

A Handful of
Cherries

Quite a few people have asked me to tell them what happened at the Brasserie Balzar, after its friends occupied it in order to protest its purchase by M. Jean-Paul Bucher, the owner of a large and (we thought) unfeeling and soulless chain of brasseries and restaurants. I've wanted to write about it for several reasons: because it sheds some light on the French struggle with change; because it touches on the differences between French and American attitudes to food, which have been filling the papers a lot lately; and because it presented me with the one moment when for a brief moment—seconds, really—I actually felt fully French. But I've also been reluctant to write about it because in the end it was a sad, typical story about the struggle for small values during a fin de siècle dominated by big money.

In plain English, we fought, and we lost. Not miserably, though, and perhaps not entirely. We saved something, if only our own amour-propre, and the solidarity of our organization, so that there is a conceivable, half-plausible sense in which, in ornamental French, we won.

The first Balzar meeting was held in June 1998, just after the purchase of the small, perfect, century-old Left Bank brasserie by Bucher. The friends of the Balzar organized a group, led by two honorable men. The first, the *délégué du personnel*, or steward of the waiters, can now emerge from behind the pathetic false mustache he was provided in my first account and appear under his real name, Claude Blanchot. The other leader was Lorenzo Valentin, a startlingly handsome and eloquent young publisher whose offices were across the street from the Balzar. We banded together a collection of regulars, the clientele—mostly writers and publishers and professors from the Sorbonne— to protect the Balzar. The first meeting was a kind of sit-down and dine strike at the Balzar itself. We infiltrated about sixty members inside to protest, and almost everyone judged it a great success.

The evening had gotten a lot of attention in the press and produced a breakfast meeting at the Balzar of our executive committee with M. Bucher himself. He freely gave any number of assurances to protect the staff, the cooking, and the distinct traditions of the place. They were, I thought at the time, both very sincerely made and utterly worthless, since he had no more obligation to keep his promises than he had to come to our apartments and cook us breakfast.

By then it was late July, though, and nothing happens in Paris in late July. (If the king could have kept things calm around the Bastille for another three weeks, France would still be a monarchy.) Right on date, August 1, everyone went one way or another: Lorenzo to Italy and the rest of the committee to one or another French resort. (All the *garçons*, as I had learned, rather reluctantly, to call them, went home too, mostly to the small towns in the Massif Central and the South and even Alsace where they came from.) The pattern of internal emigration, as described by Balzac, youth coming to the capital, remains as powerful in

France as it was a century ago. You come to Paris to make a reputation, as a writer or a waiter, intending to go home, soon, to run the local paper or to open your own brasserie on the town square, but then you don't, except in August.

We had the habit of going back to America for two or three weeks in August, to be washed over by the cold waves of American ocean and the warm spit of American opinion and to see our family. First we would go to see Martha's family in Canada (who said, Canadianly, "Oh, you live in *Paris*. How stimulating,") and then to the little shack in Cape Cod where we had first sat out and watched the sunsets and dreamed of going to Paris.

And then back home to Orly, where, bleary-eyed, airsick, after the tightly sealed flight, we would feel our hearts lift as the taxi turned in the early-morning flat white light into the porte d'Orléans, and then up the avenue du Général Leclerc, past the place Denfert-Rochereau, where I once lived as a kid (and where I could still see the window where Melissa, the baby of the six kids in my family, had once stood and semaphored to me, across the street, not to forget the *long, round* bread.) Then past the Belfort Café (where, twenty years before, I had once sneaked down for a *pain au chocolat* and my first *café serré*) and up the boulevard Raspail, where they were already setting up the *marché biologique,* and back to our apartment. "This is home," Luke said once, and our hearts skipped, because we knew it wasn't, quite, and were glad he thought it was.

The trees would already be shedding, and the streets would be filled with brown leaves, skipping across the empty boulevards. We always missed the fall coming to Paris; coming back after Labor Day is too late. Of the great argued-out differences between New York and Paris, none is more important than the simple difference that Paris is farther north than New York is. The end of August is still mostly high summer in America, at least on the East Coast, with days in the nineties and hazy sun and hardly a hint of autumn in the air. Labor Day hits Americans like a ton of bricks; we're going back to work *so soon*? And then, of course, Americans, for all their cult of summer and fussing about summer and idealizing summer have no summer at all to speak of. The two-week paid vacation, now made for the no-collar classes almost no vacation at all by the fax machine and the computer, is a small favor taken from a restless, impatiently toe-tapping employer. In France everyone—Luke's baby-sitter, the man who sells cheeses, President Chirac, Bernard Arnault, Bernard-Henri Lévy—is guaranteed five weeks of vacation by law, and just about everyone takes it. (There would be no point even for an eager beaver, overachieving tycoon to stay on the job since there would be nobody there for him to motivate.) When people say that Paris closes down in August, they don't mean the pace slackens a little. They mean it closes, like a box.

The funny thing is that the cool weather comes to Paris right around the middle of August, so that by the time everyone comes back for the *ré-entrée*, it feels like autumn, and everyone is ready to start life over. People, ordinary people, are actually fed up with their vacations and glad to get back to town. (I once saw one of the inconsolably grumpy women who works at Michel Chemin, the bakery near us, come in on the first day of September and actually grab the other inconsolably grumpy woman who works there and kiss her, fully, on the cheeks.)

|||

As soon as I was back in town, I got a call from Lorenzo, to tell me that things were going very badly at the Balzar. The waiters were nervous; they had felt abused and overtaken by events; their grievance hearing at the *tribunal des Prudhommes*—the labor court—had been postponed. It seemed that Bucher was about ready to fire everybody, or that at least was the rumor. Tour groups of Americans were being sent in by concierges of large hotels. Our only hope, it seemed, was to *médiatiser* some more and then to . . . well, to have another meeting. There was one called that week at Mme. de Lavigne's apartment over on the quai Anatole-France.

I was the only American there, and this unexceptional fact made me unreasonably self-satisfied—the Tom Paine of the Balzar insurrection (although it seemed to me that I recalled from some sixtyish piece of guerrilla theater that, bad omen, Tom Paine ended up in prison during the Terror and died drunk in New York). While I was away, the great liberal paper *Le Monde* had come out with another piece outlining our struggle to save the Balzar, by the oddly dyspeptic food writer J.-P. Quélin, the Hilton Kramer of French cuisine. Why should people whose lives are devoted to the study of pleasure be so charmless, so lacking in joy, I have often wondered? The answer is simple, I now thought. They were not drawn to their subject for pleasure; it was the *absence* of pleasure they felt that made them so tense and talky. This is the Devil's Theory of what draws critics to themes, and I am sure that it is true. The people who take natural pleasure in pictures, whom you see haunting the Museum of Modern Art at lunch hour, or eating with a copy of *Le Monde* at the old Balzar, are *completed* by the pleasure, as most of us are by sex. They feel no more need to discuss it than most of us want to discuss lovemaking; the drowsy commonplaces are, for them, the appropriate speech act, the only appropriate speech act. People who don't actually enjoy eating are the ones with the attention to look around the room—where are people sitting? Who likes what?—and absorb both the abstract system of snob values and the social comedy of it. The people who actually write well about food—M. F. K. Fisher or Seymour Britchky—are oddly abstemious, austere, even, in a way, antisensual, for the same reason that Ruskin, a man who recoiled in horror at his wife's pubic hair, could write so well about the hidden message of the pointed arch. *Not really liking it much* is a precondition of art criticism of all kinds. This is why embarrassingly, thunderously obvious thoughts—beauty counts, power matters, pictures sell for money—are often presented by critics with such shocked or plaintive intensity. All critics are food fusses, not wanting to try the green stuff, even when the

Mother-MOMA tells you it's good for you, and then announce darkly that it's poison, any child can see it is. (This is why Tom Wolfe could be both absolutely right and wrong about American art. Not wanting to eat, he alone would notice the odd order of the cutlery on the table.)

|||

At the meeting there was a general feeling that we needed to placate Quélin. We had a cross section of waiters and clients there that afternoon: Claude and Guy from the staff, and a left-wing journalist who I thought was looking at me darkly, having spotted not Tom Paine but a smoothie from the CIA.

Lorenzo led off with his usual quiet authority. He was in his usual costume: a soft black turtleneck and flannel slacks, with a scarf thrown, Little Prince style, around his throat. He has a round face, with an absolutely beautiful, warm smile. He has two registers at his command: a low, troubled one that he uses when he is reviewing the agenda and another, higher, and more plaintive one that he uses when he is exhorting us publicly, for instance when we occupy the restaurant. He outlined the problems. The waiters felt abused and uncertain because the standards in the kitchen were declining and Bucher was still letting the new manager take a chunk of their service money. "How were they declining?" someone asked. The fish was no good; the sole was being parboiled before it was grilled; someone else thought a supplier was coming in from the Flo Group with ordinary beef. "Well, I had a steak there the other night," someone began . . . but we all shushed him. The food, good or bad, was not really the *point*, we all said. The point was the spirit of the Balzar. If we did not act quickly and more decisively, the brasserie, and the *garçons'* security, would be lost. The guys had decided to stage a one-day wildcat strike, and it was important for us to support them—perhaps by occupying the Balzar the same day, perhaps on the night before. In any case, the crisis of the battle was approaching, and we could not be lazy or indecisive in our actions.

Claude spoke next. He was angry and at the same time, and for the first time, a little pleading. The *garçons* were planning to walk out on Thursday, he explained, and he hoped that we, the members of the association, would come out to support them. We would have Bucher foxed coming and going.

I could sense a reluctance to do this on the part even of our elite radical circle; this would be going beyond the politesse of our arrangement with Bucher, moving toward open warfare. "*Attention!*" someone said, a real interjection in French. "This could put us in a dangerous position." I feared too that Claude's ideas about the power of the association were greater than the power of the association deserved. I noticed that he liked to say the term *the association,* and he always referred to Lorenzo as "M. le Président."

I was becoming a little dubious, especially so because Lorenzo, for some reason, I thought, kept looking at me for ideas. I said, at last, that the only threat that had any meaning to Bucher was the threat of more bad publicity; that in effect, a boycott of his other restaurants would scare him more than anything else we could do. But I was also pretty sure that Bucher would never sell, and I feared that if the *garçons* walked out, he'd just replace them. Perhaps, I hinted, I gulped—I sensed the left-wing journalist looking at me with increasing disgust—we needed to start moving toward an exit strategy (I couldn't think of the French, so I said, *scénario de sortie,* which was more or less right). Did we have an exit strategy, aside from victory? What if Bucher held fast and didn't move? Could we get the *garçons* out in decent shape and not just blow up the Balzar, so to speak?

I was rewarded with steady, opaque looks. Having arrived at the logic of war, one of us—the American—was trying to wriggle out of it at the first sign of opposition. (I remembered what an American diplomat negotiating with the quai d'Orsay had once said to me: "It is hard enough to get them to start, and once they start, you can't get them to stop.")

Then Lorenzo and Mme. de Lavigne together raised another, stranger, and more tempting vision. What if we were to buy the Balzar? What if Bucher could be convinced that the cost to him in bad publicity and harassment was just too great, didn't make sense for his chain, and that, finally, in a moment of facesaving capitulation (but why would this be facesaving for him? I let it pass) he could sell to a group of *actionnaires*—i.e., *us*.

Lorenzo had a nice rhetorical formula for this transaction: "M. Bucher wants to join the association, but the association would like to join the Flo Group." Mme. de Lavigne had been in the restaurant business; it would not be hard to do. We could each own a little piece of the Balzar, the *garçons* too, and, run as a co-operative, a kind of writers and waiters cooperative, we could make it *rentable*.

It sounded like just about the best idea I had ever heard. Like many Americans of my generation, I am a fanatic restaurant imaginer: I think that someday I will open a restaurant called La Chanson, to serve French-American cooking: roast chicken with caramelized carrots and broccoli puree and pecan pie for dessert; then there is my favorite idea for a restaurant called Les Fauves, which would serve only game—taglietelle with wild boar, pheasant stuffed with chestnuts—or else to open—and this I was sure would make a fortune—a place to get real Montreal bagels, better than any other kind, boiled and then baked, sweet and chewy whereas New York bagels are bready and tasteless. . . .

So this was the hand that we would play, or try to play at least. We would have another sit-in at the Balzar, the night before the meeting, and we would threaten Bucher with still more *médiatisation*. The next day, independently, the personnel would stage their wildcat strike, and the two actions together would, somehow, sufficiently intimidate a whipsawed Bucher and he would crumble and sell us back the Balzar.

I can only say that at the time it did not seem like a completely crazy scenario. What we could not understand, I suppose, was why Bucher would want to buy the Balzar only in order to destroy it, why, after it had been clearly shown to him that he could not understand the institution, grasp its traditions, perpetuate its values, he would still want to hold on to it. For the money? It was too small for his chain; he had said as much himself. He could make more money in a single sitting at one of his Right Bank atmosphere factories—the vast art deco Boeuf sur le Toit, or the belle époque Julien—than he could in a week at Balzar. It wasn't as if we had anything against him personally; if he wanted to come and eat at the Balzar, we'd welcome him, anytime. But why own it only in order to ruin it? Where was the logic in that?

I suppose we couldn't realize, or could realize but couldn't accept, that the logic of business is not a logic in that sense. It's not only a narrow consideration of profits and losses, but a larger logic of, well, appetite. To buy something is to assert oneself, and to sell it, for whatever reason, is to collaborate in one's own diminishment. We were asking him to regurgitate in public, and even if we offered him the feather with which to tickle his own throat, he wouldn't want to do it. A man in his position couldn't afford to regurgitate, not in public, because then he would look ridiculous.

Anyway, we all clasped hands and swore to be at the Balzar on October 7 to reoccupy the place. Everybody had bought some food to the meeting—I recall that Claude had brought a particularly beautiful and fragrant Cantal, a wonderful cheese—and we soon broke for some wine. I buttonholed Guy after the meeting and asked him what we could really do, what the guys, the garçons, really wanted. Did they really want us to try to buy the place? He said, We want it to stay the same. To continue doing what we've always done. And to serve good food—the food isn't good enough. The food should be excellent.

This was curious, I thought. We radicals had decided that it was a red herring, so to speak, to make too much of an issue of the quality of the cooking—that wasn't the point, we insisted grandly—yet the garçons made much of it, made more of it than anything else. Some fundamental part of their métierhood is offended by the knowledge that the cuisine is being degraded. There is a real decent impulse on their part to put down a *plat* on the table with real enthusiasm: You'll enjoy this.

As I thought it over on my way home, it occurred to me that this is after all the deepest altruistic impulse that we have, food sharing being the most fundamental gesture of selflessness. I thought I was at last beginning to see the deeper motives, the real human basis of their indignation, beyond the few pennies here and there that they were losing. In the old regime they had been the tribal chieftains, the ones doing the sharing, and this more than compensated for their otherwise servile-seeming role. If they served good food, then they were practicing, if only by proxy, the primal role of the provider; if they served bad food, then they were just waiters in a restaurant. Beneath the "French" aspect of the Balzar wars—the mistrust of change that is not merely, or not merely foolishly and emptily, "nostalgic"—there was a deeper impulse, almost an instinctive one. Of course they wanted to protect their share of the service, and they wanted to keep their old working conditions. But they also were terrified of a loss of status, of being publicly shamed. To be a server at all is to dance on the edge of shame all the time. "*Sale métier*," Bemelmans's waiters famously mutter to themselves as they go in and out of the kitchen, "filthy profession," and it is easy to understand why. Bucher was reducing them to food bearers, rather than food sharers, and it made them feel as if they were being eaten alive.

|||

October came, and we occupied the Balzar again. The second *réunion* had a different feeling from the first, both gayer and angrier and more hysterical. At the first meeting the near absurdity of what we were doing had given everything an edge of comedy. *Can we really be doing this? Well, yes, we are. We are!* At the second *réunion* things seemed tougher, rockier. There were far more of us, for one thing, and not everyone could find a seat. People were waiting outside, thronged outside, trying to come in. The Balzar wars had been *médiatisé* as something amusing—a *fronde parisienne,* one of the papers had called it, a Parisian civil war. Those of us on the inside knew that the real action would take place the following day, when the *garçons* walked out, and we felt both anxious not to tip their hand and eager to let them know that we were with them.

Lorenzo was sublime. At the appointed hour he rose again from his seat, "We are here tonight not to make demands, not to protest, but to inquire," he began. "We are here to inquire of M. Bucher if, though he owns the name Balzar, if anyone can purchase its spirit. Is that spirit truly for sale? Can it be bought and sold? Or can it only be protected? We are not here to criticize the cuisine or to give M. Bucher lessons in the management of his affairs. We claim no expertise in that." Lorenzo gave a just so slightly sardonic inflection to these last words, implying that this was an expertise that one would hardly want. "But we do claim to understand the spirit of this place, the thousand tiny interchanges between the *personnel* and the place that have made it something more than a place where one exchanges money for food, and from which one would go elsewhere if more food could be had for less money. We are here to inquire about the nature of *possession,* about what it means to possess something and about who truly possesses a place: the man who owns the chairs and tables or the people who sit at those tables or those who have devoted their working lives to those tables. We want to ask: To whom belongs the Balzar? Does it belong to those who own it or to those who love it? Above all, we are here to inquire if any of us can feel at home in this place if the *personnel* of the Balzar do not feel at home in it. For they are the carriers of the spirit of this place. I say to the *personnel:* We are with you, right to the end." The room exploded in applause.

People began to rise and make seconding speeches themselves. Many of them, I am bound to report, had a slight edge of anti-Americanism, although no American was involved in this struggle, one way or another. (Apart from me, I mean, and I was there strictly as an honorary Parisian, or Quisling.)

For instance, a man rose from one of the banquettes at the end and cried, "You must let Bucher know that this is not a small war!" Applause. "Not a little brushfire that can be put out." More applause. "Let them know that this will not be the Gulf War!" Wild applause. "It will be Vietnam!" Madly enthused applause.

But after the meeting I went over to talk to this Danton, and he turned out to be a French-American businessman who lives in San Francisco. He gave me his card. Finally, and one by one, the waiters came out to bow, and we rose to our feet to applaud them. They looked genuinely touched, and we swore that we would not let them be betrayed.

|||

The next day at lunch the waiters walked out. I went over to the rue des Écoles to see what was going on and found all of them on the street, in mufti, carrying placards. Their union had put out a table, and there was a petition that you could sign to show your support for the Balzaristes. The *garçons* looked happy, and Jacques, a friend of Lorenzo's, was there with a video camera, documenting the event.

Our next meeting, in late November, was the strange one. Bucher had invited a little group of us to have breakfast with him once again, and on the eve of that meeting, we decided to have a serious meeting—an *assemblée générale* of Les Amis du Balzar. We held it, now, as serious meetings should be held, not at the Balzar or in Mme. de Lavigne's apartment, but in the classroom in a film school in the Twelfth Arrondissement, at nine o'clock at night. There was a pretty good turnout, considering, but now the alacrity and lightness had been lost, and the meeting had the air of, well, of a meeting. We all sat on school chairs, uncomfortably, and Claude, looking surprisingly uncomfortable too, droned on about the position of the waiter's grievance in front of the labor court.

Then Lorenzo took over and talked about the three plans that were open to us: We could continue to *médiatiser* and agitate about the Balzar, but that did not seem like a promising strategy, since in the meantime Bucher could simply wear us (and the waiters) down. We could attempt to buy the Balzar from Bucher—but he would almost certainly not sell. (I do not know to this day why Lorenzo had become pessimistic about this possibility, though I am sure that he was right. Perhaps he had another conversation with Bucher when they arranged the breakfast meeting.) The third possibility was to raise enough money to, in effect, start our own Balzar—a Balzar *des réfusés*, a real Balzar, under some other name, while Bucher's Balzar continued its impersonation. We all looked cheerful at this possibility, though it obviously demanded an infusion of capital. But a possible site had already been located farther down the rue des Écoles, and one of our members had long experience in the *restauration* . . . it might be done.

The conversation batted along, sometimes with animation, sometimes in a desultory way, for the next couple of hours. We pursued dead ends (could another, more sympathetic, buyer be found?) and digressions (what was the precise status of the *garçons* after the strike?) and kept circling around the central point. We needed to show Bucher that we were in earnest about opening another Balzar, in order to get him to, perhaps, perpetuate the current one. Like all public meetings of "causes," this one had a curious sideways, crab-walking momentum of its own. Somehow, the notion that we ought to show Bucher we were serious metamorphosed into the idea that the only way to show him that we were was to ask for a subscription of some real but small sum—say, six hundred francs, about a hundred dollars—from all the members of the association, which in turn metamorphosed into the idea that we ought to put the *idea* of the

subscription to a vote of the membership. We voted on this res-
olution, and it passed.

The whole thing made no sense at all, as we all knew perfectly
well the moment we left the classroom and went back out into
the cold early winter air and headed for the Métro. The sum involved was both ridiculously small—Bucher was hardly about to
be intimidated by it—and at the same time sufficiently noxious
to keep a lot of people from wanting to offer it up. (I did not look
forward to explaining to my own wife that we needed to pony up
a hundred dollars in order to open up a new brasserie.) And to
put it to a vote simply attenuated things still more. It was one of
those bizarre decisions that are arrived at in protest meetings by
a process of drift and uncertainty, in which a backwater suddenly
for a moment looks like the way to the blue ocean and then, even
when only moments later everybody knows that it's a dead end,
we still close our eyes and pretend that we are going somewhere.

I do not want to give the impression that once the drama and
steak au poivre had been removed from our movement, it lost
momentum or seriousness. The classroom was full; the debate
was intense; the purpose was firm. It was just that the strongest
part of our case was its presentation, and once we moved away
from our proscenium, there was not very much we could do. We
had moved in a single November night from ideology to politics—from what you *want* to what you do—with the usual disap-
pointing results. "We have gone from '68 to '81 tonight," a friend
sighed in my ear as we walked home. He meant that we had gone
from utopian vision and slogans to the realities of the assumption
of power, or from Mao (the make-believe French Mao) to Mitterrand.

I walked all the way home from the Twelfth, across at the
Gare d'Austerlitz and then all the way along by the river. It was a
cold night, winter really, and the few leaves left on the trees shiv-
ered sympathetically above, like waiters carrying trays.

On November 30, that Tuesday, we met with M. Bucher early in the morning at La Coupole, the vast twenties brasserie that he owns down on the boulevard du Montparnasse. It was eight-thirty in the morning—much too early, we all agreed—but that had been M. Bucher's hour, and we did not want to change it, I suppose for fear of seeming sluggish.

Bucher was as agreeable as ever. This time, though, instead of the short sleeves and open shirt that he had worn at our first breakfast together at the Balzar, he wore a suit and tie, pressed tightly over his belly. He began by smiling and shrugging and making the significant admission that maybe M. Delouche, the new maître d', was the wrong man to be fronting the Balzar. He complained again about the *médiatisation,* meaning, I think, M. Quélin and *Le Monde,* which Lorenzo agreed had been unfortunate, but then pressed on to his hard, blunt point: The *garçons* will leave with a fat envelope, and that's it.

"They drove the old owner into the bushes like a hunted animal," he says scornfully. "Not me. All this"—he meant the war of the *garçons*—"belongs to another century." He caught himself, knowing that he mustn't seem too harsh, too "liberal." "But you know, on reflection, that's why I like it. I value it. That's why I want to be a member of your organization."

He agreed, after much tender pushing by Lorenzo, to meet himself with the *garçons.* The strike had shocked him. "Ninety-five percent of my media is about Balzar and point two percent of my business. Listen, I'll talk to them, I'll try to make them happy. But if they want to leave with a fat envelope, they can leave." He swore, forcefully, that there are no tour groups admitted to the Balzar.

Then Bucher did something, amazingly, intuitively shrewd. Before he had always spoken of the alternative to his ownership as McDonald's—"Listen, if you don't want me, maybe McDonald's will take over"—and we knew this to be pure rhetoric; McDonald's was not about to take over the Balzar, in the first place, and in any case, McDonald's bashing of that kind was too generalized, too vague an ideological gesture to have any weight. It was a purely rhetorical turn, recognizable as such. But now he turned to another potential owner.

"Listen," he said, "I hear you'd like me to sell. OK. Maybe you want me to sell out to M. Conran? I'm sure he would love it." Terence Conran is the English restaurateur and furniture tycoon who a few weeks before had just opened his own new brasserie, L'Alcazar, over on the rue Mazarin. It was the first attempt by a major figure of the London cooking renaissance to establish a beachhead in Paris, and it had been getting a lot of press.

Bucher shrugged. "I think he has nothing to teach us about how to run a brasserie. I'm trying to defend a 'Franco-Français' tradition but . . ."

A little of the air seemed to pass right out of our movement at that moment. The anti-Americanism that lent a piquant, alarming note to the Balzar wars had been, as anti-Americanism most often is in France, not quite real, an abstract idea, a speech act with very few barbs in it. (Lorenzo, Claude, and I had once had a long debate, over dinner, about the relative merits of John Coltrane, whose pianist, McCoy Tyner, Lorenzo's brother had studied with, and Cannonball Adderley, favored by Claude.) Anti-Americanism in France at the end of the twentieth century is in fact in some ways like anti-Catholicism in England in the nineteenth century. It is a powerful, important, influential, official doctrine, but it is also not entirely real: English people imprecated against the Catholics and the pope, but that didn't stop them from loving Venice, traveling to Florence, worshiping Raphael, and filling their houses with Italian pictures. Even the much-publicized fusses about American mass-produced food and French peasants "trashing" McDonald's are almost pure media events. The French farmers knock down a McDonald's for the benefit of the French media, which publicize it in *Le Monde* in order to see what *The New York Times* will have to say about it the next day. Anti-Americanism has enormous life as an abstract ideological principle and a closed circle of media events of this kind, but outside of a tiny circle on the elite left and, surprisingly, a slightly larger one on the elite right, it has almost no life as a real emotion. But suspicion of the English is a permanent feature of the French psyche. Anti-English sentiment in France is like anti-French sentiment in nineteenth-century England: inarticulate but real. Those people just annoy the hell out of you. This contempt for the English, as opposed to the love-hate relation with Americans, is seen, for instance, in the almost open disdain that the French press has displayed in its investigation of the death of Diana Spencer, as it prefers to call her. Or at a more obscure level it can be seen in the magazine *Le Point,* which is usually pro-American in the neutral, hidden sense (it runs endless reviews of American music and movies and television), but when it ran a cover story on the British invasion of the Dordogne, the story was full of mistrust and contempt.

So for Bucher to say that McDonald's was coming was a mere ideological gesture, instantly seen as one. But to say that he could sell out to Terence Conran was to speak to a real, and completely annoying, possibility. Afterward, when our committee gathered in a café across the street from La Coupole, with two new members of the group—whom I didn't know but whom Lorenzo had invited along after the meeting earlier that week, Lorenzo having a good left democrat's desire to keep the leadership in touch with the masses—we all felt unhappy. The two new guys were sure that there was a *complot* of some kind, a hidden history, that was being kept from them. Discussing the possibility of our new Balzar, they also seemed unable to accept the logic of capitalism in any form, including one we would own ourselves.

Above all, they were offended by the very existence, the very idea, even in a purely hypothetical form, of Terence Conran. "I wouldn't go to England and give them lessons on making tea," one of them said, bitterly. Lorenzo, I thought, looked unsettled.

It was around that time that I finally went to have lunch with J.-P. Quélin, the biting food critic of *Le Monde*. I was almost, though not quite, an official emissary from the friends of the Balzar to him, hoping that he would tone it down a little. We went to Aux Fins Gourmets, the Basque bistro downstairs from our apartment, where I have been going for several years now and where, to my surprise, Quélin had never been.

Quélin turned out to be from central casting. (But then we are all from central casting: I' running down, without extra forethought, from the apartment, in sneakers and sweater and beige Levi's, and at my age too.) He was wearing what I have come to think of as the Uniform, the standard gear of French journalists who still see themselves as men of letters: black and beige houndstooth jacket, white cotton shirt, black knit tie. He has a perfect hatchet face, a long jaw, a clear enunciation, and he smoked American cigarettes square in the middle of his mouth. He looked nearly exactly like Ian McKellen playing Richard III.

I came in, took my table, and noticed him, thinking, This can't be J.-P. Quélin; he looks much too characteristic for that. But of course, it was, and he smiled, sardonically, and pointed: So it is you. He had invited along his editor, who turned out to be a lovely, worried-looking, square-built blonde—a mum (French writers and their editors, Frenchmen and their mums). He was brutal with the waiters and decided at last on *haricot de mouton* and a bottle of Madiran. I had sworn to have an *omelette* and no wine at all, but took the wine as a challenge to my—well, if not to my masculinity then to my Franco assimilation, my right to live in Paris and call myself a writer.

We talked about cooking and restaurants. "There is an Anglo-Saxon contempt for French food and a love for it all the same," Jean-Pierre Quélin began. I tried, tactfully, to argue that while the top heights of French cuisine remain unique—Passard, Gagnaire—the everydays might be more pleasurable now in New

York or even London. He was dubious about the second proposition but agreed about the first: They are cooking, he says, at a level of originality that defies judgment, defies criticism, defies the grammar of cuisine. (This, I think, is true. When I took my brother to L'Arpège for his birthday, we got fourteen [small] courses, mostly of vegetables—*haricots verts* with peaches and raw almonds dressed with basil and fresh mint; fresh shell beans with onion ravioli and tomato coulis—that made even the best of old cuisine look like sludge.)

We kept pouring the Madiran, and to my alarm, a second bottle followed the first. I saw the afternoon's work disappearing. In voicing my own tentative criticisms of the state of French cooking—mild and commonplace—I realized that Quélin was completely insulated from the general opinion that the new Mediterranean synthesis that reigns in New York and London is simply the thing and that the French two-tier system—three stars for the millionaires and occasions; the same old same old forever elsewhere—is defunct. He just had never heard the idea. I didn't even try to convince him otherwise, though, not that I could.

Quélin's editor left and, the bottle still there, we began confiding—no, not confiding, engaging in that level of frank, let's-call-a-Medusa's-head-a-Medusa's-head honesty that is one of the pleasures of the end of a two-bottle lunch in Paris. We shared philosophical reflections on our sons, our lives, the impossibility of journalism. "The voluptuous cruelty of filling pages," he said, "the voluptuous cruelty of filling pages is what kills us." We talked about his time in the army in Algeria, when a Breton peasant under his command tried to rape a local girl. He stopped him, and the peasant drew his revolver: "I looked death, in all its absurdity and horror, right in the face for fifteen minutes." Then we talked about our sons. The day will come when they condescend to us, when they feel themselves to be our intellectual superiors, "and in that moment of pity we will find our pride."

It occurred to me then that the paradoxes that litter French writing are deeply felt among all French literary people. The pity and pride of paternity; the absurdity and profundity of death, the voluptuous cruelty of journalism—these antinomies are not affectations but part of a real heritage of feeling. They *mean* it. In my heart, I suppose, I don't believe that something *can* be horrible and beautiful; I am too American for that, though I suppose I believe that something can be voluptuous and cruel. A child of the occupation—his father escaped twice from prison camps, to see him as a baby—and the Algerian War, he knows in his blood that it is so, that life is damnably double, whichever way it falls. It may be an affectation, but it is not a pose.

Over the third bottle—a title for a French memoir—I tried out my pet theory: that France is marked by a struggle between its pompous official culture and its matchless vernacular, commonplace civilization—and that what makes France unique is that so much of the pompous, abstract, official culture has spilled over into the popular "culture," so that every man sees himself as an aphorist, his own Montaigne in his own tower. He pointed at me again. "That," he said dramatically, "is an idea of merit. You must write it up for us in the context of cuisine." I said that I would try.

When the bill came, he handed the waiter his *carte bleu* and was told, as I knew he would be, that they don't take cards. Without looking up again at the waiter, he reached into his wallet and handed him his *Le Monde* press card. "Send it to me," he said icily, meaning the bill. The insolence was enormous. Not even an essay at a smile. Afterward, as we left, he searched out the thin, intellectual owner of the restaurant, Michel, who had been giving us the same indulgent, fixed half-smile for three years and told him that he admired his *navarin*. Michel looked at him with hungry gratitude and then at me with disbelief—*this* one brought *this* one?—and I looked back at him in quiet, sneaker-bound triumph.

That Wednesday I appeared in Quélin's column in *Le Monde,* as a *brave joyeusement américain* who had introduced him to the bistro where they still know how to master the difficult art of the *navarin,* etc. Later on that year I even made a second appearance, at Quélin's invitation, and under my own byline, explaining my theory about civilization and culture in France and even making a terrible French pun on the words *moss* and *mass.*

Quélin never again made fun of the friends of the Balzar, so I feel that this diplomatic negotiation had, at least, been well conducted. At the end of the lunch, though, I wasn't just muzzy but absolutely knocked cold by the Madiran. I went back upstairs and slept for two hours.

|||

And then it was over, all over by Christmas. One by one, the *garçons* each decided to take the "fat envelope" Bucher was offering them, and retire. They had to. There was nothing we could do. We walked into the Balzar one December evening, and everyone—Jean-Michel, Claude, Robert—was gone, gone for good. They had decided to take the fat envelope—just how fat it was I'm not sure, though it was said to be about a year's salary, in addition, of course, to their pensions—and go. Only two of the old *garçons* remained. We had lost.

Guy, who remained, spoke to me under his breath, sadly, as we shook hands, defeated. "A handful of cherries," he said softly. "They gave them a handful of cherries for a lifetime of work. What can I do? I want to work for a while longer."

I felt blue. Without the regular guys it was not the same place. They had an English menu now, and they forced it on me when they heard me speak in English to Luke. I told them to take it away and bring me the proper menu. The new *garçon* looked haughty and insulted.

I spoke to Lorenzo and Claude on the phone that week, and everyone agreed that this was the best thing for everyone: There was no sense in allowing the personnel to hang on waiting for some quixotic scheme for a new Balzar to hatch—though, they both added quickly, hatch it might, hatch it might. We rung off.

I stopped going to the Balzar. The food was fine, I was told, and I would still send visiting Americans there. But I no longer loved it, and without Jean-Pierre welcoming us, it was not the same place. Fortunately a good cookbook had appeared—by the American Daniel Young—with a couple of Balzar recipes that I liked, and I would stay home and make them for my family on Sundays: *gigot d'agneau avec flageolets* and profiteroles.

Then, one night at the beginning of May, I got a call from Claude. How was Madame and the *héritier*? Fine, fine, how was he? Oh, it was going for him. Listen, he said, the old guys had decided to come together for a night and give a dinner of their own for the people who had helped them in their fight. They would love to have us. Could we join them? Yes, of course, I said. We wouldn't miss it for the world. He gave me the date a couple of weeks off, at the end of May, and the address of a restaurant up in the Ninth, the Relais Beaujolais. The owner was a friend and was glad to be hosting the dinner.

By then Martha was already five months pregnant and very big, and it was a hot and humid night. It was a nice place, though, and we arrived at eight-thirty. There were two or three big tables set up, with familiar faces all around them. Everyone was there: Claude and Guy and Lorenzo. . . . All the *garçons* of course were in plain clothes, jeans and short-sleeve shirts mostly. There was a lot of chilled Beaujolais and a dinner of *pièce de boeuf chasseur*, roast beef in a mushroom-wine sauce.

The startling and instructive thing was that the *garçons* seemed, on the whole, happy, free, and content. They were genuinely philosophical, in the old-fashioned sense, about what had happened—meaning stoic but articulate. They could see their own situation against a broader background.

I sat across from Robert, one of the oldest of the old *garçons*, a small, mustached man in his late fifties. "A handful of cherries?" he said when I repeated, a little dolefully, Guy's comment. "Perhaps. But a handful of cherries is better than an empty hand." He was in a rust-colored short-sleeve shirt, and his mustache was turning white. "Anyway, it is only in moments of crisis that we find lucidity about ourselves—though only after the crisis is over. Still, that's enough lucidity for anyone. Anyway, it is all the lucidity that life will give you. The crucial thing is that it was *our choice*. We made it. We *chose* to leave. I'm rather old to do this. The younger fellows . . . but it's over, we made a good choice. And it was *our* choice."

We talked about more general subjects: Corsica, the Clinton affair. "We can't understand your society," he said, shaking his head, "at once so violent and so puritanical, so authoritarian and so anarchist." But of course, it turned out that he had someone, a son, in America, who was always inviting him over. He had been once and was going to go again. He liked it there.

"I love to study the problem of being," he added abruptly, and he told a long and tragic story about one of the other personnel, a maître d' who had worked at the Balzar once, whose daughter, the light of his life, had committed suicide. Her father could not stop thinking of it and talking about it, all the time, his grief so deep, while he gave orders and cleaned tables. Though I knew him, in my callowness I had never sensed the tragedy of this man.

"His problem," Robert went on gravely, "was that he could not arrive at an abstraction of himself, only at a version of *me*, a me in some other form. He could not see himself as he was, see himself from outside himself. He was trapped in himself from the failure to make himself into an abstraction."

I looked up. Lorenzo was shaking hands and I could see was being urged to make a speech, a toast, but he was politely declining, smiling and shaking his head. *La guerre est finie.*

"That's a formidable guy," Robert said, nodding at Lorenzo. "Once he is wound up, ah, he can go on brilliantly, passionately. And Claude too. We were lucky to have them."

I thought the most irritating thing about life in France, as I had described it so sapiently to the readers of *Le Monde*—the insistence on the primacy of the unspecific, on turning things into abstractions of themselves at every turn—was a gift. The civilization I had praised, and the culture exasperated me, and by civilization, I had meant small shops, and by culture, big buildings. In the end, though, the small shops were special in Paris because they were always in the shadow of the big buildings. Take the small shops away (and the streets the shops sit on and the *quartiers* that the streets sit in) and you would have nothing—not René Clair or Trenet and Lartigue or the whole of this great and beautiful bourgeois civilization. But take away the big buildings, with their abstract ideas and grand manner, and the special quality of the Parisian shops—of the brasseries and cafés, of the glass houses and glass domes—their quality of being the stage sets of a modern drama, something more than just shops, would go too. The lucidity of Parisian empiricism was bought at the price of the grandiosity of Parisian abstraction, and you couldn't have one without the other, no matter how much you wanted to or how hard you tried.

We finished dinner, and I asked the owner—who had been up on a ladder most of the night, fussing with the single unworking fan that was supposed to cool off the entire *salle*—to call us a cab. My wife was large and easily tired. But just as the owner came to tell us that the cab had arrived, Claude at last rose and began to make a presentation to Lorenzo of a single immense, earthenware tray. "A gift of friendship," he said, "of simple friendship."

Lorenzo Valentin rose to his feet reluctantly, hugged Claude, and began to sit down. "No, say something, say something," everyone said. He shook his head again. People began to pound the tables, as they had done at the Balzar a year ago. Now he was on his feet again, and I could see that he was about to begin.

It seemed like a good moment for us to slip away to the taxi, and we got up and tried to duck our heads down and go back up the stairs to the front room and the street. But Claude saw us going and cried out and called for a round of applause.

I stopped and turned and bowed. I had fallen in love all over again that night with the lucidity and intelligence of Parisian civilization, and I said, in my ornate, brutally accented, abstract French that we were leaving so precipitously simply to defend the health of one more child who would—that there would be a child who would be, to be born in Paris, and who would love Paris too—who would in some way be French. It was playing to the gallery, I suppose, but it got a round of applause, and I still tell myself they meant it.

We went out into the street, found the taxi waiting in the rain, and went home. From the street, as I helped Martha into the cab, I could hear the first murmur of Lorenzo's voice, rising in interrogation, just one last time, to inquire about the complexities of ownership, the love of a *lieu*, the hold of memory, and the meaning of possession, as it is felt both by the possessor and by the possessed.

|||

I was so overtaken by the excitement of the strike and the action, and then I was so happily filled with a sense of moral indignation, and self-righteous pleasure, that I kept away from the Balzar, and for a while I didn't miss it at all. As generations of French revolutionaries have discovered, moral self-righteousness is a very good short-term substitute for pleasure, but it wears out. Now I realize that the Balzar still exists on the rue des Écoles and that I have lost it for good, and I think about the light coming in on a spring night, and the way the waiters took the food from the oval platters to the circular plates, and the simple *poulet roti*, and how good it all was, and I miss it all the time.

Like a King

When we discovered that the child we were going to have in Paris last fall would be a girl—we already have a boy—everybody told us that we had been blessed with the *choix du roi*, the king's choice. "Why, it's the *choix du roi*!" the technician said as she looked at the sonogram, more or less in the tone of the host on *Jeopardy!* announcing the Daily Double. "It's the *choix du roi*!" said the woman in the two-hour photo place on the rue du Bac when we told her. "A little girl coming after a little boy?" said my friend Pascal, the philosopher, with evident pleasure. "Why, then, it's the *choix du roi*!"

Martha was delighted to be having a girl, however the king felt about it. She had always wanted a son and a daughter, and as she only now explained to me, one of the reasons she had been so eager to leave New York four years earlier, just after the birth of our son, was that all her friends there who had two children had two boys, and she was starting to believe that two boys were just one of the things that happened to women in New York, "like high-intensity step classes and vanilla Edensoy," as she put it. Also, she said, she was worried about having to succumb to the New York social law that compels you nowadays to name your sons exclusively after the men your grandfather used to take a *shvitz* with. In our New York circle of under-tens we already had, in addition to the requisite Maxes, a Harry, a Joe, a Sam, an Otto, and a Charlie—the whole senior staff of Benny's Market: Lowest Prices in Town. "Even if I had had another boy, at least in Paris I wouldn't have had to call him Moe," she explained.

I was pleased by the news too, of course, but a little mystified by the expression. To be brutally frank, what mystified me was why a king would choose to have any girls at all. If I were a king, I would want only boys, so that the succession would never be challenged by the sinister uncle with a mustache lurking behind my throne. Or only girls and an immortality pill. What puzzled me even more was the way the phrase, though you heard it on Parisian lips, had a slightly disconcerting air of peasants-in-the-spring ecstasy about it, the kind of thing ("*C'est le choix du roi!*") you would expect to hear set to a Trenet tune and sung by the villagers in a Pagnol film when the baker's daughter gives birth to little Lisette.

I soon sensed, though, that while people meant it, they also didn't mean it, that it was a thing you said both as a joke and not as a joke. After four years in Paris I have come to realize that this is where the true cultural differences reside: not in those famous moments when you think that a joke was meant straight ("My goodness, the *dessert grand-mère* is not made by Grandmother!"), or you misunderstand something that was meant straight as a joke ("The *tête de veau* is actually the head of a calf!"), but in those moments when you are confronted with something that is meant both as a joke and seriously. This zone of kidding overlaid with not kidding is one that we know at home. When a New Yorker passes out cigars in the office after the birth of his child,

for instance, he is both making a joke about passing out cigars—
with unspoken but quickly grasped reference to all the episodes
of *Bewitched* and *I Love Lucy* in which Darrin or Desi or some
other fifties-ish father passed out cigars—and sincerely celebrat-
ing the birth of his child. (The proof of this doubleness is that
the cigars he passes out will actually be good to smoke, while
mockery would make do with a bad or unsmokable cigar. Nobody tried to eat Warhol's soups.)

In Paris, the obstetricians all wear black. When your wife goes
to be examined, the doctor who comes out into the waiting room
is not a smart Jewish girl in a lab coat, as in New York, but a man
with a day's growth of beard, who is wearing black jeans and a
black silk shirt, like a character in a David Mamet play about
Hollywood producers.

I first became aware of this when we went to get the first of
many sonograms of the new baby. The sonogramist we had been
sent to performs in a nineteenth-century apartment in the Sixth
Arrondissement, with wainscoting and ceiling moldings and windows that open like doors. A curtain was drawn across one half
of the living room, and couples sat on two sofas in the other half,
turning the pages of *Elle* (*Elle* is a weekly in France) and waiting
to be called.

After about ten minutes the curtain parted, and the sonogram
specialist came into the room. He had on black jeans and a black
silk shirt, open at the front and plunging down toward his navel,
sleeves rolled up to the elbows. A day-old growth of beard covered his face. He smiled at us and asked us to come in. We sat
down in front of a handsome Louis XV desk—the sonogram
equipment was over in the other corner of the office—and he
asked us when the baby had been conceived. My wife gave him
the likely date.

"Was that at night or early the next day?" he asked. It took me
a moment to realize that he was kidding, and then another moment to realize that he was not, and then still another moment—

the crucial cultural gap moment—to realize that he was neither kidding nor not kidding. That is to say, he was kidding—he knew that it didn't matter—but he was not kidding in the sense that he was genuinely interested, considered that it was part of his profession to view that precise moment of passion or lust with a special tenderness. The moment of conception, the sexual act, was, in his schema, not incidental information to be handled discreetly or pushed aside altogether, as American obstetricians do—all American "What to Expect" books begin with the test, not the act—but the prime moment, the hallowed moment, the first happy domino that, falling, caused all the other dominoes that had brought the three of us together to fall, and (his eyes implied) it was our special shared knowledge that that domino had not in fact fallen but had been nudged, deliberately, and by us. Then he asked Martha to get undressed. There was, to my surprise, no changing room or even a curtain, so she did, like that. (I was the only embarrassed person in the room.) The elaborate hospital rigmarole of American hygiene and American obstetrics—the white coats, the dressing rooms, the lab gowns—is dispensed with. They make no sense, since a pregnant woman is not only not sick but in a sense has doubled the sum of her health.

We looked at the baby on the sonar screen, as though she were a character in a Tom Clancy novel. "She's pretty," he said at last. Then we got a package of fifteen or so pictures of our daughter in embryo, full of allure, as the receptionist said. The pictures were stapled, in neat, ruffled rows, into a little wallet, with sans serif lowercase type, like an e. e. cummings poem.

"In New York the obstetricians all wear white, and they all have books out," Martha said to me one afternoon. She had called up an obstetrician in New York that day, before her appointment with her French doctor. "She covered me with congratulations, and then she told me all these tests I ought to take. Week ten the CVS, then in week fourteen an early amnio, and then in weeks eighteen to twenty a targeted ultrasound to test for neural tube defects, and then I'm supposed to get genetic carrier blood tests for all these other things."

"What did the French obstetrician say when you told her that?"

"She made that 'oh' face—you know, that lips-together, 'How naive can one be?' face—said that it was far too dangerous to do the CVS, and then she prescribed a lot of drugs for pain. I've got antispasmodics, antinausea drugs, painkillers, and some other ones too. Then she told me I could drink red wine and absolutely not to eat any raw vegetables. She keeps asking me if I've had any salad. She says 'salad' the way the doctors in New York say 'uninsured.' "

French doctors like to prescribe drugs as much as New York doctors like to publish books. I suppose that it fulfills a similar need for self-expression with a pen, without having to go to the trouble of having your photograph taken with a professional yet humane grin. You cannot go into a French doctor's office for a cinder in your eye and emerge without a six-part prescription, made up of pills of different sizes to be taken at irregular intervals.

I wanted to meet Martha's doctor, who would be delivering the baby while I "coached"—I am of the Phil Jackson school as a coach; you might not actually see me doing much, but I contribute a lot to the winning atmosphere—and so I accompanied her to the next appointment. We sat in the waiting room and read *Elle* some more. By now Martha was nervous. An American friend who lives in Normandy had gone into labor a few days before, only to find that all the anesthesiologists had gone out on strike that morning. She had delivered the baby, her second, without any epidural.

"I want to go to a place where the anesthesiologists are scabs," Martha said. "Or nuns or something. I don't want to go to a place where the man with the epidural is on a picket line."

While we were in the waiting room, a man in black jeans and a black silk shirt with the sleeves rolled up, and with a Pat Riley hairstyle, peeked in and mischievously summoned one of the women in the waiting room.

"Who's that?" I asked.

"The other obstetrician," Martha said.

"Does he always dress like that?" I demanded.

"Oh, yes. He's very nice. He examined me last time."

Martha's doctor was wearing black stretch slacks, a black tank top, and a handsome gold necklace. She was very exacting about appearances. "You have gained too much weight," she said to Martha, who had in fact gained less than with her first pregnancy. "Start swimming, stop eating." (Martha says that a friend who went for an appointment two months after the birth of her second baby was told by the same doctor, "You look terrible. And do something about your hair.") We did another sonogram. "Look at her, she's pretty," the doctor said as we looked at the sonogram. "There's her *fille*," she said, pointing to the sex. Then she again counseled Martha to swim more and gave her a prescription for sleeping pills. We talked a bit about the approach of those hard, exhausting first weeks with a newborn. "Get a night nurse," she advised. "Go out with your husband. Be happy again."

In New York, in other words, pregnancy is a medical condition that, after proper care by people in white coats and a brief hospital stay, can have a "positive outcome." In Paris it is something that has happened because of sex, which, with help and counsel, can end with your being set free to go out and have more sex. In New York pregnancy is a ward in the house of medicine; in Paris it is a chapter in a sentimental education, a strange consequence of the pleasures of the body.

In America, we have managed to sexualize everything—cars, refrigerators, computers, Congress—except the natural consequences of sex. Though it is de rigueur for every pregnant supermodel to have her picture taken when she is full-bellied, it is always the same picture. She covers her breasts, she is swaddled below in some way, and she looks off into the middle distance, not dreamily, as she might when wearing lingerie, but slightly anxiously, as though she could not remember if she had left her husband's electric guitar turned on. The subject, the hidden subject, is not the apotheosis of sexuality but its transcendence into maternal instinct: babe into mother by way of baby.

In France, though, a pregnant woman is alive, since she has demonstrated both her availability and her fecundity: We Have a Winner. Though Lamaze method childbirth began here, it remains cultish and sectarian. Most women nurse for three months, no more. (It shrinks your breasts and gives you an uncomfortable accessory.) And when the anesthesiologists are not striking, they are, as our baby-sitter says, fully busy. (Two French friends of ours talk about natural childbirth: "What is the English for *accouchement sans douleur*?" one asks. "A lie," the other answers.)

The prohibition on uncooked vegetables, by the way, turns out to have a solid scientific basis. Toxoplasmosis—a mild parasitic infection that is devastating to unborn children—though it's rare in America (it's that thing you can get from cat litter), is common in France. Red wine is recommended, in turn, because it is high in iron and acts as an effective antispasmodic.

By law a French woman who is going to have a baby is guaranteed—not merely allowed but pretty much compelled—to stay four or five nights in a clinic or a hospital. In New York, when our son, Luke, was born—in the Klingenstein Pavilion of Mount Sinai Hospital—we had two days to have the baby, bond, and get out. French law is specific and protective about the rights of pregnant women. If you are a salaried employee, you get six weeks of prenatal leave and ten weeks of paid leave after the baby is born. For a third child, you get eight weeks off and eighteen more, and if you have three at once, you get, in all, forty-six weeks of paid leave. (The leave is paid, through a complicated formula, by your employer and the state.) The law is as finely tuned as a viola d'amore. There is even a beautiful added *remarque,* right there on the government document: *"Les artistes du spectacle, les mannequins des maisons de couture,"* and others who do work that is plainly incompatible with the state of pregnancy (i.e., a bigger belly) are assured of paid leave after the twenty-first week. In France, Cindy and Paulina and the rest would not just be having their pictures taken. They would already be on the dole.

The system, Martha's doctor observed once during a visit, is "royal for the users, good for the doctors, and expensive for the society." There are many rational arguments to be made about whether or not the outcomes justify the expenditures, and in any case, the level of care that the French have insisted on may be unsustainable. But the people who are being treated "royally" are ordinary people—everybody. For many, perhaps most, French people, life at the end of the century in the American imperium may look a bit like a typical transatlantic flight, with the airless, roomless, comfortless coach packed as tightly as possible, so that the maximum dollars can be squeezed out of every seat, with a few rich people up front. I am American enough to understand that this is, so to speak, one of the prices of mass travel—that there is no such thing as a free lunch, or clinic—and yet have become French enough to feel, stubbornly, that legroom and a little air should not be luxuries for the rich and that in a prosperous society all pregnant women should have three sonograms and four nights in a hospital, if they want to. It doesn't seem particularly royal to have four nights in a clinic when you have a baby or aristocratically spoiled to think that a woman should keep her job and have some paid leave afterward, even sixteen weeks, if she happens to be a mannequin in an haute couture house. All human desires short of simple survival are luxurious, and a mother's desire to have a slightly queenly experience of childbirth—a lying in rather than a pushing out and a going home—seems as well worth paying for as a tobacco subsidy or another tank.

In preparation for our own four-night stay we had first to search for the right clinic. Friends recommended two: the Clinique Sainte-Isabelle, in the leafy suburb of Neuilly, and the Clinique Belvedere, in Boulogne-Billancourt. We went to tour them. Both clinics had a pastoral, flower bed, medical but not quite hospital feel, like the sanitarium to which they pack off Nicole in *Tender Is the Night*. I liked the Belvedere best. The rooms there had a nice faded white and pale blue look, like the room in *Madeline* where she goes to have her appendix taken out and sees the crack in the ceiling that has a habit of sometimes looking like a rabbit. The cracks in the ceiling at the Belvedere were expressive too, and for a premium you could have a room with French doors leading out onto the garden. (The ordinary rooms were less grand, though they mostly had garden views too.) But what I really liked about the place were the clippings in the formal salon—the waiting room—downstairs, which was filled with dusty silk roses and blue and gold Louis XVI furniture. The clippings chronicled the birth of minor nobility in the halls of the Belvedere. A Bonapartist pretender had been born there, I remember, and also I think a prince of Yugoslavia. I liked the kingly company, particularly since it was such cheesy kingly company.

Martha, though, as we toured the clinics, kept asking gentle, pointed questions about labor relations with the anesthesiologists. Now, the anesthesiologists here—were they unionized? Did they have enough vacation time? Would the clinic manager say that they were happy with their working conditions? How long had it been since they signed a contract? Were there any, well, radicals among them, the kind of ex-Trotskyite *soixante-huitards* who might suddenly call for mass action by the workers? Eventually, we settled on the Clinique Sainte-Isabelle, which seemed to be the sensible, primly bourgeois choice of all our friends and which had a couple of full-time anesthesiologists on call, neither of whom looked like a sansculotte.

Everything was going along fine, in fact, until our meeting

with the *sage-femme*, the wise woman, or, in American, the mid-
wife. She was in yet another of the suburban clinics, an odd
Jacques Tati modern place. This meeting was brisk, and it concentrated on two essential points: breathing and lying. The
breathing bit we had heard about before—you are supposed to
breathe from the diaphragm—but she emphasized that it was
just as important, for a happy birth, to remember never to tell a
taxi driver that you are in labor. Whatever you do, she said, don't
say that you're in labor, or might be in labor, because no taxi
driver in Paris will take a pregnant woman to her clinic, for fear
of her having the baby in his car. (You can't call an ambulance because an ambulance won't go over the city line, and our clinic
was out in Neuilly.)

Then how were we going to get to the clinic? Martha asked.
(We don't have a car.) It's no problem, I interrupted, we'll simply
walk over to the taxi stand. (You can't call a taxi, because there is
a stand right across the street from our apartment.)

"I won't be able to stroll across the street and stand in line if
I'm in labor," she objected. "I'll wait in the courtyard. Just get
him to do the *demi-tour*."

At these words my heart was stricken. *Demi-tour* means literally a U-turn, but in Paris it is also a half-metaphysical possibility that exists on the boulevard Saint-Germain just across the
street from our apartment building. The boulevard itself runs
one-way, from east to west. There is, however, a narrow lane
carved out on it, for buses and taxis, that runs the other way,
toward the place de la Concorde and the quai d'Orsay and, eventually, if you turn right over a bridge, toward Neuilly and the
clinic too. Leading off this lane, at a single light about a hundred
feet from our building, there is a small, discreet curved arrow
marked on the asphalt. This arrow means that a taxicab—and
only a taxicab—can make a U-turn there and go the other way,
with the rest of the traffic. In principle, I could get a cab going
against the traffic, have him do the *demi-tour*, pick up my preg-

nant wife, and then go back against the traffic. The trouble is that, though I have sometimes succeeded in persuading taxi drivers, when we arrive from the airport, to make the *demi-tour,* I have just as often failed. "It's impossible," the cabbie will tell you, when you ask him to do it.

"No, there is an arrow printed on the pavement that advertises the possibility of this maneuver," I will say. (When I'm under stress, my French becomes very abstract.)

"I've been driving a taxi for twenty years, and it doesn't exist," the cabbie will say. Then you either give up or get hot under the collar, and neither approach helps.

If I asked a Paris cabdriver to attempt the *demi-tour* at, say, five in the morning, to pick up a very pregnant-looking woman, he would know that the only reason was that she was in labor, and to the insult of being instructed would come the injury of being asked to ruin his cab.

For the next few weeks I became obsessed by the logic and strategies of the *demi-tour.* What if I couldn't pull it off? The only thing to do was to rehearse, just as we had done in New York in the Lamaze class. So I began walking over to the taxi station at all hours of the day and night, getting in a cab, asking the driver to make the *demi-tour,* and then going, well, someplace or other. Then I walked home. Sometimes the driver made the *demi-tour,* and sometimes he didn't. I was determined to keep practicing, until it felt as natural as breathing.

We still hadn't got to the bottom of the whole *choix du roi* thing. Martha had decided to give in to the obstetrician's insistence that she start swimming, and one day, with Luke, we got into a cab to go to the pool. The taxi driver was wearing a short-sleeved shirt, and had gray hair and a lot of metal teeth. Suddenly he chuckled and said, of Luke, "Why, he speaks so well. Tell me, is it a little sister or a brother?" A sister, we said, and I grimaced and tightened inside as I prepared myself for the response, which, of course, came on cue. "Ah," he said, slapping the steering wheel. *"C'est le choix du roi!"*

I was so fed up that I said, "Please explain it to me." It was an ironic, rhetorical question. But he didn't miss a beat.

"I will be happy to explain it," he said, and he actually pulled over to the curb, near the Crillon Hôtel, so that he could speak in peace. "In Latin countries we have what we call Salic law, which means that only your son can inherit the throne. You Anglo-Saxons, you don't follow Salic law." I let the Anglo-Saxon thing go by. "For your Anglo-Saxon royal families, it doesn't matter if the king has a *nana* or a *mec*." A *nana* is a doll, and a *mec* is a guy. "But you see, a French king, under Salic law, had to consolidate his hold on the throne by having a boy. And he had to have a girl, so that she could be offered in marriage to another king, and in this way the royal possessions would be expanded, since the daughter's son would be a king too. He," he said, gesturing toward Luke in the backseat, "is your strong piece, to be kept in reserve, while she"—he gestured toward Martha's belly— "is your pawn to build your empire. That's why it's the king's choice: first a boy to hold the throne, then a girl to get another. *Tendresse* has nothing to do with it. That is why it is the *choix du roi*.

"It is very odd," he went on expansively, "because in the Hundred Years' War the king of England, as duc de Guyenne, a title he had inherited from his grandfather, was subject to Salic law too. The story of how this worked itself out in the making of the two monarchies is a passionately interesting piece of history. I recommend the series *Les Rois Maudits* [the damned or cursed kings], which is a fascinating study of this history, particularly of the acts of John the Good and what he did as an act of policy to accommodate the Salic principle. The books are by Maurice Druon, of the Académie Française, and I heartily recommend them. Passionately interesting."

We sat in stunned silence.

"Ask him does he do *demi-tours*," said Martha.

"You're wearing stripes?" she asked. I had put on a striped shirt a few minutes before, in the excitement, but I quickly changed it. I put on a suit and tie, in fact—a nice maroon cotton number—thinking that though my New York child had been born with me watching in jeans and a collarless shirt, my French kid ought to see a dad who had a touch more finish.

The drama had begun a few hours earlier, in the middle of the night, and now it was five o'clock and we were on our way to the clinic. At five-thirty, with a baby-sitter for Luke and a suitcase in hand, we were out on the boulevard. I walked to the curb, held my breath, saw that there were cabs at the taxi stand, and, head down, told Martha to wait where she was while I started across the street, preparing to ask a taxi driver to make the *demi-tour*, my moment come at last.

Far down the boulevard, a single cab with a firelight light appeared. Martha stepped out into the street, just as though it were five-thirty in the evening on Sixth Avenue, got her right hand up in that weird New York Nazi taxi salute, and cried, "Taxi!" The guy came skidding to a stop. She got in, and I followed.

"Twenty-four boulevard du Château in Neuilly," I commanded, my voice pitched a little too high (as it also tends to get in French). "Just cross the street and make the *demi-tour*," I added fairly casually, and docilely, at five-thirty in the morning, he swung the cab over to the taxi lane, on other side of the street, and did a full U-turn. He flew along the boulevard. I took the hand of my queen.

"You've got him going the wrong way," she whispered.

He was too. I waited a few blocks and then told him that I had made a mistake, could he turn around and go the other way? He shrugged and did.

When we got to the clinic, it was shut tight, no lights on at all. The advantages of a big hospital up on Madison Avenue became a little clearer. No one was answering the door, a thing I doubt happens much at Mount Sinai. We banged and cried out, "*Allô!*

Is anybody there?" Finally, an incredibly weary-looking *sage-femme*—not our own—wearing sweater and slippers, sighed, let us in, hooked Martha up to an IV, and asked to see our papers. She shuffled through them.

"Where is your blood test for the dossier?" she asked at last.

"The doctor has it," I said. "She'll be here soon."

"That the doctor has it is of no consequence," the nurse said. "If your wife wishes to have an epidural, she must have that paper."

"It's all the way back home," I protested, but of course, nothing doing. It looked as though Martha's epidural, having escaped French syndicalism, was about to be done in by French bureaucracy. Having lived in France long enough to know there was no choice, I found another taxi, rushed all the way home, ran upstairs, tore open the filing cabinet, found the paper, and then took a taxi back, setting some kind of land speed record for trips from central Paris to Neuilly. The *sage-femme* slipped the paper into the dossier, yawned, put the dossier down on a radiator, and nobody ever looked at it or referred to it again.

The labor got complicated, for various reasons—basically the baby at the last moment decided to turn sideways—and Martha's doctor, acting with the quiet sureness that is the other side of Parisian insouciance, did an emergency cesarean. It turned out that behind a small, quaint-looking white door down in the basement there was a bloc—a warren of blindingly white-lit, state-of-the-art operating and recovery rooms. They hadn't shown it to us when we toured the clinic, of course. It seemed very French, the nuclear power plant hidden in the *bocage*.

The baby came out mad, yelling at the top of her lungs. In New York the nurses had snatched the baby and taken him off to be washed behind a big glass nursery window and then had dressed him in prison garb, the same white nightshirt and cap that the hundred other babies in the nursery had on. (The next day there was also an elaborate maximum security procedure of reading off the bracelet numbers of mother and child whenever either one wanted to nurse.) Here, after the *sage-femme* and I had given her a bath, and the *sage-femme* had taped her umbilical remnant, the *sage-femme* turned to me.

"Where are her clothes?" she asked. I said I didn't know, upstairs in the suitcase, I guessed, and she said, "You'd better get them," so I ran up, and came back down to the bloc with the white onesie and a lovely white-and-pink-trimmed baby-style cat suit, which her mother had bought at Bonpoint a few days before. All by myself I carefully dressed the five-minute-old squalling newborn and took her back to her mother, in the recovery room. A day later I would walk the six blocks to the *mairie*, the city hall, of Neuilly-sur-Seine and register her birth. The New York birth certificate had been a fill-in-the-blanks, choose-one-box business, which we had filled in on our way out of the hospital. The French birth certificate was like the first paragraph of a nineteenth-century novel, with the baby's parents' names, their occupations, the years of their births and of their emigration, their residence, and her number, baby number 2365 born in Neuilly in 1999. (It's got a big hospital too.) After that, of course, would come the weeks of exhaustion and 3:00 A.M. feedings, which are remarkably alike from place to place.

But just then, looking at the sleeping mom and the tiny newborn in her arms, I had a genuine moment of what I can only call revelation, religious vision. When people talk about what it is to have a baby, they usually talk about starting over, a clean slate, endless possibility, a new beginning, but I saw that that is not it at all. A birth is not a rebirth. It's a weighty event. A baby is an absolute object of nature *and* an absolute subject of civilization, screaming in her new Bonpoint jumper. Life is nothing but an unchanging sea of nature, the same endless and undifferentiating human wave of lust and pain, and is still subject to a set of tiny cultural articulations and antinomies and dualities and distinctions and hair-splittings so fine that they produce, in the end, this single American baby lying in a French nursery in her own fine new clothes, sipping her sugar bottle. In a telescopic universe, we choose to see microscopically, and the blessing is that what we see is not an illusion but what is really there: a singularity in the cosmos, another baby born in a Paris suburb. The world is a meaningless place, and we are weird, replicating mammals on its surface, yet the whole purpose of the universe since it began was, in a way, to produce this baby, who is the tiny end point of a funnel that goes back to the beginning of time, a singularity that history was pointing toward from the start. That history didn't know it was pointing toward Olivia—and, of course, toward Salome over in the other corner of the nursery and little François just arrived, not to mention Max and Otto and possibly even Moe, just now checking in at Mount Sinai—doesn't change the fact that it was. We didn't know we were pointing to her either, until she got here. The universe doesn't need a purpose if life goes on. You sink back and hear the nurse cooing in French to the mother and child ("Ah, calme-toi, ma biche, ma biche," she says. "Be calm, my doe, my doe," but which one is she talking to?) and feel as completely useless as any other male animal after a birth and, at the same time, somehow serenely powerful, beyond care or criticism, since you have taken part in the only really majestic choice we get to make in life, which is to continue it.

Angels
Dining at the Ritz

When Martha was still pregnant, we decided to join the pool at
the Ritz hotel on the Place Vendôme for eight weeks. We had, as
I've said, thought about it once before, during our adventures at
the Régiment Rouge, but had gotten scared off by the expense
and by all those tea sandwiches on silver platters. For four years
we had been swimming at the public pool of the Sixth Arrondissement near the old Saint-Germain market, a nice place,
with families splashing in one part and solitary fierce-looking
swimmers doing laps in the other—though, like every French
public institution, terribly overcharged with functionaires, in
this case officious, functionary lifeguards. But then the same
friend who had invited us there that first time invited us to the
Ritz pool again, to spend a Sunday away from the August heat.
With Martha pregnant and more or less immobile, we weren't
able to go away anyway, even though everyone in Paris goes away
in August. (The five-week mandatory vacation is part of the in-

heritance of the old Popular Front of the thirties, one of the laws put over by the saintly Socialist leader Léon Blum.) Anyway, we couldn't go anywhere, not with Martha that big, and we were cool and comfortable there at the pool. Paris is hot in August—really, suddenly hot—and not many places are air-conditioned. Even the ones that claim to be *climatisé* are not really air-conditioned as public places are in New York. Instead a trickle of chilly air floats someplace around the baseboards.

The pool at the Ritz hotel in Paris—they actually call the place the Ritz Health Club, in English, although I think this is designed less as a concession to Americans than as a lingering sign of old-fashioned Parisian Anglomania, like calling the Jockey Club in Paris the Jockey Club—is intended to look "Pompeian" in a way that I suppose makes a strong case for Mount Vesuvius and molten lava. There is a high domed skylight, held up by painted Ionic columns with rosettes along their pillars and bordered by a bas-relief frieze of classical figures standing around in a line, as though waiting to check out of the hotel. There is a trompe l'oeil ceiling painting of old Roman bathers looking down at contemporary French swimmers, with more colored architectural drawings of Roman temple fronts decorating the locker rooms and the showers, and, on either side of the pool, two enormous murals of Romans in togas standing around on terraces, all painted in a style someplace between Victorian-Academic and New York Pizzeria.

My favorite detail at the Ritz pool is a pair of mosaics on the bottom of the pool, right where the shallow end starts to incline and deepen a little, of two comely and topless mermaids, with long blond hair—tresses, really—floating off to one side. With one hand they reach down modestly; with the other each holds up one half of the great seal of the Ritz. (Where most mermaids have fishtails that begin at their waists, these mermaids have fishtails that begin only at their shins.) These are real mosaics, by the way, assembled shiny shard by shiny shard, and they probably would be a treasure if they had actually been made by a Roman artisan and dug up by an archaeologist. The line between art and kitsch is largely measured in ruin.

Martha felt cool there, and cool matters a lot to a nine-month pregnant woman. We sat by the edge of the pool in white terry-cloth robes, surrounded by thin rich women with very high hair, who were listlessly turning the pages of magazines and occasionally going into the pool to swim. They swam like nervous poodles, with their heads held high, high, *high*—up out of the water on their long necks, protecting their perfect helmets of hair from the least drop of moisture.

We ate lunch up on the curved terrace overlooking the pool and thought, only with a little guilt, Well, this *is* nice. So we inquired and found that we could get an eight-week nonpeak hours, never-on-Sunday family membership for a lot less than it cost us to rent a cottage in Cape Cod every summer for two weeks—and in Cape Cod, we *work* all day and night, sweeping the sand out of the house and bringing up the laundry and stoking up the grill and then cleaning up the kitchen. So with a slightly nervous sense of extravagance, we decided to subscribe to the Ritz pool for the minimum off-hours "family" membership, a little joke, we assured ourselves, laid at the altar of the old Hemingway-Flanner Paris. I felt a little guilty about it, I guess— I felt a lot guilty about it, really—but I also thought that Léon Blum, all things considered, wouldn't get too mad at me. I gave it a vaguely Socialist feeling; it was our five weeks.

Since our experience at the Régiment Rouge I had been improvising exercise. For a while we had gone running with the rest of the Americans, and the French riot police, around the Luxembourg Gardens. The gardens are filled with busts and statues of writers, which make it easy to mark your progress as a runner. A half lap of the gardens, for instance, takes you right to a bust of Sainte-Beuve, the good literary critic whom Proust attacked; the two-thirds point is marked by another bust, this one of

Baudelaire; and then finally, completing the circuit, you go past the Delacroix monument, with angels looking up admiringly at his haughty, mustachioed head. At the start I could do a Baudelaire and then, after a couple of months' practice, two full Delacroix's, not bad. The trouble was that the great men seemed to look out disdainfully from their pedestals at the absurdity of Americans running today in order to run more tomorrow. Get drunk instead, Baudelaire seemed to counsel, intelligently, with his scowl. Eventually we bought a stationary bike, and I tried to do twenty-four minutes a day on it, re-creating the conditions of the New York Health and Racquet Club on Thirteenth Street, more or less in the dubious, perverse spirit of a British lieutenant wearing flannel and drinking tea at five o'clock in the Sahara. I had even bought a pair of dumbbells.

After a couple of weeks, though, Martha was too big to do much of anything, and then Olivia Esmé Claire, our beautiful little girl, was born. But we still had six weeks to work out on the membership, so Luke Auden and I kept going. I was nervous and interested. I associated the Ritz with a kind of high life that makes me uneasy, and this is not because I do not like expensive and "exclusive" pleasures, but because I do, and always feel unskilled in their enjoyment. I knew that the Ritz in Paris had once been dashing and elegant but also knew that now there was, as with so many old places of luxury, a note of unhappy rootlessness to the place. It was the capital of the non-Paris Paris. It had what we would have called at my high school bad karma. While we were living in Paris, it had been the place where Pamela Harriman had passed out—"I go badly," she had said, and went—and where Princess Diana too had left on that last car trip. English politicians in particular seemed to come to grief there; one prominent MP, I had vaguely heard, had spent a night, had it paid for by the wrong person, and lost his reputation. There was about it now, for all that it was still frequented by high-living Parisians, a note less of old Parisian high life than of new, late-century overclass big money, with big money's unhappiness about it, that high-strung video surveillance watchfulness of the very, very rich. I liked arriving at the Ritz and having a little *commis* in uniform spin the revolving door for me, but I was always worried about the way I looked when he did. I am hedonistic but not at all heedless, a bad combination. I watch the meter in the limousine, the revolving door as it spins.

Luke of course took it for granted, as children take all things. He learned to swim there, first backstroke, then "frontstroke." I felt a vague feeling of paternal pride about him, though I hadn't really taught him. Just dropped him in, really.

Then something really nice, genuinely terrific happened. Earlier that year, at the school he went to at the American Church, he had fallen in love. The little girl was named Cressida Taylor. She was the dish, the girl he had said was "quite a dish." (I had finally tracked the expression down to a three-hour compilation of Warner Brothers' *Looney Tunes* from the forties that we had bought for him. Bugs Bunny says it about, well, about a dish.) I met her at the school, and she *was* quite a dish, the most beautiful five-year-old girl I have ever seen. She had fair skin, and high blue eyes, and two long golden braids of hair, mermaid tresses, really, and an Audrey Hepburn voice, that elegant, piping voice of children who have been raised in both French and English. (Her mother was a sensible Englishwoman, and her father, I think, some kind of French banker.)

Unquestionably a dish, she was also a peach. It had been Cressida who had finally gotten Luke past the nap crisis at school, generously holding his hand when the teachers would insist that the children "take a rest" and he would go into a panic. She had come over to play a few times. (No one used the expression *play date* in Paris. Kids just came over, played, and then their mothers picked them up and took them home.) They played intensely, and there was, I thought, fondly, a kind of Gilberte and Marcel quality to their playing. They just *played,* you see, and all the other things that pass between boys and girls just passed, without comment or too much oversight from their parents. Martha was relieved at least. In love with her son, she was already worried about the woman who would take him away, and I think that she would have betrothed them on the spot, like seventeenth-century royalty, if she could have. But Cressida had left his school, and now we saw her, wistfully, only every now and again.

On that memorable Wednesday afternoon Luke and I went to the pool. Though he liked to swim, he went, to my puzzlement, mostly to take home the little shower caps that were placed all around the locker rooms. They were just shower caps, but they came in blue cardboard boxes, with the Ritz coat of arms printed in gold on them, and he would sneak home ten or eleven at a time, tucking them under his arms, hiding them in the pockets of his white terry-cloth *peignoir*, and then sticking them in his jacket—why and to what end, I was never sure.

We were strangers at the Ritz. I was nervous, self-conscious about seeming too loud or too American. "Let's kiss the mermaids," Luke would insist, every time we went swimming, and though they were scarcely five feet down, within easy dive-and-kiss distance, I never could. I was too self-conscious about splashing a lot on my way down, my flattish feet waving, and about what the ladies with the tall hair would think about it. Luke couldn't do it either, since five feet was still far too deep for him to go, but he tried, manfully, and didn't care if he splashed or not.

On this Wednesday, though, after the furtive theft of a few shower caps, and the endless irritating "Please stand *still!*" of a father changing a kid into his swim trunks, we got to the pool. Normally he couldn't wait to jump in, but now he stood utterly still at the edge of the water. I saw his small, skinny body in the madras trunks stiffen, and then he got a shy, embarrassed smile on his face and backed away.

"Daddy, look," he whispered.

"What?" I said.

"Daddy, look," he repeated urgently, still under his breath. "It's Cressida."

It was too. *And* the most beautiful thing I had ever seen, right there in the middle of the Paris Ritz pool. She was floating as elegantly as an angel, just above the mermaids, a little on her side, her long blond braids trailing in the water behind her. I think my heart stopped a little bit at that moment too.

Luke's certainly had stopped and then restarted. He leaped right in, before I could stop him, and head up—like a puppy, like a millionaire's wife—he swam out to his love in the water.

Cressida, it turned out, after a few minutes of splashing, happy greeting, was there with her best friend and constant companion Ada. (The year before, Luke had complained to me about how inseparable they were: "It's like they're twins or something.") Ada turned out to be a startling, perfect, central casting best friend, with a throaty, husky Glynis Johns–Demi Moore voice, the perfect sultry sidekick to perfect radiant beauty. They both were there with Cressida's nanny, a jolly Australian girl named Shari, who played the trombone, and whom I can describe only by saying that she looked like a jolly Australian girl who played the trombone.

The two little girls were excellent swimmers, veterans of the Ritz pool, I supposed. They splashed back and forth easily, and Luke manfully struggled after them, head up, losing it, swallowing water and coming up exhausted and clinging to the side and spitting out, his face scrunched up in misery, but then shaking his head violently ("I'm fine! I'm fine!") when I came up and, a little too paternal, a little too obvious, pounded him on the back and asked him if he was OK. Then he shot back out to the girls in the middle of the pool. Pretty quickly he worked out a good method of getting around; first clinging to the side of the pool, then shooting out in backstroke, and then going into a quick three-stroke combined breaststroke–doggy paddle over to the girls—a wonderful simulacrum of a guy who is just an easy, varied swimmer. (He swam, I realized, exactly the way that after five years I spoke French, which also involved a lot of clinging to the side of the pool and sudden bravura dashes out to the deep end to impress the girls, or listeners.)

I hovered around him, worried—I was snob enough to be tickled that he had learned to swim at the Ritz pool in Paris but insecure enough to worry about what his mother would say if I *lost* him at the Ritz pool; after all, it was, at its deep end, effectively as deep as the ocean, three times over the head of a small boy—only to have him shake me off, again and again.

I didn't mind, really. I have never seen a human being before in a state of pure liquid unadulterated joy. The little girls, to my surprise, for I had had more bitter experiences at his age, seemed to accept him absolutely as an equal and fellow diver and Ritz habitué, a *bec-fin* of this damp *beau monde*, albeit one with a bit of water in his lungs from time to time. And if his lungs *were* filling up with water, swallow by swallow, he didn't care. He just followed the red bathing suit and the blond braid, wherever they led him.

The Australian au pair and I huddled around the edges of the pool and made conversation. She had been in Paris for only a couple of weeks, she explained, had flown right over from Sydney. She seemed unperturbed, not even much interested in her surroundings, Australians being like that, I suppose: From the Sydney beach to the Ritz pool, all just water, isn't it?

After about half an hour Ada paddled over. "I want a *chocolat chaud*," she said, imperiously. She looked at me just the way that Lorelei Lee must have looked at *her* sugar daddy at the Paris Ritz, so I gathered up the children—Luke could barely speak, he was so filled with water—and we went up to the café on the terrace overlooking the pool. I strode up as boldly as I could manage to the white-shirted attendant behind the counter and ordered three hot chocolates and three cakes for the children and then a *café crème* for me and a Badoit for the Australian girl. I shuddered inside, imagining what it was all going to cost. As I say, I am hedonistic but not heedless, and like Luke, only with less fortitude, I knew that I was out of my depth and swallowing water.

After a mysterious fifteen-minute wait the attendant reemerged with the chocolate in silver pitchers and the cake—simple pound cake with lemon glaze—on silver plates and served them to the children. Ada looked bored and indifferent and demanded some more *lait chaud* for her chocolate, after she had tasted it. She soon had a chocolate mustache, but it didn't make her look like a child. She looked more like Aramis, the youngest and most imperious of the musketeers.

Luke, never a big eater, watched Cressida. I saw what there was to watch: She sipped her chocolate, daintily but not as one making a big deal about daintiness. She was just a naturally elegant sipper. I drank my coffee, gulped it, really, and thought, gracelessly enough, about the bill running up. The two girls chatted in the way children do, effortlessly and seamlessly and in this case in two languages but without actually seeming to exchange information. ("You know what? You're a *Looney Tunes*." Laughter. "No, *Oscar* is a *Looney Tunes*." More laughter, in which Luke joined.)

After the first hot chocolate had been dispensed with, Ada summoned over the waiter with a wave of her hand and said, "*Encore un chocolat chaud*"—that is, "Another hot chocolate." "Say please," I said instantly. She gave me a steady, opaque, not-only-are-you-not-my-father-but-you-couldn't-begin-to-*afford*-to-be-my-father look. But then she said please. We all went for a second round, hot chocolate and cake and bottled water, and I felt like Charlie Chaplin in *The Immigrant*—it had been Luke's favorite movie, back when he would stay home all day and watch Chaplin videos while I worked—when Edna Purviance starts ordering beans and he reaches into his pocket to count his change and finds the quarter he had picked up on the sidewalk isn't there anymore. A third round of cake followed the second round of hot chocolate—Luke left his untouched, leaving three cakes on the plate in all, which I eventually ate—and then I told Luke it was time to go.

"No," he said definitely. And the children ran back down the stairs to the pool and played some more, dodging in and out among the chaise longues. I went over to the attendant, asked for the check, and signed it, trying to feign the nonchalance of Hem ordering another bottle of Dom Pérignon for Sister Dietrich, of Dodi Fayed before his last journey.

I got him home at last, around six o'clock. Martha was mildly irascible, nursing the baby on a chaise longue near the window, all by herself all afternoon, but she melted a little when I told her the story. "You won't believe who we met at the pool today," I began. Luke seemed quietly happy, nonchalant. The improbability of the encounter simply hadn't struck him. That Cressida Taylor would be swimming in a red one-piece at the Ritz pool on the same Wednesday afternoon that we were there . . . He had no sense of the size of the world or even of Paris. His haunts were the world's haunts; his world was the world. This is an emotion shared, I suppose, only by children and aristocrats; everyone goes where we go. Where else would you expect to meet people? (I have none of it and in my heart always expect to be alone, the one man sitting awkwardly at a table in the wrong restaurant after everyone else has left it. When I see my wife and children coming down the boulevard to meet me, I am dazzled. The baby, Olivia, was, I could see, a little like me, constantly pulling away from her mother's breast to give me the same anxious, reassuring smile: *You of all people! Here of all places!*)

For the next four weeks we went every Wednesday to the pool at the Ritz, to meet Ada and Cressida and their nanny and to swim and treat to hot chocolate and cake. Although Ada was a constant presence ("I don't think I shall swim today," she would say. "She's a bit moody," Cressida would explain, unemotionally.), I could sense that a bond, a romance had begun between Luke and Cressida, in the simple sense that the unstated had emerged from the informal. I recognized the signs: It lay not in their having fun together but in their not *needing* to have fun together, in a quiet, you-here-me-there, however-deep-you-can-go-in-the-deep-end-I'll-go-deeper understanding. I remembered the words that Gilberte had said to Marcel, somewhere in Proust, I think in that beautiful section titled "Place-Names: The Name," where the two children—if they are children; I can never really figure out in Proust if they are eight or eighteen—meet at the Champs-Élysées. "Now we can begin," Gilberte says. "You are on *my* side." The two of them were on the same side too.

You are on my side. Martha and I had once always been on the same side too, and without thinking about it at all. Now, here in the city that a notion of romance, a need for one last romantic adventure, had led us to, we found that we didn't care for each other less, yet loved each other differently. Our moving to Paris, which was intended, almost too self-consciously, I suppose, to extend that feeling—to keep each other on each other's side without the fretfulness and noise of New York life, without dinner parties and gallery openings and Burmese takeout and the number 6 uptown for life—had had the unexpected effect of plopping us down in the same pool with the same hot chocolate to sip day after day after day, and this at a time when we both were already, so to speak, practiced swimmers. We began to take almost too much pleasure, I suppose, almost too much delight, in the passage of our son's first romance because it recalled to us the landscape of limitations that surround all romance, the way that romance is a thing always best allied to difficulty: the water pouring into your lungs; the trombone-playing Australian looking over your shoulder and calling you into a towel; the encumbering presence of a moody hot chocolate–addicted best friend. Martha and I had always been so close; but now we were so *near,* and that is different.

We had run away to Paris that first time, twenty years earlier, back when we had known each other for six months, and even though it would be possible to say that that first time we were merely playing at running away, since we had families and houses waiting safely for us back in Montreal, the truth is that the existence of the families and houses was what made it, weirdly, not play at all. There really was someone back there waiting for you with a towel and calling you out of the pool, and we had decided not to listen. This time running away *was* a kind of play, since there was no one to run away from save ourselves, and your self always catches up.

Perhaps in the end this is why Paris is "romantic." It marries both the voluptuous and restricted. It is not the yeses but the noes of Paris, not the licenses it offers love but the prohibitions it puts in its way, that makes it powerful. All the noes of French life, the way that each gate to each park is bounded by that endless ten-thousand-word fine-print announcement from the government announcing all the things you are absolutely *not* allowed to do in the park, contribute in some odd way to the romance of Paris. Strictness, rules, disciplines, boundaries dam the libido, as Freud knew, even when you are five, and make it overflow backward. It is the knowledge of how awkward your splashing feet will look to the rich women on the chaises that prevents you, tantalizingly, from kissing the mermaid's invisible nipple.

Sometimes now, watching Martha—watching her nurse the new baby, or just lying beside her at night and watching her sleep, practically gobbling up sleep, her brow furrowed, in her new mother exhaustion—I thought that though I knew her better than I had ever known anyone, I didn't know her now nearly as well as I had when our days were broken with the thousand small distractions of life in New York. She had been my Cressida, unique in a pool, and in Paris had had to evolve from a fantasy figure into a reality principle for a chaotic husband and a small boy and then a baby. In New York we would meet at dinner and spill out the day's discontents, and they were always discontents with other people. Our discontents now crystallized not so much around each other—we hadn't come to that quite yet—as around tiny things that we held each other responsible for and that each of us pursued with silent, independent fury. Instead of rebelling together against our common prohibitions, we nursed our little exasperations.

I, for instance, had become absolutely furious about the long hallway in our apartment, which ran all the way from the kitchen, where I cooked, way in the back, to the dining room up in front, a constant jostling corridor of plates, forgotten Évian water, and spilled spices, like a trade route in the Byzantine Empire. Back and forth we went, again and again, breakfast, lunch, and dinner. (Kitchens in Parisian apartments are always off at the back, at the end of a long corridor, since there were originally no kitchens, or else because they were for servants, who were expected to be Out There in Back.) I didn't exactly blame Martha for the length of time it took to get dinner to the table, cold, but I didn't exactly *forgive* her for it either.

Martha's exasperation, for which she didn't exactly blame me, but which she thought I might have done something about if I were a more efficient person than I am, was the absence of a decent copy shop. She looked after the bills and the dry cleaning and the rent—all the small logistics of life—and she couldn't find places where you could just go in, hand in a manuscript, and have them copy and collate it, one, two, three, just like that. They had instead machines where you had to feed in two-franc pieces, page by page. (The government discourages video rental stores in Paris, in order to protect the little repertory cinemas whose business, it's quite true, would otherwise be destroyed. I don't know who's being protected by the discouragement of Kinko-style copy shops; the remaining scriveners and clerks and copyists, I suppose.) The absence of napkins drove her crazy, too. She loved order and cleanliness, and the refusal of a French take-out shop to give more than one napkin per sandwich made her wild. "They *hoard* napkins," she would complain. "It's as though it's still wartime." New York, America, where paper napkins shower down like confetti on New Year's Eve, had become, in her memory, napkin heaven, napkin world.

One day, when I was working in my little office on the latest subject that the office at home had sent in, Martha came storming into my office.

"What's this?" she said, angry as I had ever seen her, waving a sheaf of envelopes and paper with a blue and gold crest on it.

"What's what?" I asked, though I knew, or thought I knew.

"These bills," she said, waving white paper with a blue and gold crest on it. "What is this all *for*?" she cried.

"Hot chocolate," I said weakly.

"Hot chocolate," she repeated scornfully.

"And cake," I added.

"Do you know how much this costs?" she said.

"Of course I know. But what can I do? It's Cressida."

"Say no." She looked at me darkly. "That's a lot of hot chocolate," she added suspiciously.

"It's Ada too," I explained. "She has a habit."

She walked away. I wondered if she really thought I might be having an affair at the Ritz and if, in some secret way, she wished I were.

|||

Three weeks, and then four went by, and I depended on the children's happiness to support, to float my own. Luke and I, in the *vestiaire*, would always have the same two conversations or variations on them. First we would have a sharp, pointed exchange about the nature of buoyancy. What makes people float in water? Well, people are lighter than water, I explained. If you were made of water yourself or well, metal, or something, you would sink. He thought this sounded weird, and I thought so too, actually. People certainly don't *seem* lighter than water. They seem just the opposite. People seem heavy as can be compared with water. People are *obviously* heavier than water; just touch them and then touch water. I knew it was the right answer, but it seemed as unconvincing to me as it did to him. Then we would discuss the conventions of nudity. Why was it OK to be nude in the *vestiaire* but not in the pool or around the pool? It was a matter of custom and convention, I explained, or tried to. The metaphysics of modesty was even harder to explain than the physics of floating.

I joked with him about the little girls. The sublime Ada and the glorious Cressida, I called them, and those became their names. "What means *sublime*?" he demanded, and I gave some more examples of things, besides Ada, that were scary but irresistible (though I will say right here that I have never met anyone quite as sublime as Ada).

(What *does* make things float, by the way? That they are lighter than the thing they float in sounds fine when you say it—I know it is the right answer—but it is not a convincing answer because things, however much lighter they may be than the thing they float in, are still so heavy, too heavy to keep up.)

Finally, after about four weeks of joy, Luke had to miss a Wednesday session, I forget precisely why: His class was going on a trip to a goat farm to see how chèvre is made or off to an apple farm to help press cider. They were always doing things like that. Anyway, I went to the Ritz myself, as always, feeling the eyes of al Fayed on me, in the person of the sunglassed security men who hid discreetly at the entrance. I got into my swimming suit, my body tensed for the contest to get Luke's suit on and get him pointed in the right direction, down toward the pool, and I was a little disconcerted when I found I didn't have to do it.

The girls were already in the pool.

"Where's Luca?" Cressida cried when she saw me. "Where's Luca?" She always called him Luca, in the Italian manner, and said it with that funny trans-European intonation, the accent oddly placed on the first syllable: "Where's *Loo*-ka?," just like Audrey Hepburn saying, "Take the *pic*-ture," in *Funny Face*.

He couldn't come, I explained; his school was doing something that day.

"I'm so sad," she said, and made a face. "I'm so very sad. I wanted to swim with Luca." And she swam away, inconsolable. I swam a little myself, and then I slipped away before I could buy hot chocolate for the rich little girls, half expecting to be expelled from the Ritz, a child masher, buying hot chocolate only to serve his son's romance.

I enjoyed having the Ritz to myself, for once, though, before we had to leave it. I went down to the *hammam*—that's what the French call a steam bath—and read the instructions. There were nearly as many prohibitions as those posted on the gates to the public park, although these were more varied. Translated, they read:

1. *The shower is obligatory before using the installations.*
2. *It is forbidden to shave in the sauna.*
3. *Reading of newspapers is strongly discouraged in the hammam and sauna.*
4. *Children of less than twelve years are not authorized to use the installations.*

"Obligatory," "forbidden," "strongly discouraged," and "not authorized": four ways of saying "not allowed," each slightly different, each implying slightly different penalties. Such elegant variations on the theme of No! And these intended for the rich too. *You can't do that here,* the French taste for order reaching even into the rich man's locker room. Who would want to read a newspaper in the steam bath? The ink would get all over your hand. It was like the warnings on the park gates. Who aside from a French functionary would think so encyclopedically about all the things you can't do in a park? But then only if you can't, do you want to. If you can, you don't.

When I got home, I sought Luke out right away.

"Hey, you've made quite a score with Cressida," I said. "She was just broken up because you weren't there today."

"What did she say?" he asked.

"She said, 'Where's Luca? I miss Luca, I wish Luca were here to swim.' Like that. *Nothing* would cheer her up." He seemed to take it only half in.

The next Wednesday came, and I stopped work early and went to collect the bathing trunks and towels.

"Hey, come on, let's hustle up," I said to Luke when he came home after a half day of school. "We have to go to the pool today to meet Ada and Cressida."

He shrugged. "Daddy, I don't really feel like going."

I was dumbfounded, really struck dumb.

"You don't?" I said at last. "Why not?"

"I just don't feel like it," he said, and went into his room to play.

Fifteen minutes later I tried again. "C'mon," I said, "the sublime Ada and the divine Cressida are expecting us."

"I just don't feel like going," he repeated. Then he looked up at me, a strange half-smile that I had never seen before on his face. "Daddy," he said, "what will Cressida say if I'm not there?"

"She'll say she's sad," I said, not sure where we were going.

"No, but what will she say *exactly*? What *exactly* will she say?"

Then I got it. "I don't know. I guess, 'Where's Luca? I wish Luca were here? I miss Luca so much.' "

"What else?"

"I don't know. Just like that."

"No, say exactly what she would say. Tell me *exactly* what she would say." His face was shining.

"You know." I groped. " 'I miss Luca. I wish he would come swimming with me.' " I felt vaguely as if I were reciting pornography.

"I'm not going," he repeated.

The eternal, painful truth of love had struck. Proust wasn't exaggerating, I realized. Five *was* fifteen, five slipped into fifteen— or thirty-five, or fifty for that matter, I suppose—seamlessly. He was struggling with the oldest romantic-erotic question. Was there more pleasure to be found in sharing Cressida's company or in feeling the power that he held by making her suffer from his absence? More pleasure to be found in sharing joy or in denying joy, in knowing that he now possessed the power to make her miserable, change her entire emotional state, simply by his absence?

I was already at the door, and was already turning the handle to leave, when he popped out of his room at last.

"OK," he said, "I'll go." I was glad, of course. We went to the pool, and they had a good time, though I noticed that now Cressida, ever so slightly, swam toward him. I bought a lot of hot chocolate, and everybody drank it.

I told Martha the story that night, and she seemed somehow stirred. She wanted to know what Cressida had said, too.

"Well, what exactly *did* she say?" she said. "What exactly did she say when she saw him?" His absence was alive in her too.

Was it an accident or not that we shared a bottle of champagne, our own *chocolat chaud*, that night for the first time since she had become big with Olivia, right in the living room, with Tony Bennett singing the English lyrics of our favorite old Michel Legrand song, one of the songs that had gotten us here onto the boulevard Saint-Germain, "You Must Believe in Spring"? Could it have been that her son's first thrill of sadism with a woman had reawakened her own sense of the fragility of desire, of the urge to renewal that runs through the eternal possibility that Wednesday will come and someone will *not* be at the pool, no matter how many wet Wednesdays there have been before? I don't know. There was at least for a moment present again between us the central elements of love: buoyancy, seminudity, and uncertainty, that mixture of imperfect faith and intoxicating drink that is desire.

|||

Our *abonnement* was running out that next week. From now on, I knew, we would have to cadge invitations to swim on Wednesday from Cressida and Ada and couldn't just show up as equals. But I didn't have the heart, the courage to explain to Luke that we were rubes, just visiting, trespassers of a kind. I just told Luke that we wouldn't be swimming there anymore. It didn't seem to bother him any more than our going there together had impressed him. In childhood, I suppose, you are always a little lighter than your circumstances and just keep floating. He worried more about getting his pleasures than about keeping them. He would make me promise him things, in precise order: "First we'll go to the pool, then we'll have hot chocolate, then we'll have dinner, then we'll play a game, then we'll have the Rookie story. . . ." He knew that if he didn't get a contract written down in advance, you could lose any part of it, and that worried him. On the other hand, he didn't worry that the pleasures would ever run out. Life was full of good stuff. The budget of pleasures is tighter in childhood, but the economy of pleasure at least is always in surplus.

We had one last thing to do, of course. We had tried to kiss the mermaid so many times, and we had always failed, because he was too short and I was too scared.

"Let's just *touch* the mermaid," he said wisely, this time, and we held our breaths together, and then we did.

When we were getting ready to leave Paris, I found several hundred shower caps, pristine in their gold and blue boxes, hidden in his bottom drawer.

One Last
Ride

Paris won the century, against all odds. At least we won the party, which is the next best thing to dominating the period. In London they had built a giant wheel and a giant dome and a great big rhetoric of newness to greet the next thousand years. In New York, unduly jumpy despite all the money and power, our friends' major millennial ambition seemed to be to keep out of midtown. One couple we knew had decided to drive down from the country, where they were hunkering down in Y2K alert, park on Ninety-sixth Street, go to a midtown party, and then get back in the car and get home, before the lightning struck, keeping Times Square at a safe and wary distance.

But that was New York, where everything was happening anyway, one millennial party more or less hardly mattered, everybody there was probably on to the next millennium anyway. London was more annoying. We would arrive at Waterloo Station on the Eurostar—transplanted Americans, of course, but still patriotic Parisians—and feel vaguely ashamed, cheesed off, even sort of country cousinish. Where did London come by this feeling of confidence, this sense of entitlement, all this girder and vinyl construction? My cousin Philippe, who had once wandered with me through the outer arrondissements of Paris in search of von Stroheim festivals and Dominique Sanda memorabilia, had moved to London now too and was dropping me E-mails about the progress of his fish restaurant, disparaging the provincial cooking in the country he had left behind.

Yet on the night, Paris shone, scored a clear and beautiful triumph. It had, to be sure, been a weird run-up through Christmas week. A siege of flu had struck Europe. It hit our family right in the kisser. Everyone was sick. I had been banished to the sofa, in fear that my flu would spread to the baby. (It did anyway.) I shook with the chills on the sofa all night, only to find a fevered Luke sympathetically jumping in every night alongside me. (Sympathetic? Or just so satisfied by the idea that Daddy had at last been banished from the marriage bed that he wanted to make sure that he didn't stray back?) Anyway, there is nothing so strangely comforting in sickness as the feeling of an all-elbows-and-knees five-year-old with a 103 fever, shaking alongside you on a narrow velvet sofa.

It was Christmas Eve by the time we had all recovered, and Martha and I had to crowd all our shopping into that single day, rushing from Au Nain Bleu for a two-wheeler with training wheels for Luke up to Bonpoint for a sea green tulle first dress for Olivia, and then quickly into line at Ladurée for our *bûche de Noël*. (We actually got summoned out of line, as people who had wisely ordered in advance, and got our *bûche* from an efficient but unprepossessing-looking Ladurée bakery truck, parked at the curb on the rue Royale.) Parisians are efficient Christmas shoppers, I suppose, or maybe everybody else was home sick with the flu. Anyway, the rue Royale was pretty much empty by five o'clock, and Martha and I, walking out into the pure violet and gray light of the place de la Concorde at twilight in December, had it to ourselves. The Concorde at Christmas at five o'clock has as many subtly distinguished shades of gray as a pair of flannel pants painted by Manet.

Christmas was nice. Luke liked his two-wheeler enough to want to try it out right away (with training wheels) in the little park down the rue du Bac, and after a single fall, he went right around the bust of Chateaubriand on it. The flower store on the commercial part of the street was, to our surprise, open, although there was no one minding the store. We searched a little and found the entire flower family having Christmas lunch in the little shed behind the flowers. The madame wiped her mouth and sold us some tulips and threw in some of the painted white twigs as a gift. Everyone came out to admire Luke's red and chrome two-wheeler.

On Christmas night the wind, following the viruses, socked it to Paris all over again. We woke up at five in the morning, thinking that someone was trying to push open our front door. Nobody there. It was just the wind, blowing away inside the building—blowing so strongly even in the corridors that it pressed against every door. Then we went to look out the windows and saw it blowing so hard that you felt, at least, as if you could see it, as streaking lines of force, like the pen streaks behind Superman's cape. A hundred-plus-miles-an-hour wind blew for an hour. It lifted up the awning on the café across the way, tore wooden shutters off old buildings, and even made the outer walls of our building shake—really shake, *stone* shaking, a scary sound. The winds lifted all the Christmas trees that lined the street right up and sent them blowing like tumbleweeds down the boulevard Saint-Germain. One of them still had its lights on, plugged in on a long cord, writhing and blinking.

There was a lot of damage outside Paris—the park at Versailles may be a century returning to what it was—and even in Paris most of the parks, including the little one where Luke had taken his first bike ride, were closed for a few days. But the city was more or less patched up by New Year's Eve, or Saint Silvestre, as the French more often call it. We went out for a walk at six and went back to the Concorde with the children, the baby sleeping in her *poussette*. There were wheels, small Ferris wheels, set up all along the Champs-Élysées, and then one big Ferris wheel, covered with white lights, at the Concorde—a big wheel, sure, but the same wheel they put up there every Christmas, no big London-type deal.

It was a winter evening like every other winter evening in Paris: the temperature somewhere in the forties, with a little damp mist and a white-gray sky. The whole place had a nice, easy, almost small-town flavor. People strolled. A guy climbed up the face of the obelisk in the center of the place and then climbed back down. The police grabbed him, and the crowd booed. We went home, bedtime for the kids, thinking, only a little ruefully, that with two children, the night of the millennium in Paris wouldn't be a lot different from Arbor Day in Kalamazoo: Bedtimes (and bedtime stories and bedtime stalls and bedtime nursing) rule all, even a fete that came once a thousand years. Millennial time is public time, history time; children's bedtimes are experience time, the real clock that ticks in life.

Then, at midnight, we opened our living-room windows and stepped out onto the tiny balcony outside. We had the TV on, CNN bringing the millennium from around the world. The London party, for all its buildup, seemed, we thought from watching it—and even heard from a few English friends who had called—actually a bit of a dud, with long lines and damp squibs and a nonworking Ferris wheel (our wheels were smaller, but they spun like crazy). We felt meanly, smugly glad.

Then we heard bangs from away down left down the boulevard, over by the Invalides, and a muffled roar. We looked at the television screen and saw the Eiffel Tower, all lit up. They had set up fireworks so that they began at the base of the tower, exploding in gold and violet around its piers, and then dramatically in gold bursts and haloes, working their way up to the top. As the fireworks reached the top, the entire tower turned on; twenty thousand or so small flashbulbs that had been wired to the tower went off at once, blinking hyperfast. The tiny constant explosions of the little bulbs made the tower look as though it had been carbonated, injected with seltzer bubbles. It was a beautiful sight. I thought of going out to see it firsthand, like a responsible reporter, but it was late—hey, come to think of it, it was *after midnight*—and anyway, the children were asleep. So we watched the whole thing on TV, and were proud anyway, one last virtual CNN experience, but with a living room window open, and the cold air coming in, and one ear at least hearing the muffled bangs of the real thing taking place a few blocks away.

I was still kicking myself for missing the show when about a week later Luke and I went to the big Ferris wheel for an after-school ride and stopped to buy a crepe *crème de marrons*—still his favorite Paris treat—and then decided (I decided; Luke accepted) to walk home across the Concorde bridge. We stopped to admire the searchlight that had also been placed on the top of the tower, sweeping around Paris, when suddenly the whole damn thing exploded all over again, the thousands of little flashing lights sparkling and shooting off and raising hell, just the way they had on New Year's Eve. I looked at my watch; it was five forty-seven on an ordinary Wednesday. Either an *haut fonctionnaire* in the mayor's office, following an inscrutable but precise schedule, had set the whole thing off again on the minute, maybe in honor of some visiting dignitary, or some elevator operator or janitor working in the base of the tower had thrown the switch again, just for the hell of it. Either some official in a big building had set it off, or else it was just some little guy with a taste for mischief—culture or civilization, one or the other, and you would never know which just by looking.

The tower with all its dancing lights, seen real, looked a thousand times more beautiful than it had on television, though it also looked a little as if it had been hung with a giant garland of those vulgar, blinking Christmas lights that Martha had nixed for our tree that first Christmas, when Luke was still a baby. "It looks like champagne," Luke said, and we laughed, he with pleasure at scoring a simile, and I with pleasure that the simile he had scored was, well, so French. We stood on the Concorde bridge and watched the towering, immense spire sizzle for five minutes, and then ten.

I thought: Here we were, at the end of the century and *that's* what we have to get excited, same old belle époque, fin de siècle stuff, champagne, and the Eiffel Tower? That exhausted stuff, that dead stuff. Only it isn't dead, or even really sick or, in a certain sense, even old. It's here right now, we're looking at it right now, Luke is young in Paris right now, and in that sense, the sparkling tower is the same age he is. He's going to take it with him through life, not as part of the lost glory of the French past but as part of what happened to him when he was a kid. "It looks like champagne," he said again, meaning to please me. I recalled the other night not long before when I had been trying to read one of those knotty, dense books about evolution and consciousness that are popular now and had come across an argument about whether, as a human invention, you should value more Newton's *Principia* or the Eiffel Tower. The argument, surprisingly, came down in favor of Eiffel, on the grounds that the principles of physics have a permanent general existence outside ourselves and, had Newton never existed, would eventually have been discovered by Schnewton, while the tower, in all its particulars, could have been built only in Paris at Eiffel's moment by Eiffel, even though it was, after all, only a "minor piece of romantic engineering."

|||

We went to New York first in December and then in January, to find a place to live. The forces drawing us home were pretty strong and even pretty attractive: We wanted Luke to go to a New York school, for one thing. "We have a beautiful existence in Paris, but not a full life," Martha said, summing it up, "and in New York we have a full life and an unbeautiful existence."

Luke had come to associate French, for us the language of romance and the exotic, with authority and order, with school. It was his German. Sometimes, at home, he would pretend to be Zeus and call out to his French teachers from the top of Mount Olympus. "*Oui, oui, oui?*" he would then say, mimicking their high, humorless accents as they turned their heads to look up at the god on the mountain. Then, zap, right between the eyes with a thunderbolt. He would produce what I believe is called a mirthless laugh, even with French administration at last.

Martha had at least been allowed to glimpse a proper copy shop in Paris. It was down near the rue Vavin, just outside the Luxembourg Gardens. We came across it one day, on one of our last strolls, walking home from the playground. A vast glass front, pristine, humming, superfast color Xerox machines, ten or twenty of them, right in front, eager attendants in white T-shirts, ready to collate a manuscript or laser-copy a photograph: It was her Xanadu, right there where you needed it and just as we were leaving.

When we got back, still cold February weather, we went up to the Luxembourg Gardens again, and Luke, slightly to my surprise, said that he wanted to go on the carousel. Martha sat on the little bench with Olivia, nursing discreetly. ("You can't really nurse in Paris openly," she said the other day, "the way I could in New York. I'm always putting on a scarf, and I feel people staring at me. It's not puritanical, really, more sort of the opposite. It's that baring your breast here is really meaningful and loaded.")

Luke got up on one of the beat-up and beautiful old horses. There were a couple of other kids up there too in the cold weather—Paris winter, neither bitter nor chilly nor sunny, life under the perpetual gray skies. Luke asked for a stick when the guy offered them around and held it tight, and I recalled the near baby who had come to Paris five years before.

The carousel started up, and Luke, back absolutely straight, brow slightly creased, watched the man holding the rings. His stick dipped to pick up the ring, and angled to let the ring with its little leather tag drop to its end. *One*. Once around again the second time, back straight, stick out, ring on—perfect. The carousel picked up speed, and since it has no music, the only sound you could hear was the sound of the ancient wheezing fan belt going faster and faster as it drove the horses and carriages around. Bang, bang—two more rings, picking them like cherries: back straight, stick out, unsmiling, taking one ring after another and slipping it down his wood baton.

I was unreasonably pleased and then felt a little guilty about my own pleasure. It seemed so American, so competitive; the other French fathers on the bench just sat there, watching with sober pleasure, not seeing even a carousel as a competitive sport. But as Luke whirled around, now really going fast, and grabbed still another ring—I only knew it now by the slight clang of wood on metal and the ring missing—I couldn't help myself.

"Hey, sir"—I call him sir a lot, Johnsonianly—"you're unconscious."

Luke, a blur of gray coat on the brown horse.

"What means *unconscious*?" I heard him ask, his voice clear and then fading away as the carousel whipped him around.

"It means you're doing great without even thinking about it," I called out.

The carousel was beginning to slow down now—the normal five-minute ride at an end. I saw the man's hand on the lever, bringing the ride to its close.

"Daddy," Luke said, and I thought I heard a little concern in his voice, a small edge of worry, "Daddy, I *am* thinking about it," he said, and he didn't even try for the one last ring that the man held out, before the carousel stopped for good and the man took back the stick and shook off the rings, so dearly won, to give to the next child who would get up on the carousel in the Luxembourg Gardens and give it a try.

ADAM GOPNIK has been writing for *The New Yorker* since 1986, and his work for the magazine has won the National Magazine Award for Essay and Criticism as well as the George Polk Award for Magazine Reporting. He broadcasts regularly for the Canadian Broadcasting Corporation, and is the author of the article on the culture of the United States in the last two editions of the *Encyclopedia Britannica*. From 1995 to 2000 Gopnik lived in Paris, where the newspaper *Le Monde* profiled him as a "witty and Voltairean commentator on French life," and the weekly magazine *Le Point* wrote, "It is impossible to resist delighting in the nuances of his articles, for the details concerning French culture that one discovers even when one is French oneself." He now lives in New York with his wife, Martha Parker, and their two children, Luke Auden and Olivia Esmé Claire.

ABOUT THE TYPE

This book was set in Fairfield, the first typeface from the hand of the distinguished American artist and engraver Rudolph Ruzicka (1883–1978). In its structure Fairfield displays the sober and sane qualities of the master craftsman whose talent has long been dedicated to clarity. It is this trait that accounts for the trim grace and vigor, the spirited design and sensitive balance, of this original typeface.